Leo Rosten's
Book of Laughter

ALSO BY
LEO ROSTEN

Leo Rosten's
BOOK OF LAUGHTER

ELM TREE BOOKS

The author and publishers would like to thank the following for their kind permission to reprint excerpts from their published material in this book:

McGraw-Hill Book Company for *The Joys of Yiddish* © 1968 by Leo Rosten; *People I Have Loved, Known or Admired* © Leo Rosten; *Passions and Prejudices* © 1978 by Leo Rosten. All rights reserved. Used by permission.

Victor Gollancz Ltd for *Captain Newman M.D.* by Leo Rosten.

Constable Publishers for O K*A*P*L*A*N! MY K*A*P*L*A*N! by Leo Rosten.

Author's Note
The provenance of jokes, limericks, doggerel, puns, and wisecracks is notoriously difficult, and often quite impossible, to establish with any degree of confidence, much less accuracy. I have credited the originators of such material wherever possible.
Some uncredited items may be found, in their substance, if not in their wording, in such anthologies as THE READER'S DIGEST TREASURY OF WIT AND HUMOR (1958) or THE ENCYCLOPEDIA OF MODERN AMERICAN HUMOR by Bennett Cerf (1954), both vast collections which, at times, credit different people with the same items and sometimes credit no one at all. Therefore, I hereby offer an omnibus thanks and acknowledgment to the Reader's Digest Association and to Doubleday & Company, publishers of these respective anthologies.

First published in Great Britain 1986
by Elm Tree Books/Hamish Hamilton Ltd
Garden House 57–59 Long Acre London WC2E 9JZ

British Library Cataloguing in Publication Data

Rosten, Leo
    Leo Rosten's book of laughter.
    1. American wit and humor
    I. Title
    828'.91402'08   PN6175

ISBN 0–241–11715–1
ISBN 0–241–11716–X Pbk

Photoset and printed in Great Britain by
REDWOOD BURN LIMITED, Trowbridge, Wiltshire

To
my wife,
Zimi,
who makes it all possible

WARRANTY
to the
READER

If you do not receive an amplitude of pleasure from this book, do not hesitate to return it to me, with a bill for the exact amount you paid. I will return your bill within five days.

LEO ROSTEN

CONTENTS

PREFACE

The Strategy of Humour

'Humour is the affectionate communication of insight.' I wrote
this definition almost thirty years ago. It did not, so far as I know,
cause wild cheering in the streets. I quote it now because I cannot
improve upon it.

I also said that humour is 'the chanciest of literary forms. It is
surely not accidental that there are a thousand novelists, essay-
ists, poets, journalists for one humorist.'*

The first exposure of a child to formal humour (as distinguished
from funny happenings) usually comes in the form of a riddle,
such as: 'What's black and white and red all over?' *My* first riddle,
as fresh in my mind as when I heard it so many decades ago, was
propounded by my father: 'What is it that hangs on the wall, is
green, wet – and whistles?'

I knit my brow and thought and thought. 'I give up.'

'A herring,' said my father.

'A *herring*?!' I echoed. 'A herring doesn't hang on the wall!'

'So hang it there.'

'B-but a herring isn't *green*!' I protested.

'So paint it.'

'B-but a herring isn't *wet*!'

'If it's just painted, it's still wet.'

'But – ' I summoned all my outrage, ' – a *herring – does – not –
whistle!*'

'Right,' smiled my father. 'I just put that in to make it hard.'

The joke, in every culture, is the swiftest, surest trigger of laughter. A joke is a very short short-story, carefully structured, a very
brief narrative designed to reach a comedic climax through skilful
cues, deliberate miscues, and sudden surprise.

* Preface to *The Return of H*Y*M*A*N K*A*P*L*A*N*, 1959.

To *write* a joke is much more difficult than to tell one. Just consider the arsenal of props available to you when you tell a story: the calculated pause, the ironic inflection, the ingenuous smile, the warning frown, the accented adjective, the changes in pace, in accelerated rhythm or decelerated momentum. All of these devices serve to cue and control your listeners: gestures, nods, smiles, cunning chuckles, grunts or murmurs, the gasps of affected astonishment, the moan of pretended dismay.

None of these is available to the writer of a joke. Each must be replaced by silent and nonvisual devices, devices that are far more subtle, and require far rarer skill, than the mimicry deployed by the raconteur. I, for one, find telling a story (or joke) child's play compared with writing one, for complex and frustrating road blocks impede the course of written narration. Yet the central stratagems of both forms are similar; both must use camouflage with creative cunning. What this entails is the disguising of purpose, the distribution of tantalizing but misleading 'leads', the planting of totally deceptive expectations. All of these elements must combine to explode in the surprise of that laughter Hobbes called 'sudden glory'.

Consider the multitude of questions that surround so apparently routine a matter as where to place the mundane 'he said'. Suppose I intend to use the line 'I do not think I'm ready for that.' The wholly neutral expository phrase 'he said' conveys varying overtones according to where I place it in the sentence:

> 'I,' he said, 'do not think I'm ready for that.'
> 'I do not think,' he said, 'I'm ready for that.'
> 'I do not think I,' he said, 'am ready for that.'
> 'I do not think I'm ready,' he said, 'for that.'
> 'I do not think I'm ready for,' he said, 'that.'
> 'I do not think I'm ready for that,' he said.

Suppose I am not satisfied with the flat 'said' and search for a more evocative verb. Consider the tapestry of connotations, moods, implications I can weave by using 'frowned ... glared ... chuckled ... scoffed ... murmured ... laughed ... blurted ... gasped ... shouted ... groaned ... pleaded ... (et cetera)'. Each verb injects an entirely different meaning (from amusement to menace to propitiation) into the line.

Ring Lardner made a gorgeous contribution to comedic technique when he coined the astonishing '"Shut up!" he explained'. You can manipulate readers' responses with similar incongruities:

'The man is dead as a door-knob!' he hinted.
'It's exactly five o'clock,' she wondered.
'Put down that axe!' he murmured.
'I'm going to pull this trigger and blow your goddam brains out!' he implied.

A word of warning. Dangers attend the obvious overexcitation of prose. Dramatic verbs, if not used with rigorous restraint, may call the attention of the reader to the device, which can convert a smile into a sneer. Ernest Hemingway, of course, almost never used a synonym for 'said', making the dialogue stand by itself, unaided by expository glosses. That two whole pages of unidentified dialogue might send many readers back to serialize the speakers, so to speak, in order to discover who was saying what and who was answering whom, did not seem to bother Hemingway in the least; it only confused his readers.

Because of all these mischievous ingredients, the tales in the pages that follow are of different length; they require different scaffolding and individual pacing. Some of my entries are only one or two lines long, since their humour is enhanced by the most unadorned telling; others are set in the form of unembroidered dialogue; still others take a whole page; and some I have extended beyond that, with a multitude of 'delaying' detail, to build up to a payoff that becomes all the more risible because it is so long deferred.

The first true joke I ever heard still seems to me a marvel of technique:

Three cross-eyed prisoners stood before a cross-eyed judge. He glared at the first prisoner. 'What's your name?'
'Eli Krantz,' said the second prisoner.
'I wasn't talking to you!' snapped the judge.
'I didn't *say* anything!' cried the third prisoner.*

Perhaps the best way to drive home my point is through illustration. Consider the following ways of ruining the same joke:

---

* This joke, like several others in this Preface, appears later in the text in different forms.

Version 1

Two friends, Nelly Jenkins and Marie Duval, who had been to high school together in New Rochelle, from which they both came, happened to run into each other in New York, on Park Avenue, one very hot summer day in July.

'Why, Nelly Jenkins!' cried Marie. 'Imagine meeting you here!'

Nelly Jenkins laughed, 'Long time no see.'

'You can say *that* again,' replied Marie Duval.

'What's new?' asked Nelly.

'What's new,' replied Marie, with a mischievous glance, 'is that I have just come from Dr Herman Sorenson's office – '

'Dr Herman Sorenson, the gynae*c*ologist?!' exclaimed Nelly knowingly.

'That is right,' confirmed Marie.

'I suppose you went to Dr Sorenson for your annual checkup?' suggested Nelly in a friendly, although familiar, manner.

'Oh, no,' chuckled Marie. 'I had my *regular* complete medical examination last December – '

'But this is July,' observed Nelly, 'and that's not a year from last December – '

'I *know*,' affirmed Marie, 'but you see, it just so happens that I got *pregnant* last February – '

'Pregnant?!' echoed Nelly, in astonishment. 'Oh, my. That *is* a true surprise. What wonderful news! Marie, that's absolutely fantastic! I can't say that I actually envy you – my *God*, the number of diapers alone, and the heat rashes, and the orthodontist's bills – !'

'I know. What you say is certainly all true,' agreed Marie seriously. 'But – Nelly, can you keep a secret? A very important secret?!'

'Just you try me!' challenged Nelly.

Breathlessly, Marie confided: 'Dr. Sorenson said – *I may be carrying triplets!*'

'Triplets!' gasped Nelly. 'Why, Marie Duval, that is fan*t*astic! I never before knew *any*one who has had triplets! Do you?'

'Oh, no,' huffed Marie. 'I *heard* – but that was years ago – that Sally Norton's cousin, Eileen, who lives in Ohio, had triplets...'

'I don't know Sally Norton,' Nelly disclosed.

'Well, I only *heard* she did... In fact, triplets are very *unusual*, the doctor told me,' added Marie.

'I can imagine!' chuckled Nelly.

'In fact,' gloated Marie, 'he said that triplets happen once every – *three million times!*'

'My *God!*' shouted Nelly. 'Marie – '
(Punch line will appear below)

Version 2

Two women met on Fifth Avenue. 'Guess what,' hinted the first.

'I give up,' retorted the second.

'I am pregnant.'

'Preg . . . Golly! Gosh! Gee whiz – that's wonderful!' ventured the first woman. 'Congratulations!'

'Thank you. And what's even more remarkable,' smiled the pregnant female, 'is that my obstetrician tells me there is a good chance that I will have – triplets!'

'Trip . . . oh, my *God!*' gasped the second woman. 'You must be beside yourself – but there I go, carrying on. How *do* you feel about having triplets?'

'I'm still knocked for a loop,' confessed the mother-to-be. 'Do you realize, according to my obstetrician, the statistical odds on having triplets are only one in – *three million!*'

'Lands sakes alive! Tell me – '
(Punch line will appear below)

Version 3

Two women met in the Bronx. 'Hello, Sara,' said the first. 'Say – you've gotten pretty fat! Or are you pregnant?'

'I certainly am, Cora!'

'Congratulations! That's actually wonderful.'

'What is even more wonderful,' said the mother-to-be, 'is that I – it looks like I'm going to have triplets!'

'Triplets!' gasped Cora.

'That's what my obstetrician told me!' said the mother-to-be. 'Do you realize that, according to the statistics, the odds on having triplets are one in three million!'

'Lands sakes, alive! Tell me, dear – '
(Punch line will appear in version 4)

Version 4

ELLEN: 'I'm going to have triplets!'

BLANCHE: 'Congratulations!'
ELLEN: 'My doctor tells me that the chance of triplets is three million to one!'
BLANCHE: 'My *God*, Ellen! When did you find the time to do the housework?'

The same point must be made about aphorisms, epigrams, and one-liners.

1. He has such dreadful luck that he burns a cigarette hole in the jacket of a suit which has an extra pair of trousers.
2. He's the kind of *shlemiel* who buys a suit with two pairs of pants – and burns a hole in the jacket.

1. Human beings say 'Let bygones be bygones,' but they don't really mean it.
2. No one ever forgets where he buried the hatchet.

1. Sex is very enjoyable, but humourless.
2. Sex is the most fun you can have without laughing.

Consider the universe of wit and impact that separates the following:

Version 1 A bore is a person who when he leaves a party in a living room makes the room feel that instead of containing one less person it feels like it contains one more.
Version 2 A bore is someone who, upon leaving a room, makes you feel that someone *fascinating* just walked in.

Version 1 A diplomat sends a woman a telegram that reads 'Happy Birthday' – but not 'Happy Fifty-second Birthday.'
Version 2 A diplomat never forgets a woman's birthday, and never remembers her age.

The funny story is a matchless teaching device. (The rabbis of old, in the Talmud, instruct a teacher always to begin a lesson with something amusing.) What better way is there to convey the commanding influence of 'context,' say, than in the marvellous anecdote about the artist and the model he is painting in the nude (page 30)? What more vivid way is there of describing paranoia than with the tale of the man who complains to the psychiatrist that for reasons he simply cannot understand people regard him as crazy (page 272)? What more crushing example of a 'put-down' do you know than the one about the mohel's retort to the English-

man who wants his watch fixed (page 294)? What neater example
of the Freudian slip can you concoct than the telegram on page
133?

The japeries that ignite *my* most grateful laughter are those
which are built upon so conventional and matter-of-fact a frame-
work that their climax is completely unexpected:

> 'Stella, is it true that you're going to have a baby?'
> 'Absolutely.'
> 'How wonderful! Are you hoping for a boy or a girl?'

Intercession: How many thousands of times has any of us, during a
lifetime, heard this question asked of a mother or father? But until
now has any of us heard this delicious reply:

> 'Certainly.'

It grieves me to inform you that most joke books are just not
funny; and very few are very funny. Most collections intended to
provoke laughter are simply tiresome. Often, they are in bad
taste. Nearly always, they display an irritating ineptitude applied
to exhausted jocularities. Most joke books are abominably *written*.

Humour can be crippled by the tiniest insufficiency – or excess.
The rhythm ('timing') of a joke or anecdote dictates its effective-
ness. A joke must tantalize without annoying; where the prolong-
ing of narrative tension is demanded, a joke must 'pad' without
boring; it must defer without frustrating; it must reward the
reader (or listener) with a crowning climax that is exact, immedi-
ate, and absolutely clear. The punchline of any joke is designed to
ignite the cord, carefully prepared, that explodes the bomb of
laughter; and that laughter offers the reward of catharsis: a joyous
revelation that justifies all the ploys deployed to maximize the
power of a sudden, always surprising climax.

I hope you are not foolish enough to consider humour insignifi-
cant and dismiss jokes as 'trivia'. The laughter of a people can be
as illuminating as its patterns of pride, guilt and shame. I think
humour is an isotope that locates the values of a culture. The
japery of a nation runs up and down the scale of its scorn and its
admiration, its approval or contempt.

Any collection of ethnic jokes is, perforce, a parade of its heroes,
patsies, wise men, clowns. The particular genius, or inherent limi-
tations, of any group beholden to the same preferences and
taboos is as much revealed by a sampling of its humour as by a

sampling of its IQs, indeed more so, I submit, since the IQ protocol tests only a certain kind of intelligence; it reveals nothing about
humour, judgment, affability. God preserve us from those who
have no sense of humour, for they are the scourges of human-
kind.

Now, before we set forth on our revels, permit me to remind
you of the admirable words of A. P. Herbert:

> Don't stop me if you've heard this one before. There is no
> reason why a joke should not be appreciated more than once.
> Imagine how little good music there would be if, for example, a
> conductor refused to play Beethoven's Fifth Symphony on the
> ground that his audience might have heard it before.

Accents

Perhaps because I was raised within a sea of exotic accents, in a neighbourhood surrounded by Poles, Irishmen, Germans, Bohemians, Ukrainians, Italians, Greeks, I was enchanted early on by the surprising consequences of English as spoken by the foreign-born – especially English as transformed by Jews from Russia, Poland, Lithuania, Latvia, Hungary, Romania, Austria, Germany, Egypt, Palestine... Accents added a mischievous dimension – of colour and humour – to our noble tongue. I still think dialect is one of the most endearing aspects of human communication.

L. R.

Wu Chan owned a laundry next to the New Acropolis, where Nick Matsoutas was the chef. Matsoutas, it so happened, made superb spareribs and fried rice – which is what Wu ordered every day. And every day Nick Matsoutas heaved with laughter as Wu said, 'Spallibs – and flied lice, prease.'

'Why you always raugh?' asked Wu one day.

'Because of the way you pronounce "spareribs" and "fried rice", you crazy Chinaman. Why don't you hire some American kid to teach you how to pronounce English?!'

A month later, Wu entered the New Acropolis. In a firm, confident tone, he declaimed, 'One order of spareribs, please, with fried rice.'

Nick's jaw dropped. 'I can't believe it! What did you say?'

'You heard *exactly* what I said,' sneered Wu, 'you rousy, clazy Gleek!'

Abe Tarshow had moved to a little house in New Jersey, after

thirty years of residence in the Bronx. After a year, he was returning to Manhattan for a visit. In Penn Station, an old friend, Myron
Kishner, greeted him: 'Abe! For goodness *sake*! Where in the
world have you been?'

'Hollo, Myron! Mine goodness, it's nice to see you.'

'Abe, you look like a million! Tanned, trim, no fat – '

'It's this new life. For a year now, me and my Sonya been living
in the country.'

'In the *country*?' Myron Kishner clucked several times. 'I never
would of taken you for a country type, Abe.'

'Me nider.'

'Tell me, was the adjustment hard?'

'At foist, we were lonesome. But now, we got a whole bunch
friends . . .'

'But what about the work? All the chores? Day in, day out,
doesn't a house in the country just wear you out?'

'True, true,' sighed Abe. 'It *was* hard. Then everyt'ing changed
– as soon as I got mineself a paramour.'

'You? Abe?' Myron giggled. 'A *paramour*?'

'Absolutely.'

'But, Abe . . . does Sonya know?'

'Uf cawss she knows!'

'And Abe – I don't mean to stick my nose in – but doesn't Sonya
mind?'

'Mind?' Abe echoed. 'Why should she care *how* I cut the grass?'

Welsh Romance

Lloyd Llowell llooked at Llana llonginglly. 'Llana. I llove you!'

'I llove you, Lloyd.'

'I'd llike to kiss you!' Lloyd bllurted.

'Oh. Llets!'

Sllowlly, their llips met.

It was their first kiss – and their llast, because Lloyd was drafted
the next morning. He was killled in an artilllery drilll on Llong
Islland.

Old Zeke Lumpkin and his wife were sitting on the porch of their
old home, on the edge of the Pumpkin Patch cemetery, rocking

back and forth in their chairs. The moonlight bathed the scene in silver.

'Yeah, maw,' sighed Zeke, 'it's been a long life – and, everythin' considered – a purty good one . . .'

'I sure like settin' here with you, Zeke,' sighed his wife. 'Lookin' out over the old cemetery . . . where our own two daughters are layin' . . .'

'Yup,' said Zeke. 'Sometimes I wish they wuz dead.'

To Mr Solomon Duvno, who was in the hospital after an operation, came Ellis Twersky, secretary of their synagogue. 'Sol,' said Ellis, 'I am bringing you the good vishes from our board – that you should get vell soon, comm back to the congregation, and live to be a hondred and tan years old – at least!'

'Oh, that's nice,' said Duvno. 'Vary nice.'

'*Nice?* Listen, Sol. That vasn't just a simple "get-better and goom-bye" from the board; it vas an official *rasolution* – '

'My!'

' – pessed by a vote of fourtin to saven!'

Scene: Toodle's Club, Mayfair

'Chadwick, old boy,' said Lord Effingham, 'may I have a word with you?'

'Of course, old man,' said Chadwick.

'Chadwick, old bean, I *do* hate to embarrass you, but I'm shaw you'll understand . . .'

'My dear Lord Effingham, fire away.'

The tenth earl cleared his throat. 'Well, then . . . I *say*, Chadwick . . . did you sleep with my wife last night?'

'Not a wink, old cock. Not a wink!'

Effingham beamed. 'Awfully decent of you, old chap. *Awfully* decent.'

The Reverend Selkirk from Aberdeen was visiting the Holy Land. He was especially moved by the Wailing Wall, where a long line of men, draped in prayer shawls, holding small prayer books, were swaying back and forth, murmuring their ancient prayers. Then the Reverend Selkirk noticed a man far from all the praying ones, standing alone before the wall. He had no prayer shawl, no prayer book; he was not swaying back and forth. Indeed he was not praying at all, it seemed; he stood erect and made gestures. . . .

The Reverend Selkirk walked over. '*Shalom*, friend. I dinna mean to be intrudin' . . . D'ye come here often, then?'

The figure turned. '*A*very day! Two o'clock, exactly, I am in this same place – for toity-vun years awready!'

'Och, mon! Therty-one years, is it? And how long d'ya pray?'

'Pray?' the Jew echoed. 'Who prays? I'm not praying. I talk to God, blessed be His name. I esk His advice.'

'Ay . . .' The reverend hesitated. 'I'm nae wantin' to pry, friend, but – what type o' advice?'

'All types. What should Israel do about Jordan? Who I should vote for? How I can convince my wife we should move to a smaller apartment? Should I let our daughter marry that no-good Shmuel Yavno?'

'My! . . . An' what does the good Lord tell you?'

'Ha!' the Jew snorted. 'Nothing! In toity-vun years – not vun void! . . . Mister, it's like talking to a *vall*!'

ᔕ

Stockholm: Borggren Department Store

Time: 5:55 P.M.

Throughout the store, on every floor, the ringing of a bell is heard.

VOICE (over loudspeaker): Five minutes to closing. . . . All shoppers, please note: store closes at six.

GUARD (at door): Olie. Hey, Olie.

SECOND GUARD: Ay?

FIRST GUARD: Olie, it's no good.

SECOND GUARD: What's no good?

FIRST GUARD: Bell. Ring, ring, ring. Every night the same. And still, every night, *some* dummy is the last one out.

ᔕ

The learned Viennese healer, Dr Leopold Lochmacher, said to his patient, 'Mrs Rhinebeck, zis terror you feel about lightning and t'under. . . . Zese are natural phenomena. Zey are not directed against *you*. Ze next time zere is a bad storm, and you begin to shake and shiver, do – do like *I* do.'

'What,' quavered Mrs Rhineback, 'do you do, doctor?'

'Ze moment I detect a storm, I crawl unter ze bed, put pillows over ze ears, and cry until zat goddamn trauma goes avay!'

◎

THE MAN WHO COULD SPEAK
EIGHT FISH DIALECTS

Scene: Gluckstern's Supreme Seafood

The waiter, a veteran fish-server of thirty years' standing, served 'Today's Special' with a flourish to a meek little man, a customer new to the piscatorial fare for which Gluckstern's Supreme was famed. 'So enjoy,' said the waiter, starting off – when he stopped short; for the meek little man had leaned over the plate, close to the flounder, and was whispering! To the fish!

The waiter exclaimed, 'Mister – !'

But the diner held up a silencing hand, now turned his *ear* close to the flounder, listened, nodded, turned to whisper something to the fish again, then listened again. . . .

The waiter could contain himself no longer. '*Mister!* What are you *doing*?!'

'I am talking mit de fish.'

'You talk to *fish*?!'

'Soitinly. I know eight fish dialects. I talk Flonder, Carp, Selmon, Pike, Vhitefish – '

'B-but what do you talk to them *about*?' the waiter goggled.

The little man said, 'Vell, take dis little flonder. Ven you put him in front of me, I leaned over and said, nice, polite, "Hollo dere, little flonder. How do you feel?" He said, "So-so." So I esked, "Fisheleh, vhere do you come from?" So he said, "Peconic Bay." So I esked, "*Nu*, how is everyt'ing in Peconic's Bay?" So he looked me straight in the eye, cold, and said, "How should *I* know? It's been *years* since I vas dere!"'

◎

Mr Fortescue, tossing and turning in an upper berth, could not get to sleep because, from the berth below, came a woman's mournful muttering. '*Oy* . . . am I toisty. . . . *Oy*, . . . am I toisty . . .'

On and on went the lament, until Mr Fortescue got out, crawled down the ladder, padded the length of the Pullman car, filled two paper cups with water, brought them back, and handed them through the curtains to the passenger in the lower berth. 'Madam, here. Water!'

'God bless you, mister! Thank you . . .'

Fortescue crawled back into his berth. He was on the very edge of somnolence when, from below, came the suspiration: '*Oy* . . . vas I toisty . . .'

At dinner, Señor Tilliera, a visitor from Brazil, said, 'My wife ees a wonderful woman. We are very, very hoppy, except for thees one thing: we hav no children.' He sighed. 'My wife ees – unbearable.'

Tilliera saw the others glance at each other and hastened to correct himself. 'What I mean: she ees inconceivable.' And when *this* brought amused exchanges, he exclaimed, 'Ah, no, no! My wife ees impregnable!'

At a meeting of the Parent-Teacher Association in Rego Park, the chairperson, Mrs Leona Potenik, said, ' – And now we come to the most important part of our meeting: the suggestion, from the board of trustees, that the salaries of our teachers should be adjusted entirely on a merit basis. Not length of service, age, degrees in education. Only merit. . . . Who would like to lead off the discussion?'

Up stood Mrs Rabinov.

'Yes, Mrs Rabinov?'

'Vat I have to say is straight, plain, and simple,' said Mrs Rabinov. 'Salary shouldn't matter if teachers are single *or* merit. Treat them just the same.'

Moke Scrogg's battered, fenderless, overladen jalopy, bearing Oklahoma licence plates, chugged up the George Washington Bridge. At the toll gate, Moke said to the attendant, 'Howdy.'

'A dollar and a quarter,' said the attendant.

Moke pushed back his weather-beaten hat, took the match from between his lips, and said, 'Giss Ah'll take et.'

Little Italy: New York

Dr Parelli examined Mr Mavocci's complete record – cardiogram, pulse rate, X-rays, blood count. . . . 'Mavocci, you no *seek*. But is not so good you *condition!*'

'What I should do?' anxiously asked Mavocci.

'What you hava to do is changa – changa whola way life. Ata you age, no more smoke, no more drink, no *dissiparsi* with the woman. . . . If you do alla thees – will be besta t'ing in world for you!'

Luca Mavocci had turned paler and paler. And when Dr Parelli finished his disheartening litany, Mavocci croaked. '*Dottore* . . . what is *nexta* best t'ing in world?'

⌒

Abner Gormitsky, having made a good deal of money in his leather works, was considering his wife's suggestion that they move from Central Park West to one of the tonier parts of Long Island. ' – and Abner, if we do that, I think we ought to change our name . . .'

After some weeks, the Abner Gormitskys became the Alexander Gormans, and they bought a fine mansion in Oyster Bay and furnished it with antiques. Their friendliness made friends for them easily, and their hospitality was so gracious, their cuisine so excellent, that the Gormans soon shone on the social scene. Indeed, they were invited to become members of the emphatically non-Jewish St Andrew's Country Club.

The trustees gave a huge welcoming dinner at the club for the newly elected St Andrewians; four couples: the Townsend Fillmores, the Clyde Watson-Setons, the Harley Hammonds, and the Alexander Gormans.

And there, at the head table, the liveried servant serving Mrs Gorman spilled an entire bowl of St Germain soup in her lap.

'*Oy!*' cried Mrs Gorman – but swiftly added, ' – whatever *that* means!'

⌒

Scene: Grocery store

'Are you the owner here?' asked Mrs Pozener.

'I am the owner here,' said Mrs Kadinsky.

'So – eh – how much is this' – Mrs Pozener pointed to a plump pickle in a tray on the counter – 'pickle here?'

'That pickle is a nickel,' said Mrs Kadinsky.

'A *nickel* for this pickle?' Mrs Pozener sniffed. She pointed to another, smaller pickle. 'So – how much is that pickleleh?'

'That pickeleh,' said Mrs Kadinsky, 'is a nickeleh.'

⌁

MRS ORLANDO: Hey, Carlotta! What you do? Almost I no reco'nizin' you! You grow seex inches ina one week? Or – eh! – you wearin' a weeg?!

MRS SALAZAR: *Sí.*

MRS ORLANDO: Imagine! Nobody could guess.

⌁

On Purim eve, finding himself in Tokyo on business, Mr Rubinoff asked the Japanese hotel clerk: 'Excuse me. Would you happen to know if there is a synagogue – here – in Tokyo?'

'Synagogue?' replied the clerk. 'Ah, so. *Is* synagogue. Reave hotel – ralk down street two brocks, turn reft – banzai! – is synagogue.'

So Mr Rubinoff left the hotel, walked two blocks, turned left, and there – lo and behold! a Star of David was on a door, and under it a small sign:

CONSERVATIVE SYNAGOGUE

Michio Myako, Rabbi

Mr Rubinoff entered. It was indeed a synagogue. The rabbi, the cantor, all the worshippers were Japanese. The Purim services had begun, and Mr Rubinoff happily joined in.

When the services were over, he went up to the rabbi and said, 'Rabbi, I am from America. I just want to tell you how happy I was to be here tonight.'

The Japanese rabbi beamed. 'Is honour! . . . But excuse, prease; you a Jew?'

'Certainly.'

'That's funny,' said the rabbi. 'You don't rook Jewish.'

⌁

Scene: Yorkville, New York City

Dr Schapentaur adjusted his head-mirror, turned off the overhead light, and directed the beam of a small flashlight into the left eye of Christian Yorgen ... then into the right eye.... 'Herr Yorgen,' said the doctor, 'I see nozzing wrong. ... How long you said you are seeing green spots in front your eyes?'

'Six-saven monz, Herr Doktor.'

'Did you go to ophthalmologist?'

'No, doktor.'

'Optometrist?'

'Alzo no.'

'Vell, Herr Yorgen, haf you seen any ozer doktor?'

'No. Only zose green spots.'

'Mrs Smolinsky,' said the doctor earnestly, removing the stethoscope from his ears, 'when did you last have a complete physical examination?'

'Must be ... let's see ...' Mrs Smolinsky screwed up one eye '... so long ago, I dun't even remember.'

'A year ago, five years ago?' the doctor insisted.

'Could be fife ...'

'Mrs Smolinsky, how many doctors have treated you – '

'Not vun!' exclaimed Mrs Smolinsky. 'I alvays pay!'

See also: **English Language, Freudian Slips, Goldwyniana, Jews, Just Jokes, Languages: Pitfalls**

Actors

The most important thing in acting, the one crucial factor is *honesty*. Absolute honesty ... Once you learn to fake that, it's a cinch.

John Wayne demonstrating facial isometrics, based on the technique of Calvin Coolidge.

Harvard Lampoon

The eternal triangle: An actor, his wife, and himself.

A well-known actor met a friend on Sunset Boulevard. 'Larry! How wonderful to run into you! Did you hear about the sensation my latest film is causing? Such reviews I've never seen in all my years on stage and screen. One critic said I'm sure to get an Oscar. Two directors said my performance will rank with—but forgive me, Larry. Here I go on rattling all about myself, and not a *word* about you. . . . Tell me, Larry, how did *you* like the film?'

An actor of more than ordinary vanity asked a friend. 'I sometimes wonder if my fans – you know how they admire my pictures – will still love me after my career – well, begins to go downhill?'
   'Of *course* they do,' said the friend.

Modesty: The artifice of actors, similar to passion in a call girl.
JACKIE GLEASON

See also **Hollywood, Reviews of Note.**

Advertisements

Note: Anyone who reads advertisements as a hobby, as my wife does, is certain to get an interesting (albeit curious) view of the economy, professions, unemployment, and any number of other matters. Here are some dandy examples.

AUTOMATIC BLANKET
Ensure sound sleep with one of our authorized
dealers.

BED FOR SALE
Four-poster, over 100 years old. Perfect for antique
lover.

Send no money. You will be bilked later.

FINE FURNITURE
At sensible prices. Antique, Colonial, and
Temporary.

TO ALL OUR PATRONS
This week, the Saturday matinee will be held on
Tuesday instead of Thursday.

Testimonial in advertisement: 'I used your soap two years ago and
have not used another since then.'

NOTICE
GNANASAMUNTHAMURTHI NAICHER intends to change
his name to Gnanasamunthamurthi Moodley, reports
the government *Gazette* in Durham (India).

'You can fool some of the people all the time, and all the people
some of the time, but you can't fool all the people all the time.'
That is the idea on which our business has been built up.

Rev Jarvis has spoken in the largest Baptist
churches in America. To miss hearing him will be
the chance of a lifetime!

Expert Stenographer: Wants work at home. Anything awful considered.

GIVE US YOUR DIRTY CLOTHES
Ladies! If you drive by our new launderette
and drop off your clothes, you will receive
very swift attention!

'Do you think advertising gets results fast?'
  'You bet I do.'
  'Can you prove that?'
  'Sure. On a Tuesday, one of my clients advertised for a night
watchman. That night his safe was blown open.'

ROOM WANTED
Young, sentimental, loving male. Loves to play. Wants Room and
Board with loving female. Cannot pay rent, but offers true love,
constant company, and 24-hour protection. Will serve as escort to

and from classes if desired. Will keep you warm all night long. Allows you complete freedom to date others. Call EG 4–6627.

DO NOT CALL unless you are truly interest in giving a home to this adorable puppy.

URGENTLY WANTED
BY MACHINE TOOL FACTORY
Male parts handlers
Box 132

'Bathing suit. 50% off' turns out to be topless, and 'Simple, elegant coat-hanger' turns out to be a nail.

DAVID FROST *and* ANTONY JAY

VIRGINIA BEACH
Comfortable apartments. Short walk
to beach. Daily or Weekly. Attractive
germs.

The strike committee met in a bra near the factory, a locale which created more drinking than discussion.

WANTED
Tamer lion, by lion tamer.

Ad in *Variety*

LIFE AND DEATH MATTER
Important Notice: If you are one of the hundreds of
parachuting enthusiasts who bought our course
entitled *Easy Sky Diving in One Fell Swoop* please
make the following correction:
On page 8, line 7, change 'state zip code' to 'pull
rip cord.'

See also **Applications, Bloopers, Radio and TV, Graffiti, Headlines That Haunt Me, Conversations I Cannot Forget, Movie Marquees, News Items That Haunt Me, Signs**

Advice

When a man comes to me for advice, I find out the kind of advice he wants, and give it to him.

JOSH BILLINGS

THE SIX COMMANDMENTS OF SATCHEL PAIGE
1. Avoid fried food, which angers the blood.
2. When your stomach disputes you, lay down and pacify it with cool thoughts.
3. Go light on the vices, like carryin' on at night in Society, 'cause the social ramble ain't restful.
4. Avoid running at all times.
5. Keep your juices flowin' by janglin' gently as you move around.
6. Never look back: something might be gainin' on you.

The only thing to do with good advice is pass it on: it is never of any use to oneself.

OSCAR WILDE

Always do right: this will gratify some people and astonish the rest.

MARK TWAIN

Never buy something you don't want merely because it is expensive.

OSCAR WILDE

Gretchen Plattenring, a sturdy, pleasant Swiss maiden, had been taking flute lessons since she was a child. Her idol was the celebrated flautist Pierre Bronteaux.

When the great Bronteaux arrived in Zurich for a series of concerts, Gretchen summoned up enough nerve to write him

```
Dear Maestro,

    Ever since I am small girl, you are my
idol.  I hear your every recording.  I
dream of also playing flute for you-and
receiving honest opinion.  That will mean
whole world to me!
```

```
    To answer, please-by phone 72-60, or
to mail address below.

                    Your admirer
                    Gretchen Plattenring
                    Flat D
                    196 Zwingli Strasse
```

To Gretchen's surprise and delight, the phone rang the next morning. 'Here is Klaus Umglick, Maestro Bronteaux's secretary. Please you come to Hotel Hofburg, eleven o'clock. Suite Three twenty-two, bringing flute, music, *und so weiter.*'

Promptly at eleven, an excited Gretchen knocked on the door of Suite 322. Pierre Bronteaux's secretary admitted her. 'I am Klaus Umglick. Now, Fraulein Plattenring, you must go into next chamber. Maestro awaits you. He is sitting by window. His eyes are closed. Do not talk to him, as he does not wish any distracting. He is already concentrating – entirely – on you . . .'

'Herr Umglick,' said Gretchen nervously. 'I should maybe *tell* which composition I play?'

'No, no.' sneered Umglick. 'The maestro know *every* composition for flute. You yust go in, bow, put sheet music on stand near piano – and play.'

Gretchen Plattenring entered. It was a fine room with an imposing chandelier, a grand piano – and, at the high French window, seated in a huge wing chair, facing her, his chin low, his eyes closed, was none other than Pierre Bronteaux.

Gretchen bowed her homage, put her music on the stand next to the piano, placed her flute to her lips, and began to play. . . . She played from Mozart's *Magic Flute* and from Debussy's *Afternoon of a Faun.* After each selection, she paused, glancing toward the large wing chair. But the maestro simply nodded and waved a finger, as if to say, 'Next piece . . .'

Gretchen played from Chopin and Boccerini.

Pierre Bronteaux sat expressionless.

Gretchen played pieces from Vivaldi and Stamitz. Still Bronteaux made no reaction.

Finally, Gretchen blurted. 'Maestro, shall I play more?'

The maestro opened his eyes. 'No, *merci.*'

Gretchen hesitated. 'What is your opinion? For my future – what I should do next?'

Pierre Bronteaux said. 'Get married.'

An unmarried southern belle asked her mother. 'But, mama, what can I give Charles? He simply has *every*thing!'

Mother smiled. 'Encouragement, my dear. Just give him encouragement.'

See also **Criticism, Fan Mail, Graffiti, Ingenuity, Kibitzers, Old Saws Sharpened, Sarcasm, Signs**

Answering Machines

When the recording machine at one executive's office went on the blink, his secretaries answered the phone: 'Hello. This is four-one-two, two, five, nine, two. Our answering machine is out of order. This is a real person talking.'

The man on the phone cried desperately, 'What do you mean "This is a recording?" *You* phoned me!'

When George Minter dialled Essex 8–6433 he heard, 'This is a recording. Essex-eight, six, four, three, three is not a working number. You have dialled the wrong recording.'

The chief executive of an international corporation so hated being disturbed at his home, fifty miles from the city, that he talked this message into his answering machine. 'This is Brentwood-six, nine, nine, oh, seven. If that is the number you wanted, leave your name and number. If Brentwood-six, nine, nine, oh, seven is not the number you dialled, hang up, try again, and don't be so goddamn stupid!'

See also **Computers**

Anti-Semitism

Mrs Chauncey Ashley III telephoned the headquarters of the infantry base near Great Oaks, her ancestral home. 'This is Mrs Chauncey Ashley the Third, and with Thanksgiving coming up, I thought it would be nice for us to have ten of your fine enlisted men share our family feast.'

'That's very kind of you, Mrs Ashley.'

'There's only one thing – I'm sure you understand: my husband and I prefer not to have any Jews...'

'Madam, I *quite* understand.'

When her front door bell rang on Thanksgiving Day, Mrs Ashley, dressed to the nines, hurried to the door herself. She flung it open. '*Wel*come to Great – ' She stopped, aghast.

Under the great portico stood ten smiling black soldiers.

'Omigod,' gasped Mrs Ashley. 'There has been a terrible mistake!'

The black sergeant said, 'Oh no, ma'am. Captain Finkelstein *never* makes a mistake.'

∽

When Herr Doktor Oskar Dorfman, associate professor of brain surgery in the University of Vienna's medical school, was denied promotion to a full professorship, a colleague confided to him: 'I was present when we discussed the promotion. You must never repeat what I shall tell you, Oskar—but you were turned down because – well, because you are a Jew.'

Doktor Dorfman nodded glumly. 'I suspected as much.... Who got the professorship?'

'No one yet, Oskar. A special committee, headed by Wolfgang Bloeringen, is searching for the right man.'

That night, after considerable thought, Dorfman sat down and wrote the following letter:

> Dear Prof. Wolfgang Bloeringen:
>
> Permit me to make a hearty recommendation for the vacant chair in Brain Surgery at the University: Rudolf Heffelklinger.
> I have known Herr Heffelklinger for seventeen years and can testify that he is

remarkably conscientious in the performance
of his duties, and exceptionally efficient
in how he performs them.   Furthermore,
he does not drink, works extremely hard,
and is happy with a relatively modest
salary.

Herr Heffelklinger, I should add, is
not an MD.   But he meets your primary
qualifications for the Professorship in
Brain Surgery; he is not a Jew.

Faithfully yours,
Oskar Dorfman, MD

P.S. Herr Heffelklinger can be reached at
1726 Kaiserstrasse, the same building in
which I have lived for the past seventeen
years.   He is the janitor.

Scene: Berlin, 1936

A Jew, crossing the street, accidentally bumped into a burly Storm
Trooper.

'*Schweinhund!*' snapped the Nazi.

'Goldberg,' bowed the Jew.

∽

Yorki Brastonyovich, commissar of education in Novgorod, came
to the elderly rabbi, one of the few Jews left in the region, and
said, 'It is well known that you Jews employ a special form of
reasoning, called Talmudic, which explains your cleverness. I
want you to teach it to me.'

'Ah, Comrade Commissar,' the old rabbi sighed, 'I fear you are
too old for that.'

'Nonsense! Why?'

'Well, when a Jewish boy wishes to study Talmud – we first give
him an examination. It consists of three questions. Those lads
who answer the questions correctly are admitted to the study of
Talmud: those who can't, are not.'

Yorki Brastonyovich glowered: 'Give me the exam!'

The old rabbi shrugged. 'The first question in the exam is: Two
men fall down a chimney. One emerges filthy, covered with soot;
the other emerges clean. Which one of them washes?'

'The dirty one, of course,' sneered Brastonyovich.

'Wrong, commissar. The clean one washes.'

'The *clean* one washes?' Brastonyovich was all astonishment. 'Why?'

'As soon as the two men emerge from the chimney,' explained the rabbi, 'they look at each other, no? The dirty one, looking at the clean one, says to himself, "Remarkable! To fall down a chimney and come out clean!" But the *clean* one, looking at the dirty one, says to himself, "We certainly got filthy coming down that chimney!" So *he*, the clean one washes . . .'

'Ah,' Brastonyovich, '*Very* clever! . . . Now let's have the second question.'

'The second question,' sighed the rabbi, 'is this: Two men fall down a chimney. One emerges filthy, covered with soot: the other emerges clean. Which—'

'That's the same question!' exclaimed Brastonyovich.

'No, no, commissar, please. This is an entirely different question.'

'Very well,' glowered Brastonyovich. 'You won't fool me. The one who's *clean* washes!'

'N-no,' sighed the rabbi.

'But you just told me—'

'That was an entirely different problem, commissar. In this one, the *dirty* man washes. Look: the two men look at each other. The one who is clean sees the dirty one and says, "My! How dirty *I* must be!" But then he looks at his own hands. He sees that he is *not* dirty. . . . But the dirty man, on the other hand, looks at the clean man and says, "Can it be?! To fall down a chimney and emerge so clean?" So *he* looks at *his* hands, and he sees that *he* is filthy. So it is he, the dirty one, who washes . . .'

'Clever, Jew,' muttered the commissar. 'Very clever. . . . Now the third question?'

'Ah, the third question.' The rabbi hesitated. 'The third question is the hardest of all.'

'Ask it! Ask it! You will not fool me again!'

'Very well.' The rabbi stroked his beard. 'Question three: Two men fall down a chimney. One emerges clean, the other – '

'But that's the same question!' cried Brastonoyvich.

'No, no, commissar. The *words* may be the same – but the problem is entirely new. . . . Which man washes?'

'The dirty one!' snapped Brastonyovich.

'Wrong,' murmured the rabbi.

'The clean one!'

'I'm sorry,' said the rabbi. 'Wrong again . . .'

'Then what is the right answer?' seethed Brastonyovich.

'The right answer,' said the rabbi, 'is that this is a cuckoo examination! How can two men fall down the same chimney and one come out dirty and the other come out clean? . . . Anyone who doesn't see that at once will, I'm afraid, never be able to understand Talmud.'

&

Gerhart Kleinschmitt did not like Jews. He also did not like Frenchmen, Italians, Englishmen, and Puerto Ricans. He especially did not like Frenchmen, Italians, Englishmen, and Puerto Ricans if they were Jews, too.

When the Norman Pivniks moved next door to Gerhart Kleinschmitt, in Hammond, Indiana, he was not happy. He made snide remarks to Mr Pivnik, obscene phone calls to Mrs Pivnik, and declared their little puppy a public menace.

One night, when the Pivniks were away, Kleinschmitt pried the little tin oblong (a *mezuzah*) off their front doorjamb and hurried home. He slid the cover off the *mezuzah*. Inside there might be dire evidence of some conspiratorial group. Fingers trembling with excitement, Gerhart Kleinschmitt opened a tiny scroll – on which was printed:

**HELP! HELP! We are prisoners in
Gerhart Kleinschmitt's *mezuzah* factory**.

&

In Leningrad, two KGB agents saw old Boris Glatkoff on a park bench – reading a book.

The first KGB agent asked, 'What is that book you are reading?'

'A book about grammar,' said Glatkoff. 'Hebrew grammar.'

The second KGB agent sneered, 'Why bother, Jew? We'll never let you go to Israel.'

'Well,' sighed Boris, 'I think that in Heaven, they speak Hebrew.'

'What makes you think you'll get to Heaven? Suppose you go to Hell?'

Boris shrugged. 'I already know Russian . . .'

See also **Behind the Iron Curtain, Communism, Jews, Russia**

Aplomb

Mendel Kissenbaum, aged seventy-three, assembled his three children and said, 'Dear children, I want to make an announcement to you. The life of a widower is very, very sad. It is ten years since your dear mother passed away. I want my remaining few years to be a *little* happier. So – well, I have decided to get married. To a very fine girl, a good cook – '

'"*Girl?*"' echoed Mendel's son Morton.

'Papa, did you say "*girl*"?' asked Mendel's son Ira.

'That's right.'

'*Papa!*' cried Mendel's daughter, Miriam. 'How old is this girl?'

'Nineteen.'

The room shook with the exclamations of astonishment and outrage. 'Papa, you are seventy-three!'

'It's a scandal, a *scandal!*'

'Papa,' cried Miriam, 'How can you even *think* of such a thing?! Aren't you *ashamed?*'

Mendel Kissenbaum cleared his throat. 'Why should I be ashamed? Children! Take hold of yourselves. After all, when I married your mother she was not even eighteen!'

Arthur Rampolovski, the internationally known concert pianist, was in his apartment on Central Park West, rehearsing furiously for his concert that night. He had issued strict instructions to his wife and Beulah, the maid: under no circumstances was he to be interrupted; he would see no callers, answer no phone calls, refuse all interviewers until the following day. . . .

The phone rang. Beulah swiftly lifted the receiver. In a low voice she murmured, 'This ez th' Rampolovski raisedence.'

'Hello,' came an agitated voice. 'Here is Mrs Czernov! Mrs Valdmir Czernov! It is emorgency! I *must* talk to maestro! At once!'

'M'z Czernov,' said Beulah, 'the maystrow ain't here.'

'What? *What* you say?' the woman demanded.

'Ah sayd, the maystrow ain't *in*.'

'And who are you?'

'Ah'm Beulah, the maid.'

At this point Rampolovski struck a loud, soaring arpeggio

'Look here, you maid!' the indignant caller snapped. 'I can hear the maestro playing. In foct, he is playing Tchaikovsky's First Concerto – '

'Oh, no, ma'am,' cried Beulah. 'No, that ain't maystrow. Thess me – jest dustin' the keys!'

$\backsim$

Scene: China Sea
Aboard H.M.S. Plantagenet

Midshipman Stacy, the Communications Clerk, knocked on the cabin door, on which a sign read:

```
        MEETING IN PROGRESS
     NO UNAUTHORISED PERSONNEL

          Hilary Staunton-Quade
          Captain
```

A buzz of earnest voices came from the cabin.

Midshipman Stacy rapped louder.

A disapproving lieutenant opened the door. '*Do* you not read English?'

'Yes, *suh*,' the midshipman faltered. 'But this m-message just came through, from the CQC, Fleet Manoeuvres. "Urgent!" For Captain Staunton-Quade.'

'Enter.'

There were a dozen men around the table, pouring over a huge map.

Stacy snapped to attention before Captain Staunton-Quade, saluted smartly, and barked, 'C-compliments of Leftenant Noland, suh! Urgent cable for CQC, Fleet Manoeuvres!'

Captain Staunton-Quade scarcely looked up, so intent was he in perusing the naval chart. 'Read it . . .'

'B-but, suh – '

'Just *read* it – aloud,' the captain repeated.

Stacy cleared his throat:

```
     To: Captain HMS Plantagenet
     From: Commander in Chief, Fleet Manoeuvres
     Your last three successive movements are
     without a doubt the most stupid, futile,
     transparent tactical follies I have wit-
     nessed in forty-one years at sea.
                                        COC
```

A hush had fallen upon the assembled brass and braid.

Captain Staunton-Quade drew erect, placed a monocle over his right eye, and said, 'Midshipman, take that cable back to Leftenant Noland – and have it decoded.'

See also **Can You Believe It?, Chutzpa, Diplomacy, Put-downs, Squelches, Stratagems, Texans**

Appearances

Only shallow people do not judge by appearances.

OSCAR WILDE

'Father Bryan, Father Bryan!'

'Yes, Mrs McGillicuddy?'

'I do believe me poor daughter's husband – Davey O'Shea – has been unfaithful to her!'

'Faith, an' that would be a terrible thing, Mrs McGillicuddy!' said Father Bryan. 'Are ye sure o' that?'

'Well,' huffed Mrs McGillicuddy, 'just you look at their baby, father. Does he bear the faintest resemblance to Davey?!'

$\backsim$

She has a winning smile, but a losing face.

BOB HOPE

Paris: Latin Quarter

Michelle Fauver, a pretty painting model, skipped up the stairs to the studio of Jacques Benoit, for whom she was posing in the nude. She entered the atelier with a bright, '*Bonjour*, M'sieur Benoit.'

'*Bonjour*, Michelle,' he sighed. 'No, no, *chérie*, don't undress. I'm not feeling up to snuff this morning. I don't feel like working. Sit down. Let's have some coffee. We'll get back to the painting tomorrow.'

They were having coffee, chatting about inconsequential matters, when Benoit suddenly froze. Footsteps were heard coming up the stairs. The painter listened, slammed down his cup, and said, 'My wife! Michelle, quick – take off your clothes!'

It was was Mr Kreyber's first trip to Israel. And after a few days, passing an optometrist's office, he dropped in. 'Doc,' he said, 'I'm having trouble reading, ever since I got here. Maybe it's the climate, maybe an allergy, maybe I need stronger reading glasses.'

The optometrist said, 'Let's see what we can do.' He asked Mr Kreyber to sit on a stool before a large optical chart. 'Now, sir, just read the letters on the bottom line.'

'Those tiny, *teeny* letters?!'

'Yes, if you can. Try.'

Mr Kreyber squinted hard. 'Nope, I can't.'

'Then try the next line up. The letters are larger.'

Mr Kreyber stared, narrowed his eyes, and shook his head. 'Sorry . . . no . . .'

'Then try the top line. The letters are quite large.'

Again Kreyber stared, squinted, and shook his head.

The optometrist frowned. 'Listen, mister. Do you realize you're almost *blind*!'

'Me? No, no, doc,' said Mr Kreyber earnestly. 'I just never learned to read Hebrew.'

See also **Accents, Can You Believe It?, Evidence, Hanky-panky, News Items That Haunt Me**

Applications

Note: What is true of Advertisements (*supra*) is also true of job applications. Personnel *mavens* have encountered the following:

> *Name:* Hortense Dressler
> *Sex:* Not yet

> *Denomination preference:* I prefer 'Jimmy'.

> *Marital status:* Eligible.

Reasons for wanting to become a teacher: June, July, August.

Person to notify in case of accident:

> Doctor, ambulance, or anyone nearby.

> *Beneficiary:* Melba Farwell.
> *Relationship to you:* Very nice.

Accident report

> *Condition of driver of other vehicle:* Poor.

How many people in department, broken down by sex:

> Drinking is more of a problem with us.

Insurance policy application

> *Beneficiary:* Alice P. Moody.
> *Relationship to you:* Miserable.

$\backsim$

'Your job application, Miss Cooley, looks quite good – but may I ask one question? You say your reason for leaving your last job was sickness.'

'Yes, sir.'

'Was the sickness serious, Miss Cooley?'

The pretty young girl thought for a moment. 'I never asked him.'

'*Him?*'

'My boss said he just got good and sick of me.'

$\backsim$

Name:	Violet Andrews
Address:	832 Eustace Way
Date of Birth:	Feb. 7, 1959
Weight:	6 pounds, 10 ounces
Height:	20 inches
Colour of hair:	None

Name:	Rinaldo Piaccelli
Address:	166 Mulberry St.

Length of residence: 29 feet

See also **Advertisements, Can You Believe It?, Graffiti, Signs**

Arabs

The sheik in his diaphanous kaffiyeh and embroidered slippers came into the women's dress department of I. Magnin's posh emporium in Beverly Hills. The saleswoman asked, 'May I help you, sir?'

He waved regally. 'I wish to inspect your garments.'

'Certainly sir.' She escorted the glittering figure down files and files of clothes racks, chattering away.

Finally, the oil prince stopped. 'Ah, *this* style I like. Very fetching . . . I'll take this lot.'

'"Lot?"' echoed the saleswoman. 'Sir, there are seventy to eighty dresses in this particular style – '

'Very good. Deliver them to this address.' He handed the bewildered clerk his card.

'But, sir – these dresses are different sizes!'

The sheik said, 'So are the ladies.'

Art

Sign in antique shop   **If you don't know what you want, we have it.**

Sign on music store   **Bach at 2 (Offenbach sooner.)**

Button worn by a Greenwich Village English major:

MARCEL PROUST

IS A

YENTA

There once was a sculptor named Phidias,
Whose judgment in art was invidious.
He carved Aphrodite
Without hint of a nightie,
Which outraged the ultra-fastidious.

Norwich Neo-Ultra-Abstract Gallery
175 Pine Street
Cleveland, Ohio

Dear Sir or Madman:

ᕦ

An *avant-garde* art gallery in Kensington was having a showing of
the latest Ultra-Abstract-Anti-Representational paintings of
Zoltan Ferrucci, plus the Symbolic-Neo-Neo sculptures of Nadya
Medveskovna, plus the Anti-Expressionist-Spectrum wire assem-
blages of Horton Corander-Nolting.

An American tourist from Texas sauntered about the gallery,
then stopped before a small, oblong, white panel, in the centre of
which was a tilted black prong. The Texan lady studied this *objet
d'art* for a while, then signalled to the gallery owner. 'I find myself
interested in this one.... *Very* provocative. I may buy it, for my
husband.'

'Madam – '

'Very *orig*inal. What does the artist call it?'

'The artist doesn't call it anything – '

'Ah, these geniuses. How they *hate* ordinary names...'

'Madam – '

'What would *you* call it?' asked the Texan lady.

'I, madam, believe that the most appropriate name would be:
"Light switch".'

ᕦ

Mr and Mrs Emmanuel Nudelman, taking a fiftieth-wedding-
anniversary trip to Paris, went to the Louvre. Past all the master-
pieces they slowly sauntered, marvelling at the display of genius.
'Look, Manny,' said Mrs Nudelman, stopping in front of a huge
Renaissance painting called *The Child in the Manger*.

'Colours ... beautiful,' said Mrs Nudelman. 'Although dark,
still very rich...'

'True,' said Mr Nudelman.

'You know what the scene is about, Manny? What it shows?'

'Certainly I know what the scene shows, Stella.'

'So why are you standing there with such a puzzled expression?'

'I have on a puzzled expression, because I can't figure the whole thing out!'

'What's to figure out?' asked Mrs Nudelman.

'What's to figure out, Stella, is this: here is a family living in a *stable*, with animals, the floor is *dirt*, covered with straw, and the little baby is naked...'

'So?'

'*So*, how could they afford to have their picture painted?!'

Arno Kunudsen, having made a fortune in toothpicks, began to buy *objets d'art* for his mansion in Oslo. He went off to the galleries of Berlin, Paris, New York.... When he returned to Oslo, it was with four large paintings, all by the same artist, the ultra-abstract-reductionist Arkady Jakolski.

Kunudsen held a reception to show off his treasures. The paintings were hung in successive rooms: the parlour, the library, the conservatory, the salon. Arno Kunudsen shepherded his guests from one room to the other: 'This the artist calls *Night Journey*.... Here, ya, is Jakolski's *Summer Storm* ... Here, yoost look: *Flaming Horse by Sea*....'

The only thing puzzling about the great Jakolski's canvases was their titles – each canvas was simple enough: a large surface, completely blank – save for a dot of blue. For *Night Journey*, the dot was in the upper right-hand corner. For *Summer Storm*, the blue dot was in the lower right-hand corner. *Flaming Horse by Sea* consisted of a dot in the upper left-hand corner....

'Now, Arkady Jakolski's latest composition!' Kunudsen ushered his guests into the salon. 'Yoost admire...' On a long wall hung a long oblong canvas, twice the size of the other three, and all white; but this painting contained *two* blue dots, in the exact centre. 'Jakolski's masterpiece!' exclaimed Kunudsen. '*Soul Reborn!*... Ay? So eloquent ... composition ... Jan Islak, tell me. What you feel?'

Jan Islak cocked his head to one side, narrowed his eyes, then murmured. 'Arno, ay wonder ... is it not too *busy*?'

∽

Laurence Alford had his easel set up in Regents Park and was painting a sylvan scene. Over his shoulder two cockneys, Howie and Harry, mufflers around their throats, were gravely watching.

After a while, Alford rested. 'Well, now,' he said to his observers. 'I should like your opinion, please. You, sir?'

'Blimey!' said Howie. 'Right bloody wonderful, Oy says. What about you, 'arry?'

'Loikwise,' said Harry. 'Guv'nor, how long'd you 'ave t' study t' do somep'n loike this?'

'To tell you the truth, sir, I never studied painting at all,' smiled Alford.

'Then,' said Howie. 'It'd 'ave t' be somep'n you – you inherited. Roight?'

'N-not necessarily,' said Alford. 'Take a fine painter like Tintoretto. Did you ever hear of Tintoretto's father?'

'Can't say as Oy 'ave.'

'Or Tintoretto's mother?'

'Naw.'

'Well there you are!' beamed Alford.

The two Cockneys looked at each other, then Howie said, 'T' tell you th' bloody truth, guv, we ain't never 'eard o' Tintoresky neither.'

Astronauts

In the debriefing of one of the first astronauts to return to Andrews Field from outer space, a psychologist asked, 'Can you tell us what was the very last thing that went through your mind just before lift off?'

'You bet,' said the hero. 'What kept running through my mind was the thought, "Every goddam part of this vehicle was supplied by the lowest bidder".'

∽

'Hey, grampa! You're alvays so cynical. Did you hear that we put a man on the moon!'

'Sure, sure.'
'Grampa, that feat cost ten billion dollars!'
Grampa cocked his head to one side. 'Including *meals*?'

'And on my sixty-fourth orbit,' said the astronaut, 'I made another
prayer.'
'*Another?*'
'Well, from that spot it's just a local call.'

Bachelors

Bachelor   A man who tries to avoid the issue.

A man who comes to work each morning from a
different direction.

SHOLEM ALEICHEM

Unlanded gentry.

OGDEN NASH

A man who has no children to speak of.

A man who is crazy to get married—and realizes it.

Bachelors are usually broad-minded:
in fact, they don't think of much else.

A bachelor never met a woman he couldn't live without.

He seems too good to be true – and isn't.

LOUIS SAFIAN

Hilary Follard, a very shy Englishman, was taking a cruise on the
SS *Frontenac*. At the table next to his, he noticed an extremely
attractive American woman. . . . The orchestra began to play a

popular tune, and from different parts of the dining salon, couples drifted on to the floor.

The Englishman glanced toward the American woman yearningly, but she was absorbed in her food. Follard's waiter leaned over him. 'And your entrée, sir?'

Follard said, 'I *say* I wonder if – well, could you do me a *very* great favour? . . . Do you see that charming lady? Well, could you be a good chap' – he slipped a pound note into the waiter's palm – 'and ask her – for the next dance?'

The waiter said, 'Anything to oblige, sir.'

Follard watched out of the corner of his eye. He saw the waiter go to the table, bow, and whisper to the American woman. She smiled, nodded, and rose. They glided on to the floor together.

In County Sligo

'Teddy, m'boy, do y' realize y're approachin' the fortieth year o' your birth and y're still a bachelor?'

'Ay, realize it I do.'

'But Teddy – in all them years, did y' not *once* think of tyin' the connubial knot?'

'Ay, many toymes,' said Teddy. 'An' that's why I stayed single.'

See also **Hanky-Panky, Just Jokes, Shadchens**

Banks

AT THE BANK

GIRL: Please give me change for this one hundred dollar bill.

TELLER: Of course – oh-oh. Miss, this is a fake one hundred dollar bill.

GIRL: Omi*god*! I've been raped.

A Texas billionaire made out a cheque for a huge sum of money. It bounced. Stamped on the cheque was:

INSUFFICIENT FUNDS

– under which was written:

Ours, not yours.

Sign on president's desk: **In this bank, 'No' is
a complete sentence.**

STROM: I'm phoning to ask if you got the cheque I sent you.
BIRKETT: Twice.
STROM: Twice?
BIRKETT: Once from you and once from the bank.

The Chase Manhattan Bank's memorable advertising campaign is
built around the slogan:

YOU HAVE A FRIEND AT CHASE MANHATTAN!

'Tis said that a sign in the window of the nearby Bank of Israel
reads:

– BUT HERE YOU HAVE RELATIVES!

TV Announcer in Biloxi, Mississippi

... So save a part of your pay cheque each week. Come into
Fidelity Bank. Save for the good things in life: a home, a new car, a
trip, a broad.

```
                    Bank of Powhatan
                    Powhatan, N.Y.
                    September 26


    A.D. Rogers
    112E. 47 St.
    New York, N.Y.

    Dear Sir:

        I have been examining your account,
    notably the sizable loans you have made
    since January 4.  You are now overdrawn
    $3,874 as well.
```

> May I suggest that we go back to the
> very pleasant relationship that existed
> between us before January 4-in which you
> banked with us.

>   Yours,

>   L.O. Morton
>   President

See also **Business**

Barbers

Sign in window of Hair Salon

FOUR BARBERS
Constant Discussion

To the fetching manicurist in the Ritz Barber Shop, Sheldon Caster, a compulsive skirt-chaser, smiled, 'When do you quit work?'

'Seven o'clock.'

'Well, how about you and me having dinner...'

'Sir, I'm married.'

Caster shrugged. 'Maybe your husband won't be home early.... Why not phone? Ask him.'

'Ask him yourself. He's just stropping his razor to give you a shave.'

Scene: Palermo Tonsorial Parlour

Marcello, the snappy barber, whipped the white cover around the new customer and asked, 'Okay, *commendatore*, a niza haircut, eh?'

'No,' said the stranger icily. 'Ia joost come in for a estimate!'

In a barber shop   **TO MEN OVER 40**

> **Don't worry about losing hair;**
> **think of it as gaining face.**

Sign in barber's window

> **During vacation of owner, a competent**
> **hair-stylist will be here.**

Behind the Iron Curtain

Stasya Korjagov, honoured for his exceptional productivity as a coal miner, was rewarded by his local Communist Party with a free tour in a group of twenty-four Heroes of Soviet Labour. To his friends, Korjagov promised he would send picture postcards from each country the group visited.

Here are the postcards Stasya Korjagov sent:

From Warsaw: Greetings from Free Poland.

From Berlin: Greetings from Free Germany.

From Prague: Greetings from Free Czechoslovakia.

Then there was a hiatus – not a word for eighteen days. At last came a postcard, postmarked Vienna, with this message.

> At last!
>   Free Stasya!

ᘐ

Yuri Pridlykev, the last Jewish engineer in the Kiev office of the Soviet Commissariat on Electrical Energy, had been ordered to move to a minor post in the faraway, godforsaken Siberian outpost of Stredna-Kolymsk. His parents, in tears, were watching him pack. 'I'll write every day,' said Yuri.

'But the censorship,' wailed his mother. 'They'll watch every word. They'll open every letter. Yissel,' she said to her husband, 'you must make a secret code – '

'No, no, codes are dangerous. Yuri, I have an idea. Anything you write in black or blue ink, we'll know is true. But anything you put in red ink, we'll know is nonsense!'

A month passed; then from Stredna-Kolymsk came a long letter – all in blue ink!

> Dear Mama and Papa,
>
>   I can't tell you how happy I am here in this workers' paradise! We are treated like kings. I live in a fine apartment- and the local butcher has meat every single day! There are many concerts, theatre, movies-all free. And there is not one tiny bit of anti-Semitism!
>
>   Your loving son,
>   Yuri
>
> P.S. Now that I think about it, there's only one little thing you can't find in Stredna-Kolymsk: red ink.

In Budapest, two strangers stood admiring a beautiful new automobile that was parked on Embassy Row. 'What automobile!' said the first man. 'How refined. How magnificent. Historic triumph for Communist engineering!'

The second man growled, 'It not Soviet car! It Cadillac. *American* car! Don't you know American car when you see one?'

'Sure. . . . But I don't know you. . . .'

The Communist journal *Izvestia* recently announced an important change in editorial policy.

NOTICE
TO ALL READERS

It is rumoured, by certain comrades who have been deceived by filthy capitalist-imperialist propaganda, that legitimate complaints from loyal members of the proletariat are not being published in the democratic Communist press. We intend to squelch these false baseless rumours once and for all. Starting immediately, we are instituting a

WORKERS' COMPLAINTS COLUMN.

It will appear three times a week. We will print the unedited letters of workers with a legitimate grievance – about their pay, conditions of labour, their supervisors.

Send in your Letter of Complaint now!

Important: Be sure to sign your letters. Print address and next of kin.

~

Lev Bryshkov stood before the three judges in Uzbek.

' – And your punishment is ten years of hard labour in Siberia! Have you anything to say?'

Lev cleared his throat. 'Comrade Judges, *tovarichi*. The United States is a terrible, decadent, capitalist country. It savagely exploits the proletariat. Hunger, unemployment, racism defile every corner of that reactionary land. Is that not right?'

'Right!' the three judges assented as one.

'Then why not, Comrade Judges, send me there?'

~

Pravda: The Russian paper that runs contests for political jokes, first prize being thirty years.

IRVING R. LEVINE

~

Medical circles are abuzz with the news from Warsaw: Dr Jaczi Gredzinczki just announced he has performed history's first successful transplant of an appendix.

~

Mrs Czernik marched into the leading toy store in Poznan. 'My son is having a birthday tomorrow. I want to buy him a fine bicycle.'

'We have no bicycles,' said the manager.

'*What?* A big toy store without bicycles?'

'We have only *tricycles*,' said the manager.

'Tricycles are for little boys. My son is twelve years old! You expect him to ride a tricycle?'

'Psst.' The manager beckoned Mrs Czernik to one side. 'Buy the tricycle, and don't worry. Before the week's over, one wheel is absolutely sure to drop off.'

An English tourist came out to the best hotel in Warsaw and looked about for a taxi. None was to be seen. He walked several blocks and saw a cab, parked at the curb. The Englishman said, in accented Russian, 'Driver, are you free?'

'No. I'm Polish.'

See also **Communism, Russia, Stratagems**

Bloopers, Radio and TV

Here, collected with profound gratitude down many years, are some choice boo-boos, boners, malapropisms, and spoonerisms cheerfully committed on American, Canadian, and British radio/television programmes.

L. R.

'Good evening, ladies and gentlemen of the audio radiance.'

' – and when the Queen arrives you will hear a twenty-one sun galoot.'

'We take you now to Rome, where we will hear the Christmas greeting from His Holiness, Pipe Poess the Fifth.'

'It is a privilege to present to you now the distinguished Virgin of Governor's Island.'

'You have been listening to a message by our Honourable Minister of Wealth and Hellfire.'

'I am very happy to speak to you over this nationalwide hick-up.'

'The first thing the doctor has to do when a baby is born is he has to cut the biblical cord.'

'Don't fail to miss tomorrow's double-header.'

' – this company is America's largest producer of alceminum, magnoosium, and stole.'

' – and at Fonseca's Pharmacy you can be sure of having your prescriptions filled with scare and kill.'

'This news roundup has come to you through the wild-world facilities of the Appoicated Sess.'

See also **Boo-Boos, Freudian Slips, Goldwyniana, Malaprops, Old Saws Sharpened, Typos**

Boasts

Al ('Alkali') Crawford, a Texan, driving down a great flat desert in Israel, spied a tiny house in the distance, with a neat picket fence. An old man, wearing a skullcap, was leaning on the fence.
    Alkali stopped in front of him. 'Ha there . . .'
    'Hollo.'
    'You speak English, friend?'
    'Oh, sure.'
    Alkali put out his hand. They shook hands. Then Alkali said, 'You own this little house?'
    'Yes.'
    'Man, what in the world do you *do* way out here to hell an' gone?'
    'Oh, I raise up chickens.'
    'Mmh. And how large is your property?'
    'Well,' said the Jew, 'in front, it's a good eighty fitt—and in back, must be a hundred, a hundred and ten, at *least*.'
    Alkali grinned. 'Well, sir. I'm not aimin' to brag, but you just might be innerested to know that back home, on *my* ranch, I get up and after breakfast I get in m' car, around nine AM, and I start to drive – and I drive and drive and drive, and I don't reach the end of m' property until six o'clock that night!'

'Tchk, tchk!' sighed the Israeli. 'I once owned a car like that.'

Strom Germond, a loyal son of Texas, was visiting Washington, DC. At a dinner in his honour, Strom boasted of the wonders of his beloved state – and of his own riches. 'Now, I know some of you folk will find this hard to believe, but it jest happens I have *five hundred* head of the finest St Gertrudis cattle!'

Another Texan spoke up. 'Oh, come off'n it there, Strom. I know heaps of Texans own five hundred head of cattle!'

Germond drew himself up in *hauteur*. 'In their *freezer?*'

ROTH: People say you always act like such a wise guy, Goldfarb. As if you knew everything!

GOLDFARB: Not *every*thing. But it happens I know a lot, so people are jealous.

ROTH: You know anything about – tennis?

GOLDFARB: Why shouldn't I know about something as simple as tennis? What makes you ask?

ROTH: Because my boy Sheldon has begun to take lessons from a pro.

GOLDFARB: For what position?

The Erwin Schlangers, just returned from a Marco Polo All-Expense Tour around the world, were regaling their friends in Milwaukee with tales of their travel. 'China?' Erwin replied to one question. '*Far*. Also crowded. And we never got any of that great food they serve big shots.'

'India?' Gerta Schlanger answered someone. 'You could *die* from seeing such poverty, misery, sickness – and those crazy *cows* dumping on the sidewalks . . .'

On and on came the questions, and the candid answers of the voyagers.

'Venice? Okay if you like water instead of streets.'

'So Madrid? You seen one bullfight you seen them all.'

'Paris? Mi*god* is that town expensive! And the traffic is so noisy you can't hardly sleep.'

'In Rome,' said Mr Schlanger, 'you can't cross a street. Those drivers are *mur*derers. And the whole town smells . . . gasoline fumes, bus fumes, garbage ... But still, it was a high spot – on account of, as Gerta will tell you, we had an audience with – the pope!'

'Hey!' 'Wow!' 'That must of been some thrill! ...' 'Tell me, Gerta, what was your impression?'

'*Him*,' said Gerta Schlanger, 'I liked. *Her*, I didn't.'

It ain't bragging if you really done it.

'DIZZY' DEAN

See also **Kibitzers. Put-downs, Squelches, Texans**

Boo-boos (from the Press)

1.   A verbal mistake: a *faux pas*.
2.   An embarrassing error.
3.   A blunder.
4.   (Originally) Accidental loss of bowel contents by a baby or child.

This euphemism rocketed to public attention around 1949–1950 as a trademark of a the comedian Jerry Lewis in nightclub and television skits with his then partner Dean Martin.

Boo-boo began as a parent's/nurse's code word (like BM) for a child's 'accident' in diapers or panties. It was, because expressive and amusing, inevitably taken up by children.

Boo-boo became popular among radio and television performers for it was a funny sounding, indispensable label for any *faux pas*:

'In front of the whole class? What a *boo-boo*!'

'If I don't get to a men's room fast, will I make a *boo-boo*!'

Among Gentiles in the Bronx and other boroughs, the tympanic *boom-boom* served as the genteelism for 'bowel movement'.

from my *Hooray for Yiddish!*

The bride was wearing a gorgeous old lace gown that fell to the floor as she came down the aisle.

Despite the many delays, the game began promptly 35 minutes late.

Mr and Mrs Walter F. Hill announced the coming marriage of their daughter Helene. No mate has been selected for the wedding.

The area in which Miss (Jane) Russell was injured is famed for its beauty.

At this point the gallery of golf fans deserted the champion to watch Miss T—, whose shorts were dropping on the green with remarkable regularity.

In a club magazine

> The three-day outing is climaxed
> by a huge picnic, which practically
> doubles the town population each year.

When the baby is done drinking it must be unscrewed and laid in a cool place under a tap. If the baby does not thrive on fresh milk it should be boiled.

As for this puzzler: 'Was it he you were talking to?' or 'Was it him you were talking to?' Mr Lewis says the correct sentence would be: 'Was it he to whom you can also say it was she I were talking.' However, he adds, was thinking about.

'Her dark hair is attractively set,' said Miss Fryn, 'and she has fine fair skin – but,' she admits ruefully, 'it comes out in a mass of freckles at the first sign of sin.'

Dr N— had another patient in the same apartment house, so he figures he could kill two birds with one stone.

In a pharmacy window: On every prescription,
                           we dispense with care.

The banquet began with a vote of thanks to the chairman who had resigned, for his contribution.

In a firm voice, the bride then repeated . . . 'to love and to cherish, in sickness and in health, for poorer or richer, until debt do us part.'

'Those shoes? I only use them for street-walking.'

'Why some parts of the Grand Canyon are a mile deep – and two miles high.'

'They better not fool around with that A-bomb. It's dynamite.'

'He wants to be cremated, because he doesn't believe in death.'

'Oh, did he make a wrong mistake!'

'A girl of seventeen is much more of a woman than a boy who is seventeen.'

'The heroine has to be like Julius Caesar's wife – all things to all men.'

'She is a middle-aged child.'

'Do you wake up feeling tired and lustless?'

'You get just what you pay for – and you don't pay very much.'

'It strikes me as funny, don't you?'

'In exactly thirty seconds, it will be approximately one fifteen.'

'Her father was a civil serpent.'

from my Rome Wasn't Burned in a Day

Usher: 'May I sew you to your sheet?'

Singer: 'I have dedicated the next song to our queer old dean.'

Texan: 'That blow-hard? He's the biggest lamb dyer in Texas!'

Churchgoer: 'Excuse me, ma'am, but is that pie occupewed?'

See also **Advertisements, Bloopers, Radio and TV, Can You Believe It?, Churches, Freudian Slips, Headlines that Haunt Me, How's That Again?, Typos**

Bores

Bore:
Someone who, upon leaving a room, makes you feel that some-one fascinating just walked in.

Someone who talks, when you want him to listen.

AMBROSE BIERCE

We often forgive those who bore us, but we cannot forgive those whom we bore.

ROCHEFOUCAULD

He deprives you of solitude and doesn't provide you with com-pany.

The new patient, a most proper Englishman of forty or so, sat down opposite Dr Cruikshank. 'Now Mr Fotheringdale,' said the doctor, 'what brings you to consult me?'

'Can't say, really,' said Mr Fotheringdale, 'except – yes – prob-ably hope. Sheer hope, I daresay. Mmh. Yes. Hope. That you can – perhaps – give me some measure of relief...'

'Relief? From pain, sir?'

'Oh, no. Nothing as *dram*atic as pain, doctor.... It's – well, to be perfectly frank about it, it's a – it's this *fright*ful habit I have...'

Dr Cruikshank waited.

'Had it since I was at school. Caused a bit of trouble there, I might say.... Then I was in the services. Four years.... Saw a bit of this rum old world, I did – '

'About the habit that distresses you ...' the doctor gently inter-jected.

'Ah, yes. Sorry. This habit – quite simple, really. It's – talking.

That's all. Just talking . . . to myself, I mean. All day long. And in my sleep. Talk, talk, talk. Been going on like that for years and *years*. Talk . . . talk . . .'

'My dear Mr Fotheringdale,' said Dr Cruikshank easily, 'that is not such a worrisome thing. A good many people, I'm sure you know, talk to themselves . . .'

'Oh, yes. I daresay. Quite so.'

'Then why does it upset you?'

'Well, sir, they may talk and talk . . . but . . .' Fotheringdale sighed.

'Yes?'

'But I very much doubt, doctor, whether *any* one of them, any- where in the world, is as completely, unutterably, unrelievedly *boring* as I am.'

See also **Just Jokes, Psychiatrists, Shlemiels**

Business

Myron P. Walton, the most successful salesman on the insurance company's staff, was especially skilful in using the telephone. Prospects often agreed to Walton's suggestion that he come to their home to discuss a policy.

One day, Walton called a number on his list of prospects. 'He- vo,' came the high, thin voice of a child.

'Hello, there,' Walton chuckled. 'And what's *your* name?'

'Jamie.'

'Are you a boy or a girl, Jamie?'

'I'm a *boy* . . .'

'That's nice. Jamie, can I please talk to your father?'

'He's not here.'

'Then could you put your mother on the phone?'

'She went with my daddy.'

'Well, is there someone else there I can talk to?'

'Would you like to talk to my sister?' asked Jamie.

'Fine. Can you call her to the phone?'

'Okay.'

A long silence ensued. Then Walton heard the little boy's voice again. Mister?'

'Yes, Jamie?'

'I can't lift her out of the playpen.'

⌒

Andrew Hamilton struck it so rich in London, that on an impulse he sent his father in Dundee a magnificent fur-lined overcoat – and soon after telephoned the old man. 'Well now, dod, an' how'd – '

'Andy, lad, that coat is a very marvel! The fur is fine as a wee one's bottom. And *warm*! By all the saints, Andrew, m' old mackintosh is not fit to be worn next t' it!'

'I'm so glod, dod – '

'But y' should na be spendin' mooney like that, lad. That coat must cost three hoondred pounds!'

'Do na worry, dod. I got it wholesale. It cost me but two.'

Several weeks later, Hamilton received this letter from his dear dad in Dundee:

> Andrew, my boy-Send five more of the same
> coat. I sold mine for two-fifty.
>
>   Dad

⌒

A beggar knocked on the door of the rich man's house at six thirty in the morning. There was no answer. He knocked and knocked again.

The rich man opened his window and cried down. 'How *dare* you wake me up so early?'

'Listen,' said the beggar, 'do I tell you how to run your business? Don't tell me how to run mine.'

⌒

'Hello there, Chuck. Ain't seen you in ages.'

'Yeah. How're you, Steve?'

'Moving along, moving along. Tell me, Chuck, how's your plumbing business?'

Chuck wrinkled his nose. 'Don't ask!'

'Oh,' Steve paused, then, with a bright smile, added, 'Hey, for this time of year, that's not bad!'

⌒

Gershon and Velvel, old friends, went fishing off the coast of Fort

Lauderdale. It was a marvellous day, and the fish were biting. Suddenly, a tropical squall darkened the sky, the clouds dropped a ton of rain, and the waves smashed the boat. Soon Gershon and Velvel were floundering in the boiling waters.

'Gershon?!' shouted Velvel. 'Are you okay?'

'Velvel!' gulped Gershon. 'I'm okay.'

'Don't try to swim to shore!' cried Velvel. 'It's too far! Float! Do you hear me?'

'Yes!' cried Gershon. 'I'm floating! But Velvel – can *you* float alone?'

'*Gottenyu!*' wailed Velvel. 'Is this a time to talk business?!'

∽

One morning, every office at IBM headquarters bore the now-famous admonition on one of its walls:

THINK

The next morning the executives arrived to find, beneath the sign, this addition:

OR THWIM

∽

'Fifaty cents a roll?' exclaimed Mrs Barbella. 'Cilento, acrossa street, he is ask onaly forty!'

'So you go acrossa street anda buy.'

'Today, Cilento isa sold out.'

'Mrs Barbella, when *I* ama sell out, I charga only t'irty cents!'

∽

Jim Fadden, of the Peerless Employment Agency, telephoned Mr Langley, president of Langley Textiles. 'Mr Langley, I hope you can verify a few facts given to us by a client who used to work for you and is now looking for a good job.'

'What's your client's name?' asked Langley.

'Hardwick. Bob Hardwick.'

'I remember him. What do you want to know?'

'How long did Hardwick work for your firm?'

After a pause, Langley said, 'About two weeks.'

'*What?* Hardwick said he'd been in your employ for four years!'

'That's right.'

Sign in cashier's office: **There is no such thing
as petty cash.**

See also **Banks, Chutzpa, Clothes, Hotels, Ingenuity, Salesmen, Stock Market, Stratagems**

Can you believe it?

There were only two automobiles in the state of Ohio in 1895. They collided.

JOHN TRAIN, True Remarkable Occurrences

Five thousand people were polled by *Collier's* magazine (May 1949) and asked:

What is bought and sold on the
New York Stock Exchange?

Sixty-four per cent replied:

Livestock

RADIO GEMS

'MEN! For Christmas, give your wife a gorgeous Gruen!'
(Repeat, increasing tempo, until light dawns.)

'And now, folks – stay stewed for the nudes!'

TRUE TALE

MRS CHARLES LARKIN
ROUND HILL ROAD
GREENWICH, CONN.
DENVER CONFERENCE GREAT SUCCESS. ARRIVE NEW YORK
TONIGHT. MEET ME AT OPERA 8.15 HAVE GOTTEN TICKETS.
LOVE.

CHARLIE

Mr Larkin arrived at the opera, where he met his wife – plus eight friends.

Her telegram clearly said:

HAVE GOT TEN TICKETS

Suppose you are driving through the back country of Iraq one fine spring day. And suppose you see (as you will) that the faces of all the calves are purplish in colour, all the chicks are green, all cows' udders are red, and all bulls' dangling testicles are blue.

You would blink, of course, and look again, and swear off the hard stuff, but the astonishing colours would not disappear.

Why? Because superstitious natives in Iraq think that fearful gods demoralize the fornication of animals, thus freezing their fertility. Each spring, therefore, the natives paint their precious livestock in colours to outwit the ancient demons. The colours are dictated by tradition. I do not know what effect the painting has on the animals; it certainly enchants tourists.

from my The 3:10 to Anywhere

From a newspaper I received the intriguing news that a Mrs Elizabeth Hammond, of Gillette, N.J., owns a pet nine-hundred-pound elephant, called Mignon, who sleeps in the living room, turns on the TV when bored, and blinks lamp lights on and off to signal that she is going to sleep.

The neighbours think that Mrs Hammond is bereft of cranial marbles, but her husband and children have accepted Mignon as just another revelation of the lady's love of animals, which include a pet lion cub, three dogs, a horned owl, a bobcat, and a python twelve feet long.

Mrs Hammond used to train animals for their debut on the stage of the Metropolitan Opera. Perhaps the most startling aspect of all this *mishegoss* is that Mignon, who was born in Thailand, has developed a passion for roast beef sandwiches.

from my Passions and Prejudices

In the lounge of an old inn in the Cotswolds, I browsed through a country weekly. One item still haunts me: a letter addressed to the Dean of the Augustinian Order in Guisborough, England, had been returned to its sender with the address crossed out and this correction written by some local minion in Her Majesty's Royal Post Office:

> This monastery was
> dissolved in 1540.

**NATIVES IN NEW GUINEA
DISTURBED BY MANNEQUIN**
Port Moresby, New Guinea, Dec. 19 (UPI) – The appearance of the first mannequin in a store window in New Guinea's primitive eastern highlands has created havoc among natives.

Hundreds of natives in the town of Goroka have gathered outside the store's display window for days, wailing and conducting dances to honour the dead, in the belief that the dummy is a corpse.

See also **Appearances, Embarrassing Moments, Evidence, News Items That Haunt Me, Snafus, Texans, True Tales, Waiters**

Characterizations

He has dined in the finest homes in England – once.

OSCAR WILDE

His mind is open – so open that ideas simply pass through it.

F. H. BRADLEY

He is a man without a single redeeming defect.

DISRAELI (of Gladstone)

He could not see a belt without hitting below it.

MARGOT ASQUITH (of Lloyd George)

He gave her a look you could pour on a waffle.

RING LARDNER

He had all the backbone of a chocolate eclair.

THEODORE ROOSEVELT (*of William McKinley*)

'I may not know much, but I know chicken-shit from chicken salad.'

LYNDON JOHNSON (*of a speech by Vice-President Richard Nixon*)

'One good thing about being president. Nobody can tell you when to sit down.'

DWIGHT D. EISENHOWER

He is by all odds the most interesting man he has ever known.

L.R.

He is one of those people who would be enormously improved by death.

H. H. MUNRO ('*Saki*')

You can lead a horticulture, but you can't make her think.

DOROTHY PARKER

(He respects nothing and nobody.) Why, I once heard him speak disrespectfully of the equator.

SYDNEY SMITH

He is every other inch a gentleman.   REBECCA WEST

He has not an enemy in the world, but none of his friends like him.

OSCAR WILDE

While he was not dumber than an ox, he was not any smarter either.

JAMES THURBER

Her cooking suggested she had attended the *Cordon Noir*.

L.R.

He wasn't hostile to facts; he was apathetic about them.

WOLCOTT GIBBS

He is insane, but he has lucid moments, when he is merely stupid.

HEINRICH HEINE

His judgment is so poor that he runs a risk every time he uses it.

EDGAR WATSON HOWE

There's someone at every party who eats all the celery.

FRANK ('KIN') HUBBARD

I despise the pleasure of pleasing people whom I despise.

LADY MARY WORTLEY MONTAGU

If not actually disgruntled, he was far from being gruntled.

P. G. WODEHOUSE

'When you're as great as I am, it's hard to be humble.'

MUHAMMAD ALI

The butler entered the room, a solemn procession of one.

P. G. WODEHOUSE

On the stage, he was natural, simple, affecting; it was only when he was off-stage that he was acting.

OLIVER GOLDSMITH

He charged nothing for his preaching, and it was worth it.

MARK TWAIN

See also **Put-downs, Repartee, Sarcasm, Squelches, Wit**

Chelm

Chelm (pronounce the *Ch* as in the German 'Ach!' or the Scottish 'loch' – as if expelling a fishbone from the roof of your mouth) is a Jewish mythical town, in which all the inhabitants are fools, simpletons, dumb-bells. Chelm is the Jewish equivalent of the legendary Gotham, whose wisemen were idiots.

〜

The most popular fad in Chelm is a game called 'Guess Who?' Any number of players can play. The rules are simple. One player leaves the room: the others must guess who it was.

〜

The elders of Chelm decided to give Yussel, the perennial indigent, a face-saving job. 'Yussel, we will pay you two zlotys a day. Sit on the hill outside our little village every day, from dawn to sunset.'

'Two zlotys!' exclaimed Yussel ecstatically. 'What do you want me to do there?'

'We want you to be our lookout – for the approach of the Messiah.'

'Pssh,' cried Yussel, slapping himself on the cheek. 'The Messiah! And if I see him coming, what should I do?'

'When you see him, you run back to the *shtetl* as fast as you can, shouting, "The Messiah! The Messiah! He is coming!"'

Yussel's face lighted up just thinking of the glory.... Every morning he greeted the dawn from the hill outside Chelm. He did not budge. He brought a bag of black bread and radishes and cheese, and a little container of tea, to nourish him during the day. And not until sunset did Yussel leave his treasured post.

One day, a year later, a traveller approached the little village and noticed the figure sitting on a hill. '*Sholem aleichem*,' called the traveller. 'What are you doing on this hill?'

'I am waiting for the Messiah. It's my job. I sit here all day, every day!'

The traveller suppressed a smile. 'Confidentially, how do you like this job?'

'Ssssh!' Yussel looked about. 'Frankly, it doesn't pay much – but it's steady!'

〜

The rabbi of Chelm visited the prison, and there he heard all but one of the inmates insist on their innocence. So he came back, held a council of wisemen, and recommended that Chelm have *two* prisons: one for the guilty and another for the innocent.

⌒

'How just is the Lord,' said a sage from Chelm. 'He gives the food to the rich – and the appetite to the poor!'

⌒

The sages of Chelm began to argue about which was more important to the world: the moon or the sun. The community divided into two passionate camps. The reigning wiseman then ruled: 'The moon *must* be more important than the sun, because without the light of the moon our nights would be so dark we could not see anything. The sun, however, shines only by day – which is when we don't need it!'

⌒

In Chelm, after many years of research, they finally invented an entirely new brand of parachute. 'People all over the world will be talking about the Chelm parachute!' boasted an elder. 'It is unique!'

'What,' asked a visitor, 'makes it unique?'

The elder laughed. 'What makes it *unique?* Mister, it's the only parachute in the world that is guaranteed to open *every time* on impact.'

⌒

Two Chelmites were discussing the wonders of scientific research. 'Listen,' said Minkus, 'let's you and me do an experiment. Maybe it will make us famous!'

'Fine,' said his brother Shlomo, 'What should we experiment about?'

Minkus looked around. On the sleeve of his brother's jacket he saw a flea. Carefully, he reached out, caught the insect, tore off one of its legs, and, putting his mouth close to the flea, said, 'Jump! . . . Jump! . . .' and nudged the insect. The flea did just what Minkus had ordered. Minkus spent the day ordering the flea to jump – and the flea jumped each time.

'That's wonderful,' said Shlomo.

'Tomorrow,' said Minkus, 'we'll teach him to jump *backward.*'

The next day, Shlomo tore another leg off the flea, chanted, 'Back! Back!' and nudged the flea from the front. After several hours, the flea had learned to jump backward. . . .

On the third day, Minkus removed a third leg of the flea, and called 'Circle! . . . Circle!' nudging the flea to rotate on its axis. But the flea did nothing. Minkus removed the fourth leg from the flea and cried 'Circle! Circle . . .' The flea remained motionless.

'Aha! You've done it!' cried Shlomo.

'*Done* what?'

'You've proved that when you remove the legs of a flea it destroys his sense of hearing.'

Sleep faster: we need the pillows!

THE WISDOM OF CHELM

Things were getting worse (and worser) in Chelm. Jobs were virtually nonexistent. Food was running low. To find some solution, the elders met. After prolonged analysis they decided that the best hope for Chelm was for the town to develop and sell a new brand of beer.

After considerable experiment, they produced a liquid they thought not bad—and sent a gallon to a famous brewmaster in Prague, with this letter:

O Worthy Brewmasters:

Seeking to help our poor, we have produced a beer that we can sell. We are humble folk, not known, so it would help our cause if a famous brewer such as you praised our potion.

May the Holy One, blessed by His name, speed your answer.

The Elders of Chelm

A week later came the answer from Prague:

Your horse has diabetes.

In Chelm (so 'tis said), one night a citizen ran to the fire station, yelling at the top of his lungs: 'Theatre! Theatre! Help! Theatre!'

In Chelm, they go to the dentist to have their wisdom teeth put in.

See also **Dummies, Nebechs, Shaggy Dogs, Shlemiels**

Children

Scene: The Porch of a Summer Hotel in the Catskills

The two women were rocking back and forth, gazing at the lovely sunset.

'And how many children,' asked Mrs Alpert, absently, 'do you have?'

'No children,' sighed Mrs Minkoff.

'*No* children?!' blinked Mrs Alpert incredulously. 'Tell me, Mrs Minkoff, if it's not too personal, what do you do for aggravation?'

ᧈ

Childhood: That wonderful time when all you had to do to lose weight was to bathe.

KIM MCGINNIS

Mrs Botnick and Mrs Krasnitz had not met in years. 'Tell me,' asked Mrs Botnick, 'whatever happened to your son?'

'My son – what a misfortune!' wailed Mrs Krasnitz. 'He married a girl who doesn't lift a finger around the house. She can't cook, she can't sew a button on a shirt; all she does is sleep late. My poor boy brings her breakfast in bed, and all day long she stays there, loafing...'

'How terrible,' said Mrs Botnick. 'And what about your daughter?'

'Ah, my daughter!' beamed Mrs Krasnitz. 'She married a man, an angel! He won't let her set *foot* in the kitchen. He gives her a full-time maid, a cook, and every morning he brings her breakfast in bed! And he makes her stay in bed all day...'

ᧈ

A universe of aspiration lies in the heart-felt cry of a Jewish woman at the seashore:

'Help! Help! My son the doctor is drowning!'

ᧈ

> The saddest words of tongue and pen:
> We just sold the buggy; then –

Mrs Kotchin and Mrs Mishkin sat rocking on the porch of the Villa Lipshitz, a Catskill resort, when a young man approached.

'*Gottenyu!*' exclaimed Mrs Kotchin. '*Look* at that boy! Did you ever see such a big nose? Such shifty eyes? Such a crooked mouth?'

In a freezing voice, Mrs Mishkin replied, 'It so happens, you are talking about my son!'

'Well,' said Mrs Kotchin, 'on *him*, it's becoming!'

See also **Famous People (as seen by Children), Kids' Stuff, Mothers**

Churches

On church bulletin board

Today's Sermon

HOW MUCH CAN A MAN DRINK

with hymns from
a full choir

On church bulletin board

Sermon Sunday Feb. 6:
Change Your Wife Through Prayer.

The Tuesday Night Ladies Club had a nice time at the church after their pot-luck supper. For the first time in several months all the members were pregnant.

Church bulletin

Miss Marcia Devin sang 'I Will Not Pass This Way Again', giving obvious pleasure to the entire congregation.

Correction

The sermon at the Presbyterian Church this coming Sunday will be

There Are No Sects in Heaven.

The subject was incorrectly printed in yesterday's edition of the *Clarion* as

There Is No Sex in Heaven.

Notice on church bulletin board

Sunday. Rev. M. Farnsworth will talk on:

ETERNITY AND YOU

**Come early – if you want to be sure of
getting a seat in the back.**

See also **Bloopers, Radio and TV, Boo-boos, Clergy, Faith, God, Heaven,
Prayer, Religion**

Chutzpa

Chutzpa

The quality demonstrated by the man who, having killed his
mother and father, throws himself on the mercy of the court –
because he's an orphan.

Note: Challa, pronounced with a rattling *kh*, is a Jewish bread,
greatly favoured for Sabbath eve. It is a braided white-bread loaf,
glazed with egg white.

A beggar came to the back door of the Meiselman house and
knocked.

Mrs Meiselman came to the door. 'Can I help you?'

'Can you help me?' the beggar repeated, with a bit of scorn.

'You sointinly can. Lady, I am *starving*. Two days already, not a piece food – '

'Oh, you poor man!' said Mrs Meiselman. 'Come in, come in. Sit down. On the table is some rye bread and some *challa*. Start – I'll make you something.'

The shnorrer fell upon the soft, sweet, ever-so-tasty *challa*.

'Uh . . . listen,' said Mrs Meiselman. 'There is some good *rye* bread there, too.'

'I know.' More slices of *challa* were wolfed down.

'Mister . . . The *challa* is much more expensive!'

'Lady,' observed the beggar, 'it's *worth* it.'

Two friends met on the street in Dublin. 'Terence, me boy, how nice it is t' see ye, 'specially since you owe me ten-pound-six.'

'Eamon, me old friend, I know. I'll give ye the money firrst thing t'morrow.'

'"T'morrow, t'morrow. It's procrastinatin' ye are, Terence. Last moonth, ye said ye didn't have th' money. Last *week*, ye swore ye simply could not pay. Last Friday, ye will recall, ye said ye were out of funds – '

Terence cut in. 'Enough, Eamon. Are ye forgettin' that *each toime I kept me word?!'*

Pincus, a *nebech* if ever there was one, blubbered to his boss, 'Mr Fiddelman, I absolutely can't live on the salary you're paying me! My wife has been nagging me – have to ask for a raise – of t-ten dollars a week more!'

The boss shrugged. *'Nu?* So okay. . . . You got it.'

It was an overjoyed Pincus who hurried home that night with ten dollars more than he had earned the week before.

Next week, he opened his pay envelope – and his face fell. He rushed into the boss's office. 'Mr Fiddelman! Mr Fiddelman! What h-happened to my *raise*?!'

'Your raise?' echoed Fiddelman. *'Gevalt*, Pincus. *Again* you want ten dollars more?'

The phone rang in the office of Joel Greenberg, owner of La Plage Sportswear.

'Hello,' said a woman's voice. 'This is Mrs Feitelman. Would you please call my husband to the phone?'

Greenberg frowned. 'Who's your husband?'

'Shimon. Shimon Feitelman.'

'Does he work here?'

'Sure. He's a presser.'

'No pressers are working today, lady. They're all on strike!'

'I know,' said Mrs Feitelman. 'That's why I asked if you would call him to the phone. He's on the picket line. He's the one carrying the big, big sign.'

ↄ

The Internal Revenue agent walked into Feinberg's Fancy Deli and asked for the owner. 'I am Milton Feinberg,' said one of the men behind the counter.

The IRS agent flashed his identification. 'I have a question about your income tax returns.'

They sat down at a corner table, where the IRS man opened his briefcase, pulled out a folder, spread its contents before Feinberg, and said, 'I call your attention to this section – Professional Expenses, tax-deductible.'

'My expenses are very big,' said Feinberg.

'But not *this* big,' said the revenue agent. 'Look. Right here, under "Business Expenses" you list five trips to – Israel!'

'Right.'

'Five trips to Israel? Those you call "*Business* expenses"?!'

'Certainly.'

'How can a small delicatessen justify – '

'What do you mean "justify"?' Feinberg drew himself up. 'We de*liver*!'

ↄ

The beggar knocked at the back door of the cottage in Falkirk. Mrs MacDougald came to the door.

'Mum, could a poor mon ask y' f'r a piece o' cake?' He wiped his nose with the back of his sleeve.

'Cake, is it?' bristled Mrs MacDougald. '*Cake* y' have the gall to ask for, mon? A piece o' plain bread is nae good enough for you?'

The beggar raised a conciliatory hand. '*Usually*. But, mum, y' have t' bear in moind that t'day is me birthday.'

‿

Marvin O. Winkler, owner of Delectable Dresses, en route to
Israel from New York, was obliged to make a business stop-over
in a certain Arab country. The customs officer at the airport studied
Winkler's passport carefully, went through his suitcases twice, re-
examined the passport, the picture of Winkler, the visa, and
addressed him bluntly: 'Mr Winkler, frankly – are you a Jew?!'

'Nope,' said Winkler.

'You certainly *look* Jewish.'

'So do you,' smiled Winkler. 'So do nine-tenths of the people in
your country!'

The official, taken aback, stammered. 'W-what is your religion,
sir?'

'I,' said Winkler, 'am a Seventh Avenue Adventist.'

‿

A *chutzpanik*, having dined very well in a restaurant, now smoking
a fine cigar, asked to see the owner. When the owner came to the
man's table, the diner said, 'My friend, I greatly enjoyed your
food. But I haven't a penny to my name. Wait: don't be angry! I
have an idea: I am, by profession, a beggar. I happen to be extremely talented. Why, I can go out – and inside of an hour I can
raise the entire amount I owe you. But naturally, you can't trust
me to come back? I understand. You'd be well advised to come
with me – not let me out of your sight? But a man like you, a well-
known restaurateur, can't be seen in the company of a man who is
begging, right? So, I have a simple solution. I'll wait here – and
you go out and beg, and when you have raised the price of this
dinner and cigar, come back. I promise not to leave until then.'

See also **Aplomb, Groucho, Ingenuity, Jews, Repartee, Retorts, Sarcasm,
Squelches, Stratagems, Waiters, Wordplay**

Clergy

Old Seamus McCord was dying, dying. For two months he had
lain in his bed, and the number of times that Father Morphy had
come to comfort him were beyond counting. One fierce winter

night, with the thermometer below twenty and a howling wind blowing the snow and rattling at the shutters, old Seamus called out, 'Mrs McCord . . . Mrs McCord . . .'

His wife was at his side in a flash. 'Yes, me darlin'?'

'Mrs McCord,' breathed the old man, 'my time has come for sure now. Before this night is done I shall be in the bosom of the Lord . . .'

'Oh, Seamus, Seamus . . .'

'Mrs McCord,' murmured the old man, 'go to the phone . . . and call the rabbi around the corner . . . Kaminsky is his name. . . . Beg him, in the name of the Lord, to hurry over . . .'

'Rabbi Kaminsky?!' echoed his wife. 'Seamus, 'tis mad you are! Sure you must be wantin' me to call Father Morphy!'

'Nay, nay . . . the rabbi . . .' His eyes closed.

Mrs McCord clasped her hands and gazed toward heaven. 'Oh God, forgive this poor soul – ravin' so . . . Why, in the hour of his passing, would he want a rabbi?'

One of Seamus McCord's eyelids lifted. 'Because I don't want a *priest* to come out on a godawful night like this!'

The car of Rabbi Golden was stopped at the traffic light, waiting for the red to change to green, when the coupe driven by Father Mitchell crashed into him.

At once, traffic cop Kelley hastened over. 'Well now, father . . . How fast would you say the good rabbi was going when he backed into you?'

See also **Churches, Faith, Heaven, Prayer, Rabbis, Religion**

Clothes

Sign at chic fashion boutique:

OUR PANTS LEAVE YOU BREATHLESS

The dowager came into Kolitsky's Fashion Emporium and said, 'I want to try on that dress in your window.'

'If you want to, you want to,' said Mr Kolitsky. 'Personally, I think you'd feel more comfortable in the dressing room.'

○

A man hurried into Minkoff's Cleaning Emporium. 'Can you press this suit while I wait?'

'Soitinly,' said Mr Minkoff. 'I got a nice little waiting-place behind that curtain.'

'Good. How much do you charge?'

'Four dollars.'

'Four dollars?' exclaimed the man. 'You must be crazy. Why, in Florida I can get a suit pressed for only a dollar and a half!'

'Is dot so?' Mr Minkoff stroked his chin. 'And how much is the plane fare?'

○

Sign in girdle department of western store:

Unlike the government, we give aid to overdeveloped areas.

○

Ian Crombie stumbled along the street in Inverary, limping, moaning, and groaning. Mrs Dumfree stopped him. 'What is the matter, mon?'

'M' shoes,' said Crombie. 'These shoes. Instruments of torrture, they are!'

'Why d' y' wear them, then?'

'*Why*, woman? I'll be tellin' ye. M' business couldna be worse. I owe money t' th' bonk, th' grocer, th' landlord. I have a doughter so ugly, it would be a miracle she iver married. M' wife nags me day oon night. I coom home each night, look at th' bills and at m' wife 'n doughter – ooon I could kill m'self! So I take off m' shoes. Woman, th' viry moment these shoes is off m' feet, it's th' only thing makes life woorth livin'!'

Communism

Two dogs met in West Berlin. 'How do you like life in this decadent, capitalist city?' asked the dachshund.

'So-so,' waffled the borzoi.

'What's wrong with it?'

'Well, in East Berlin I get meat that is soaked in the finest vodka. My doghouse has an electric heater in it. Once a week I see a cultural movie.'

The dachshund scratched his chin. 'If that's the way you live in Communist East Berlin, why do you come to West Berlin so often?'

The borzoi frowned, 'Every so often I have this need to bark.'

∽

The ardent Communist explained to his son, 'You see, under capitalism, Man exploits Man. But under Communism, it's exactly the opposite!'

∽

At the bar in the great lounge of the United Nations, the chief USSR delegate, Nikita Ordzhonokidz, raised his glass to his American and British guests. *'Tovarichchi*, please to join me in fine toast: to Alexander Voloshov Chamainsky, fine Communist!'

The three men drank. Then Lord Stanway, the delegate from Britain, cleared his throat. 'Forgive me for being *fright*fully dense, old boy . . . but who *is* Alexander Voloshov – '

'Alexander Voloshov Chamainsky was big Rossian genious! Inwanted electric. Inwanted movies. Inwanted raddio. Also television. In foct' – Ordzhonokidz raised his glass again – 'Chamainsky was almost as big inwantor-genious as Grischa Ivanovich Yamporkov! I now toast you: Communist Grischa Yamporkov!'

Again the three glasses were raised and the contents drunk.

'Um . . . Sascha,' said the American delegate, 'I hate to ask, but – who was Yamporkov?'

Growled Ordzhonokidz, 'You don't know who is Grischa Yamporkov? Yamporkov inwanted Chamainsky!'

∽

Georgi Maystrovich, the Commissar of Agriculture's representa-

tive, came, on a special tour of inspection, to the Commune of
State Farm 78 in the Kharkhov zone. 'And what are your estimates
of the tomato crop for this season?'

'This season, Comrade Maystrovich,' said the chairman of the
local commune, 'the tomatoes will be so large and juicy, the
department in Moscow will be overjoyed!'

Maystrovich wrote a few notes in his notebook. 'And how *large*
will the crop be, comrade?'

'How large? Why if all the tomatoes we pick are put into one
pile, it will make such an enormous mould that it will practically
reach the feet of God!'

'Stop that!' snapped Maystrovich. 'What sort of nonsense is
this? Communists know there is no God!'

The chairman nodded. 'And there aren't any tomatoes either.'

The Chinese Security Police officer, accompanied by two soldiers
with rifles and bayonets, hammered on the rickety door of the flat.
'Police! Open the door! At once!'

The door was opened from the inside, creaking on its hinges, by
a barefoot man in a frayed jacket and old blue pyjamas.

The Security officer stepped into the room. Eight persons lay on
old mattresses in the sunless, airless room. 'I have come for Wu
Zung-Ko.'

Someone coughed, someone grunted, but no one said a word.

'Does Wu Zung-Ko live here?' the officer bellowed.

Silence.

'You!' the officer addressed the barefoot man who had opened
the door. 'What is your name?'

The old man bowed. 'Wu Zung-Ko.'

'Then why,' the officer glared, 'didn't you say you lived here?'

The old man bowed again. 'Do you call *this* living?'

See also **Behind the Iron Curtain, Diplomacy, Russia**

Computers

At the Hokumora-Fijo display room in Tokyo, the long-awaited electronic marvel, the KZ9–6444, was being demonstrated to the foremost mathematicians and philosophers in Japan. The savants hovered over the elaborate display screen as numbers, fractions, equations, cosines, curves, graphs, tables flashed and popped. After some time, lights brightened, a bell rang, and on a huge screen above the KZ9–6444 appeared an equation consisting of thirty-two integers, four vectors, seventeen sines . . .

The scientists buzzed with wonder and admiration. 'Is amazing!' 'Hard to berieve . . .' 'Banzai . . .'

And the senior scientist in the group, the revered Professor Mikio Chimoru, said, 'Honolable correagues, do you learize it would take one hundled matematician, wolking ten hour a day, over sixty-two year to make mistake rike this?!'

The great Technion Institute in Israel perfected an electronic translator, a machine that could with blinding speed render the text of any one of twenty-two languages into any one of the others.

The marvellous machine was returned to the laboratory for improvement when this sentence from the New Testament was fed into it:

> *The spirit is willing, but the flesh is weak.*

– and this answer, in Russian, popped up:

> *The vodka agrees, but the meat smells bad.*

Scene: A Computer Shop in London

'Is this electronic device any *good?*' the salesman echoed. 'My dear Mr Shelling, this is a most *remark*able machine. It is, in fact, so efficient that our firm guarantees that it will cut your workload in half!'

'I say!' exclaimed Mr Shelling. 'You're not simply puffing the product – to make a sale?'

'*Mister* Shelling! A written guarantee accompanies each of our

DR-209s, precisely stating that the instrument will cut an executive's workload by fifty per cent!'

'By Jove! In that case, I'll take two of them.'

∽

After all the passengers were belted in, and the aircraft reached its flight path of thirty-two thousand feet, through the loudspeakers came this:

> Good morning, ladies and gentlemen. Thank you for flying Eagle Airlines. We shall be flying at a height of thirty-two thousand feet. Our present ground speed is six hundred and thirty miles per hour. So lean back and relax, read, take a nap. This plane, the JX-802, is the latest, most modern model. It is the safest aircraft anywhere in the world. All our operations are governed by the finest computers, which guarantee that nothing can go wrong – nothing can go wrong – nothing can go wrong . . .

See also **Answering Machines**

∽

Please read this couplet with care:

> Under a lamp the nude is vain
> Broccoli is often blind.

And scan a second:

> Life reached evilly through empty faces.
> Space flowed slowly o'er idle bodies.

These lyrical *pensées* are not the work of an idiot, or a brave bard. The couplets are the first to have come from a digital computer.

The method for producing poems is quite simple. The programmers simply feed a basic vocabulary into the memory bank of their robot, making sure there is an ample assortment of parts of speech (verbs, articles, nouns, adjectives, prepositions, adverbs).

I was so carried away by visions of odes-via-randomization that, owning no digital computer, I decided to conduct an experiment of my own. I wrote one hundred winged words on one hundred slips of paper, making sure that about twenty per cent of the words rhymed. Then I distributed the slips among twelve separate envelopes – marked, respectively:

Openers
Articles
Adjectives
Nouns
Adverbs
Verbs
Adjectives
Nouns
Conjunctions
Articles
Verbs
Nouns

I reached into the envelopes, in the same sequence as I had listed the categories above, and picked one slip out of each envelope. When I had extracted twenty words, I arranged them in four lines. *Voilà:*

On bright pumpernickel gravely twinkle
Sweet daffodils and a stately pickle,
Where shrill brassiers shyly hide
Broken dreams inside insides.

I am sending this to the Pulitzer Prize jury.

I now made a second venture into verse-via-envelope – this time adding a few verbs to my Openers. The slips I pulled out formed this pregnant thought:

Hail the hair artichoke!
Torquemada's frog will gloat.
Can lunatics like noodle toys?
Angels have no adenoids.

My third dive into poesy produced:

How deftly pink suspenders sigh
A pox on clavichords that lie.
Hark, hark! The dawn barks Gosh!
And pregnant mice sell succotash.

Do you want to scale Parnassus, too? It's easy. Just follow the rules I've given you. Choose glowing, gleaming words. Don't worry about gibberish. You may hit upon something as throat-grabbing as this, my latest madrigal:

> Swish green albino dust
> Through avatars unborn
> And circumcise the circumscribed
> Circumstance: Juno stabbed the rooster.

I have read that over many times. It is very beautiful, and makes no sense.

from my Passions and Prejudices

Conscience

Conscience

That part of the psyche that dissolves in alcohol.

H. D. LASSWELL

The small inner voice that tells us someone is watching.

H. L. MENCKEN

The mother of invention.

The conscience does not stop you from doing anything; it just keeps you from enjoying it.

Conscience is what makes you feel bad about feeling so good.

L. R.

Conversations I Cannot Forget

'Why, Becky Sorkin!' cried her friend Rachel. 'You're pregnant?! Right?'
  'Right,' smiled Becky.
  '*Mazel tov!*'
  'Thank you.'
  'So tell me, Becky, do you want a boy or a girl?'
  Becky said, 'Certainly.'

Judge Napier was very, very cross-eyed. And one day, by a fluke of fate, three cross-eyed hooligans stood arrayed before his bench.

Judge Napier studied each of the men with obvious distaste. Then he asked the first hooligan. 'What's your name?'

'Martin Gordon,' replied the second.

Snapped the judge: 'I wasn't talking to you!'

Cried the third hooligan: 'I didn't *say* anything!'

'Mr MacIntosh,' the young man said, 'I coom t' ask f'r your kind permission. I – I make so bold at t' ask ye if I may marry your doughter, Megan.'

'Well, well, lad,' said Mr MacIntosh. 'Afore I say a worrd – lad, have ye seen Mrs MacIntosh?'

'Aye, sir,' said the young man. 'But – I still prefor your doughter.'

See also **Accents, Groucho, Martians, Restaurants, Squelches, Waiters**

Courts

Eighty-year-old Augostina Hernandez appeared in Naturalization Court where the judge asked her: 'How many states are there in the United States of America?'

'Feefety.'

'Good. Who was our first president?'

'Jorge Washington.'

'Mmh. . . . Do you believe in overthrowing our government by subversion or violence?'

Mrs Hernandez thought a moment. 'Violence.'

JUDGE: Now, Mr Mansfield, how long have you known the defendant?

MANSFIELD: Over twenty-five years, Your Honour.

JUDGE: And in your opinion, do you think the defendant is the kind of man who would steal the money the plaintiff alleges he stole?

MANSFIELD: Uh . . . how much was it?

☞

The attorney for the defence, famed for his skill in cross-examination, leaned close to the star witness for the prosecution, one Melvin Prosker, and, in the smoothest of voices, crooned: 'Now, Mr Prosker, you have testified that it was night – moreover, a very dark night – and that you were almost two blocks from the scene, yet you clearly saw my client, so you allege, beat Clarence Hyslop over the head with his cane. . . . Is that correct?'

'Yes, sir.'

'Mr Prosker,' smiled the attorney, 'please tell the court and this jury: how far can you see at night?'

Prosker leaned back. 'I don't know for sure.'

'You don't *know?*' sneered the attorney. 'Well, make a guess.'

Prosker leaned forward. 'How far is the moon?'

☞

In a courtroom in Tel Aviv, old Mr Eisenstat was on the witness stand.

The prosecuting attorney was peppering him with questions – all of which Mr Eisenstat answered, quite politely, quite steadily, but with a lowered head, and in such a low voice that it was almost impossible to hear his answers clearly.

Judge Fanster leaned forward and said, 'Mr Eisenstat, you simply will *have* to speak louder – much louder. And please address – not your chest – but the jury! Do you understand?'

Mr Eisenstat nodded, raised his head, and said to the jury, '*Shalom*, jury.'

☞

'Mr Caravello, how long after you put the phone down did she come into your store?' asked Mr Marsh, the plaintiff's lawyer.

'I tinka five meenut.'

'Are you sure of that, Mr Caravello?'

'Oh, *si, avvocato*. Fiva meenut.'

'It couldn't have been eight minutes?'

'Oh, no.'

'Or three minutes?'

Mr Caravello shook his head emphatically. 'I say fiva meenut.'

Mr Marsh smiled. 'Well, sir, let's test the accuracy – the reliability of your time sense.' He pulled a snap-case watch out of his pocket. 'When I say "Start", begin your estimate. When five minutes have gone by, say "Now!" Do you understand what I mean, Mr Carvello?'

'*Certamente*. . . . *Si, si.*'

'Ready? . . . Start.'

The courtroom was hushed as the seconds went by, the minutes . . . on and on. . . . Time suddenly seemed to stretch out. And when some spectators in the courtroom were sure Mr Caravello was far past the stated time, he sighed and now, '*Alora!* . . . Now!'

Mr Marsh looked at his watch. His jaw dropped. 'My Lord. Five minutes – *precisely* five minutes.'

The judge leaned forward. 'May I congratulate the witness on the remarkable accuracy of his time sense?'

'*Grazie*,' said Mr Caravello. 'Eesa easy, judge. On wall, behind the *avvocato*, is beeg clock . . .'

⌒

Mrs Alexander Dinerstein was on the witness stand. The judge asked her: 'You are Hilda Dinerstein?'

'Yes. Your Honour.'

'The wife of Alex Dinerstein?'

'Yes, sir.'

'And what does your husband do, Mrs Dinerstein?'

'He is a manufacturer.'

'Children?'

Mrs Dinerstein blanched. 'My God, *no*, Your Honour! Luggage.'

⌒

'Now, Miss Flinner,' said the judge, 'Will you please tell the court precisely what the defendant said to you?'

The young, blonde, buxom charmer blushed furiously. 'It was *very* vulgar, Your Honour.'

'We are all adults here, Miss Flinner.'

'I – I just can't make myself say something so – so filthy!'

The judge thought for a moment and handed the girl a pencil and notepad. 'Very well. Just write down the man's words and we'll pass them around the jury.'

The girl bit her lip as she wrote down nine or ten words and handed the paper to the judge. He read the paper and gave an involuntary whistle. 'You mean the defendant actually asked you – this?'

'Yes, Your Honour.'

'Bailiff, circulate this paper among the jury.'

The bailiff handed the note to the foreman, who read it, gulped, and passed the indecent proposal to the number two juror, who read it, dropped his jaw in disbelief, and passed the note on to a woman juror, who barely read three words before she paled, closed her eyes, and passed the words on to the next juror. So it went, juror after juror reading, flushing, turning pale, swallowing. . . . The note reached the last member of the jury, who had been dozing off throughout. He read the note, looked up, nodded to the witness, and, with an expression of bliss, placed the paper in his pocket.

See also **Evidence, Lawyers**

Criticism

From a book review

However, this is not a book to be tossed aside lightly. It should be thrown with emphatic force.

A Boston book review:

I have no doubt that this book will fill a much-needed void.

Critic

A man who boasts he is hard to please, when nobody tries to please him.

AMBROSE BIERCE

A person who surprises an author by informing him what he meant.

WILSON MIZNER

Mr—— apparently writes his plays for the ages: the ages between six and twelve.

GEORGE JEAN NATHAN

Of the play, *I Am a Camera:* I no Leica.

Of the play, *Dreadful Night:* Sure is.

'The opening of this play? It was anything but exciting. I've seen more carryings on at the opening of an umbrella.'

ᔆ

An aspiring, unsuccessful writer sent his latest four-hundred-page novel to a publisher in Boston.

It was returned without comment, he thought, until he happened to turn to the page preceding the first page of the story. There was the usual epigraph.

> All the characters in this
> story are fictional. They bear no
> resemblance to any person, living
> or dead

In the margin, a blue pencil had scribbled:

> How true.

ᔆ

Greek tragedy:

The type of drama where the hero says to his sister, 'If you don't kill Pa, I will.'

SPYROS SKOURAS

From a movie review in the New York T——

> There is Richard Burton growling and growling
> and endlessly chewing the lips, ears, and neck of
> Elizabeth Taylor as the faithless wife of a dull
> ambassador, with whom he is having a clandestine
> affair.

I am glad in a way, that Mr Burton was endlessly chewing the ears and neck of Miss Taylor as the faithless wife of a dull ambassador, because it probably wouldn't be fun to chew her neck as anyone else. But who is the ambassador with whom Burton is having a clandestine affair?

from my Passions and Prejudices

See also **Goldwyniana, Reviews of Note, Sarcasm**

Curses

Note: Anglo-Saxons may well marvel over the opulent curses used in Mideastern cultures, where oral maledictions are a popular art form.

Among Jews, swearing is rare but cursing is common. By 'swearing' I mean the venting of frustration or anger in obscene phrases directed at no one in particular; by 'cursing' I mean the invocation of calamity (pain, injury, death) upon someone – hoping that God, though not directly asked to do so (indeed, usually asked *not* to), will direct his wrath upon the one cursed, in the form requested. For example: '*Damn* this hammer!' is swearing; 'May he be buried in the ground and bake bagels – God forbid!' is cursing.

The elaboration of Jewish curses reaches staggering heights of picturesqueness: 'May his intestines sound like a music box!' 'May he own a hundred houses, and in each a hundred rooms, and in each room a hundred beds; and may he go from bed to bed night after night in search of one moment's sleep!'

I, for one, am awed by such ingenuity in the catharsis of disaffection.

L. R.

May you spend many hours in a soft chair: your dentist's.

I would like to treat him like a treasure: bury him with care and affection.

May God grant him so much breath that he should always be able to ask what the weather is like – outside.

May his navel turn dizzy.

May all your daughters become well known – to policemen.

May he grow sick from satisfactions.

May his buttocks fall off!

Let bunions grow *on* his bunions, and on his carbuncles should grow boils.

May all your teeth fall out – except one: to get toothaches.

Your wife should eat *matzos* in bed, so you get insomnia from the crumbs.

May the seven seas not be enough for your enemas.

May you own five ships of gold – all wrecked.

May a child be named after you soon. (Ashkenazic Jews were forbidden to name a child after a living person.)

May you gain twice as much brains, so you can be a halfwit.

May you become very famous – in medical history.

Like a beet should he grow – with his head in the earth.

Let onions grow in his navel.

Your healthy days, spend on your back – your sick ones, on your feet.

May cramps parade through your bowels.

May all your relatives move in with you.

May you need a prescription.

May you leap up with joy – over an open manhole.

May all his baths be boiling hot, and all his women icy cold.

May everything you fry stick to the bottom of the pan.

May all your shoes be too short.

May you dance with joy, and skid into a sewer.

BUT REMEMBER:
A curse does not arrive as fast as a telegram. (Don't take curses too seriously.)

adapted from my Treasury of Jewish Quotations

See also **Insults, Sarcasm**

Cynics' Dictionary

Adolescent: A teenager who acts like a baby when you don't treat him like an adult.

Applause: The echo of a platitude.

AMBROSE BIERCE

Artificial insemination: Copulation without representation.

Playboy

Aspersion: An Iranian donkey.

Autobiography: A book that proves that the only thing wrong about its author is his memory.

Babies: The worst feature of any new baby is its mother's singing.

FRANK ('KIN') HUBBARD

Bachelor: One who treats all women as sequels.

Bore: One who has the power of speech but not the capacity for conversation.

Calories: Weight lifters.

Centimetre: A parking meter that takes pennies.

L. R.

Champagne: The drink that makes you see double but feel single.

Charm: The ability to make someone think that both of you are wonderful.

Civilization: The progress from shoeless toes to toeless shoes.

Coincide: What you should do when it starts pouring.

Cold War: Hot peace.

Conscience: The thing that feels bad when everything else feels good.

Courtesy: Acceptable hypocrisy.

AMBROSE BIERCE

Critic: One who goes along for deride.

L. L. LEVINSON

Demagogue: A man who preaches doctrines he knows to be untrue to men he knows to be idiots.

H. L. MENCKEN

Dinosaur: A colossal fossil who had no *mazel*.

L. R.

Disco: A din of iniquity.

Eccentric: A man too rich to be called crazy.

L. R.

Egotist: One more interested in himself – than in you.

AMBROSE BIERCE

Eternal triangle: Diapers.

L. L. LEVINSON

Etiquette: Yawning with your mouth closed.

Fanatic: A man who does what God would do – if He only had the facts straight.

FINLEY PETER DUNNE

Flattery: The applause that refreshes.

Florida: A place you go to in winter, and usually find it.

Forger: The man who gives a cheque a bad name.

Fortress: A fort – with breastworks.

Fjords: Bodies of stjll water between steep cljffs in Njorway.

Friendship: An emotion so sweet, steady, loyal, and enduring that it lasts an entire lifetime – unless asked to lend money.

MARK TWAIN

Glamour: That indefinable something about a girl who has a large bosom.

ABE BURROWS

The capacity of a woman to get more out of a dress than she puts into it.

Gossip: The only time people dislike gossip is when you gossip about them.

WILL ROGERS

The person who doesn't gossip has no friends to speak of.

Guillotine: The one sure cure for dandruff.

Guilt: One of America's most abundant resources.

Hobson's Choice: Mrs Hobson.

L. R.

Home: The place where you can scratch any place you itch.

Housing development: Where the builder tears all the trees out of the plot, then names the streets after them.

Humorist: Someone who knows how to feel pretty good about feeling pretty bad.

DON HEROLD

Hypochondriac: One who enjoys poor health, then complains of feeling better.

Hypocrisy: A hypocrite is someone who – but who isn't?

DON MARQUIS

Idealist: One who upon observing that a rose smells better than a cabbage concludes that it will also make better soup.

H. L. MENCKEN

Imagination: What prevents us from being as happy in the arms of a chambermaid as in the arms of a duchess.

SAMUEL JOHNSON

Inconceivable: What happens when an irresistible force meets an immovable object.

L. R.

Insomnia: The inability to sleep even when it's time to get up.

Ireland: A country with so little sense of compromise that a girl has to choose between perpetual adoration and perpetual pregnancy.

GEORGE MOORE

Justice: Injustice is not hard to bear; it's justice that really hurts.

H. L. MENCKEN

He'd wash his hands in blood to keep them clean.

ELIZABETH BARRETT BROWNING

Kleptomaniac: Someone who can't help helping himself.

HENRY MORGAN

Laissez-faire: The theory that counsels those determined to do good by (or for) others: 'Don't just do something; *stand* there.'

Llama: The animal that resembles a camell.

L. L. LEVINSON

Los Angeles: Ten suburbs in search of a city.

A fine place to live, if you're an orange.

FRED ALLEN

Luck: The only explanation for the success of people we hate.

Marriage: Marriage makes two one; but you never can tell which one is the one.

L. SAFIAN

It's a mutual partnership, if one remains mute.

Love parsonified.

Masochist: Some one who is only happy when miserable . . . (See *Sadist*).

Maybe: The preamble to hope.

Middle-aged: Someone twelve years older than you are.

Money: The thing that keeps people from calling you 'Hey, Mac!'

Motel: The place where we exchange good dollars for bad quarters.

Mummies: Egyptians who were pressed for time.

L. L. LEVINSON

Murderer: Someone presumed to be innocent until he is proved insane.

Reader's Digest

News: Anything that makes a man say, 'For heaven's sake!'

Operas in English: About as sensible as baseball in Italian.

H. L. MENCKEN

Optimist: Someone who thinks things can't get worse – after they get worse.

Parking space: An unoccupied place on the other side of the street.

Pawnbroker: A man who takes an interest in everything.

FRED ALLEN

Peace: Time-out.

L. R.

Pessimist: One who feels bad whilst feeling good out of fear he'll fear worse if he feels better.

TED ROBINSON

Platitude: An observation too true to be good.

AMBROSE BIERCE

Politics: That which makes strange postmasters.

FRANK ('KIN') HUBBARD

Popularity: To be popular, ask people for advice. Don't *do* anything about it; just ask.

L. R.

Pornography: Obscene records you play on a pornograph.

Professional men: Slaves to conventions.

Changing Times

Puritanism: The haunting fear that someone, somewhere, may be happy.

H. L. MENCKEN

Railways: Saturday afternoons, although occurring at regular and well-foreseen intervals, always takes this railway by surprise.

W. S. GILBERT

Rare volume: A returned book.

Reformer: One who doesn't realize how much worse things can be made.

One who wants his/her conscience to be your guide.

Rules of War: The rules that make it illegal to hit below the toes.

L. R.

Sadist: Someone who positively refuses to beat up a masochist.

L. R.

Someone who sends get-well cards to hypochondriacs.

Saloon-keepers: I never said all Democrats are saloon-keepers; I said all saloon-keepers are Democrats.

HORACE GREELEY

Sarcasm: Barbed ire.

L. L. LEVINSON

Scotsman: A man who, before sending his pyjamas to the laundry, stuffs a sock in each pocket.

Screens: The wire mesh that keeps flies from getting out of the house.

Secret: What we tell everybody to tell nobody.

Slander: To lie, or tell truth, about someone.

AMBROSE BIERCE

Snobs: People who talk as if they had begotten their ancestors.

ALFRED ADLER

Spring: The season of balls: tennis, base, charity, and moth.

adapted from L. L LEVINSON

Suspicion: The emotion that creates what it suspects.

C. S. LEWIS

Switzerland: Beautiful but dumb.

EDNA FERBER

Tears: A copious discharge of hydrated chlorine of sodium from the eyes.

AMBROSE BIERCE

Television: The device that brings into your living room characters you would never allow in your living room.

RED SKELTON

The electronic device that intersperses gory slaughter with the brushing of teeth.

The reason for ten thousand new brands of cereals that make noise.

The place where show-biz illiterates can express their ill-informed opinions.

The stage for plays about psychopathic adolescents and homicidal nymphomaniacs who are tragically trapped in immense riches.

L. R.

Tact: Thinking all you say without saying all you think.

Thief: A man with a gift for finding things before you lose them.

JOE E. LEWIS

Tourist: Someone who goes three thousand miles to get a picture of himself in front of his car.

Truth: It is hard to believe that a man is telling the truth when you know you would lie if you were in his place.

H. L. MENCKEN

Waiter: A representative of the leisure class.

War: The worst thing about war is that it kills the wrong people.

Yawn: A silent shout.

G. K. CHESTERTON

Zeal: A nervous disorder that affects the inexperienced.

AMBROSE BIERCE

See also **Graffiti, Groucho, How's That Again?, Ingenuity, Sarcasm, Wit**

Death

At his wife's gravesite, in Montparnasse Cemetery, Paris, Alfonse Raimeau wept copiously. And just as copiously wept Gaston Chamford, the late Mme Raimeau's lover. In fact, Chamford wept with such feeling that Raimeau put his arms around Chamford's shoulder, saying, 'Contain yourself, my dear Gaston. Don't take her passing so hard.... I promise you, I'll marry again...'

Cemetery:

An isolated spot, usually in a suburb, where mourners swap lies.

AMBROSE BIERCE

Cremation: All men are cremated equal.

Sign on Halstead's Funeral Home
January 9
We are undergoing extensive alterations. Our facilities will be closed for one month.

THE MANAGEMENT
(cont'd)

Sign on Halstead's Funeral Home

February 9
We are now open for business.
Thank you for waiting.

THE MANAGEMENT

On funeral parlour   Must you be going?

Money refunded if not completely satisfied.

Cremation: For people whose attitude to death is one of grave doubt.

Francis J. Quimby, aged forty-seven, was reading his morning paper, the Dublin *Bugle*. He turned, as was his habit, to the obituaries – and there, to his astonishment and horror, he beheld:

FRANCIS JOSEPH QUIMBY

and under that:

> Francis J. Quimby, president of the Q. & R. Building and Loan Society, died last night of a sudden heart attack. He was 47. He leaves his wife, two children, his mother . . .

Fuming in rage, Quimby telephoned his lawyer. 'Aloysius! Did y' read this mornin's *Bugle*?'
'That I did, sir. Who is it callin'?'
'What do you mean "Who is it?" Do y' not recognize my voice? This is Frank. Francis Quimby!'
'*Francis?*' cried the lawyer.
'Hisself! And I want you t' start a suit against that goddam newspaper! For falsehood, embarrassment, psychological grief t' me and me loved ones – '
The lawyer hesitated. 'Francis – where are you phonin' from?'

Mr Smithers entered the offices of his fraternal society. 'Mr Barnes,' he said to the secretary. 'I want to make funeral arrangements for my dear departed wife.'

'Your wife?' frowned Mr Barnes. 'Don't you *remember*, Mr Smithers? . . . We buried her last July. . . .'

'That,' sighed Mr Smithers, 'was my first wife. I am talking about my second.'

'Second? I didn't know you had married again. . . . Congratulations!'

The mourners filed past the coffin, some sobbing, some sighing, and Mrs Thomson murmured, 'Look at him. How peaceful he looks . . . how relaxed . . . so tanned . . . so healthy . . .'

'Why not?' replied the widow. 'He just spent three weeks in Arizona.'

See also **Epitaphs**

Dentists

Dentist The greatest Yank of all.

A dentist bores you to tears.

'How much will such an extraction cost me, doctor?'

'Fifty dollars,' said the dentist.

'For a few minutes work?' exclaimed the patient. 'Isn't that a lot of money to charge?'

The dentist nodded amiably. 'Well, if you want, I can pull the tooth out very, very slowly.'

On dentist's tombstone

> Stranger, approach these bones with gravity:
> Dr Brown is filling his last cavity.

Sign in Istanbul   ***American Dentist***

Room 203
Teeth Extracted by Latest Methodists

Dr Monte Gershman was an excellent dentist, and a compulsive joker. 'Your teeth are in fine fettle,' he would tell a patient, 'but your gums will have to come out.' (That was far from original with Monte, but whenever he sprang the line upon an unsuspecting patient, Monte would chortle and chuckle and shake with delight.)

One day a new patient, Mrs Marbury, well dressed, condescending in her manner, came to Dr Gershman's office.

'May I ask who referred me to you?' asked Monte.

'Oh, one of my friends. She said you were Jewish. And I think you Hebrews make the best doctors and dentists.'

'Really?'

'I suppose it's something in your blood. Now, doctor, I want to warn you in advance. I will not pay any bill I find excessive. I have a lawyer who approves or disapproves every one of my bills.'

'Fine,' said Monte. 'Now, Mrs Marbury, open ... open your mouth, wider.... Great Scott, madam! You have the largest cavity I have ever seen in twenty years of practice! ... *The largest cavity I have ever seen in twenty years –* '

'*I heard* you, doctor!' snapped Mrs Marbury. 'There's no need to repeat yourself.'

'*Repeat* myself?' Monte asked with surpassing innocence. 'Mrs Marbury, that was the *echo*.'

See also **Doctors**

Diets

Fat   Energy gone to waist.

There's a divinity that ends our shapes.

                                                          L. R.

'Did you say you're a light eater?'
  'Absolutely.'
  'But, man – you must weight over two hundred pounds!'
  'Two twenty.'
  'And you claim you're a light eater?'
  'Absolutely. As soon as it's light, I start eating.'

Overweight: Just desserts.

                                 When you diet
                                 Please be quiet.

KATE: I haven't seen you in *years*. What's new?
JANE: Well, since we last met I've gotten rid of one hundred and
    eighty-two pounds of ugly, stupid fat.
KATE: Good lord! How?
JANE: By divorce.

Diplomacy/Diplomats

Diplomacy: A blend of protocol, alcohol, and Geritol.

                                            ADLAI STEVENSON

Diplomat

A man who never forgets a woman's birthday, and never remembers her age.

One who acts disarming, when his country is not.

At a UN meeting, a French delegate, pulling his chair up to the
table, accidentally touched the thigh of the Russian female to his
left. The Frenchman, smiling, was most gracious in his apology.
  The lady turned to the Russian diplomat on *her* left and whis-

pered something in his ear. The diplomat got up, left the meeting, and hurried out to a phone. He was gone for an hour. When he returned, he leaned over to the lady and whispered in her ear. She leaned toward the French delegate and murmured, 'Your place or mine?'

See also **Ingenuity, Tact**

Doctors

I said to the doctor, 'I have this ringing in my ears.'
He said, 'Don't answer.'

JOEY BISHOP

The sign on the Medical Centre door read:

LAWRENCE DUNCAN, M.D.
Brain Surgery

F. B. CARNOT, M.D.
Psychiatry

S. RANGOFF, M.D.
Proctology

Under this, someone had added:

*Specialists
in
Odds and Ends*

My doctor is a family physician. He treats my family and I support his.

PHYLLIS DILLER

My doctor told me I had low blood pressure, so he gave me my bill. That raised it.

ALAN KING

'So how do you feel, Mr Bohrod?'

'I feel absolutely terrible, doctor. I feel so bad I honest-to-God hope I'm really sick!'

'What a strange thing to say, Mr Bohrod. Why do you hope you're really sick?'

'Because I certainly don't want to feel this terrible if you tell me there's nothing wrong with me.'

> A witty young man with a hernia
> To his doctor said, 'Gol dernia,
> While improving my middle
> I don't want you to fiddle
> With parts that don't concernia.'

Old Sam Clayborn had spent a dollar on a sweepstake ticket. His number won a million dollars. Clayborn's children did not know how to break the fantastic news to him. 'He has a bad heart,' said his son. 'The surprise could kill him!'

'Let's ask dad's doctor,' said Clayborn's daughter.

They phoned the doctor, told him the news, and described their dilemma.

Said the doctor, 'Let me handle it. I'll come over.'

So Dr Frungler 'dropped in' on the Clayborns and was shown to the old man's bedroom. He made casual conversation with Clayborn for a bit and then, in the most offhand manner, asked, 'By the way, I hear you bought a sweepstake ticket. Is that so?'

'Yes, I did,' quavered Clayborn.

'What's the amount, if – by some miracle – you win?'

'One million dollars.'

Dr Frungler laughed amiably. 'That certainly is a lot of money. . . . Have you thought of what you'd do if – oh, I *know* the chance is very, very slim – you won that much money?'

'Doc, I sure have thought of that. In fact, I put it in my will. If I win a million dollars, half goes to you.'

Dr Frungler dropped dead.

Victor Borge discourses with particular fondness about an uncle who keeps discovering cures for which there are no diseases.

☞

Dr Noah Slocum, the distinguished surgeon, carefully cut open the patient's abdomen, parted the skin, sponged the flowing blood, adjusted the haemostats – and out flew two butterflies. They began circling the large lamp over the operating table.

Surgeon, nurses, anaesthetist stared at the butterflies. Then Dr Slocum exclaimed, 'I'll be goddamned! He was telling the truth!'

☞

My doctor is a very generous man. He gave a patient six months to live – and when the man couldn't pay his bill, my doctor gave him another six months.

HENNY YOUNGMAN

☞

Waldo Stirling told his wife: 'Th't new doctor, by Binnie Road – they say he does charge two pound ten th' first visit, thin one pound five after that.'

'Ay?'

'So Ay'll fool th' mon,' Waldo chuckled. 'Ay'll go in and say, "A fine morning, t' ye, doctor. Here Ay am ag'in!"'

When Stirling returned from the doctor he looked anything but triumphant.

'So what hoppened, darlin'?' asked his wife.

'What hoppened,' said Waldo glumly, 'is Ay went in an' very cheery sang out, "Holloo, doctor. Here Ay am ag'in!" So he bade me disrobe, which Ay did. And when he finished examinin' me, he said, "Ay now, Mister Stirling. Just ye continue taking the med'cine Ay recommended bifore . . ."'

☞

My doctor is terrific! Some doctors will treat you for a broken arm and you'll die of pneumonia. If my doctor treats you for a broken arm, you die of a broken arm.

MOREY AMSTERDAM

☞

For the first time in her life, Mrs Flaherty went to a gynaecologist.

After taking her medical history, he said, 'Now, please go into the next room and take off your clothes.'

'My *clothes*?' gasped Mrs Flaherty.

'Yes.'

'Listen, doctor, an' does your good mother know how y' make a living?'

My doctor said I was sound as a dollar. That scared the hell out of me.

RED SKELTON

Dr J. Ritter and Dr N. Schacht, both obstetricians, shared an office. One day some joker printed under the names:

24 HOUR SERVICE ... WE DELIVER

'How *are* you, Higgins?' smiled Dr Nayland, the distinguished obstetrician. 'Haven't seen you in a long time. Are you still writing those funny little "filler" paragraphs for the *News*?'

'Yep,' said Higgins. 'What about you, doc? Are you still delivering those funny little people?'

The new patient, Yvonne Dupree, was a most ravishing woman.

Dr Martin said, 'Miss – or is it Mrs Dupree?'

'Mrs. But I'm divorced. Twice . . .'

'Please take off your clothes and get on the examination table.'

Yvonne Dupree blushed furiously. 'Doctor, you must excuse me. All my life, I've had this – this absolute *revulsion* about undressing in front of anyone. Even before my husbands – I made them turn off the lights first.'

Dr Martin cleared his throat. 'I'll be glad to turn off the lights.' He snapped the switch on the wall. 'Go ahead, madam. Just tell me when you're done.'

After a few minutes Mrs Dupree called, 'Okay, doctor. . . . Where shall I put my clothes?'

Dr Martin's voice was sweet as honey. 'Over here. On top of mine.'

Diagnosis: What a sick person must make before he can determine which specialist to call.

Dr Solaway had been in practice for more years than anyone could remember. The faith of his patients in his skill was boundless. His bedside manner was as reassuring as his office manner, which had become legendary in his neighbourhood.

One day a distinguished, grey-haired man came to Dr Soloway's office for a check-up. Dr Soloway spent a full hour on his examination, then said, 'Your blood specimen and urine analysis won't come back from the laboratory until Tuesday. But from everything I've seen, your vital organs are in *excellent* shape. Absolutely. In fact, to me you look like a man who will live to be seventy-eight years old!'

'That's nice,' said the patient.

'"Nice?" Only "nice"?! My God, man, do you know how few people who come to this office are as healthy as you?! By the way, my nurse didn't write your age on your interview: how old *are* you?'

'Eighty-one.'

'See?' cried Dr Soloway. 'What did I tell you?!'

See also **Psychiatrists/Psychoanalysts/Psychologists**

Drink/Drunks

A saloon can't corrupt a good man, any more than a synagogue can reform a bad one.

A drunkard smells of spirits – but so does the bartender.

YIDDISH SAYING

Q: In what month of the year do Swedes drink least?
A: February.

Newscaster in Louisville, Kentucky

> Authorities announced that the Pelican Club, where the unfortunate incident occurred, will have its leer and bicker licence revoked.

In Third Avenue saloon: If you must drive your man to drink, please drive him here.

Hangover: The wrath of grapes.

The most unpleasant thing about him is that when he isn't drunk, he's sober.

W. B. YEATS

Sign on brewery: The Beer that Made Milwaukee Jealous.

On a bottle of Japanese 'Scotch', in Tokyo: This whisky made from finest grape, by appointment of His Majesty King Elizabeth.

In a bar on the Bowery: Not responsible for ladies left over thirty seconds.

Two men, blissfully boozy, paused before a newsstand, to read the headline:

MAN WANTED FOR ARMED ROBBERY IN BROOKLYN

'By gosh and by golly,' said the first man, 'if that job was in Manhattan, I'd take it!'

Paddy Gilhooly, walking down a crowded street in Belfast, suddenly keeled over. At once a crowd collected, firing suggestions.

'Call a doctor!' cried one man.

'Give the poor soul air!' cried another.

'Fynted, has he?' exclaimed a little old lady. 'Then give him a stiff shot o' whiskey.'

'Call th' police!'

'Nay, jist open his collar – '

Gilhooly sat up. 'Shut up, ye nincompoops, an' listen to th' little old lydy!'

Scene: A Saloon in Stockholm

The brothers Jorgensen, identical twins, always dressed exactly alike. One night they went to a saloon. A man at the bar took one look at the Jorgensens, his eyes popping, and cried, 'Godamighty, only two drinks of Aquavit and I be seein' things.'

'No you're not,' grinned one Jorgensen.

'My brother and me,' smiled the other, 'we are *twins*.'

The barfly gasped, 'All *four* of ye?!'

DOCTOR: I'm afraid I can't do any more for your husband, Mrs Windsor. Has he tried Alcoholics Anonymous?

MRS WINDSOR: I suppose so. Percy will drink *anything*.

Cohane and Driscoll, old friends, came out of a Dublin saloon in a fine state of euphoria. As they stumbled along, humming aimless tunes, Driscoll stopped short. 'My, my, my, my. Liam Cohane, will y'not look at that! A beautiful, *beau*tiful bug – on the branch of that bush?'

Cohane hiccuped. 'Bug, is it? What kind o'bug?'

Driscoll blinked and said, 'Sure, and 'tis a ladybug.'

Cohane gasped. '*Lady* bug, did y' say? By all the saints, Seamus, y'have the eyesight of a telescope.'

Mr Schaffner was on his way home, walking from the subway station to his flat in Astoria, when a drunk came out of an alleyway, a gun waving in one hand and a bottle in the other. 'Take a swig – of thish – mister – or I'll – ' He pointed the gun at Mr Schaffner.

The terrified commuter took the bottle with trembling hands, drank, cough, retched. 'Migod, that's the most *awful* stuff – '

'Right!' beamed the boozer. 'Now you hold the gun...'

See also **Just Jokes, Shaggy Dogs**

Dummies

As Prokovnick started up the stairs to his flat, the janitor grabbed him. 'Listen, Prokovnick! Your wife – she's in bed – *with your best friend!*'

'What?!' boomed Prokovnick. 'I'll tear that swine limb from limb!' He charged up the stairs.

In a few minutes, Prokovnick returned, 'Hey, janitor. What's the matter with you, telling me my wife is in bed with my best friend? Why, I never laid eyes on that guy before in my whole life.'

Harry Farkel, leaving for lunch, handed a batch of bills to his new secretary and said, 'Miss Tobin, please total these.' At the door, he added, 'And make sure you're right, Miss Tobin. Check the addition three times.'

When Farkel returned at two thirty, his secretary handed him the batch of bills, plus a covering sheet of figures, smiling, 'Here you are, Mr Farkel. All done.'

'Oh, good, Miss Tobin. Did you check your results like I said?'

'Yes, *sir*. Three times.'

'Thank you.'

'On the top page, Mr Farkel, you'll see all three answers.'

Nelda Petersen, the new maid at the Lawrence Hansfords, seemed able, though she admitted she had never worked in so fine a mansion before.

As Mrs Hansford was having lunch, she heard Nelda answer the phone, 'Hansford residence.... Ay, y' can say that again!' and hang up.

Some time later, the phone rang again. Nelda once more lifted the receiver. 'Hansford residence.... Et certainly is!' and hung up.

Around the cocktail hour, the phone rang and Nelda answered. 'Hansford residence.... You don't have t' keep telling me!'

At this point, Mrs Hansford asked, 'Nelda, have you been getting calls from a friend?'

'Oh no, ma'am.'

'Then what on earth is going on?'

'It sure beats me, ma'am,' said Nelda. 'I pick up the phone; someone says, "It's long distance from Portland," and I keep sayin' "Et sure is!"'

⌒

The new secretary, Miss Selzer, was very pleasant and seemed eager to work. Mr Rackman, her employer, was pleased. As he went out to lunch, he said, 'Miss Selzer, remind me to call Dr Boris Yablon the minute I come back.'

'Is his number on our office phone list?'

'No. Look him up in the telephone directory.'

When Mr Rackman returned from his lunch date, he said, 'Miss Selzer, get me Dr Yablon.'

'Very soon, sir. I'm still working on it . . .'

'You're still working – on *what*?'

'His number,' smiled Miss Selzer. 'I'm already up to the *K*'s.'

⌒

Five men were playing poker at Latski's apartment . . . when Latski leaped to his feet, crying, 'You're cheating! Bleifeld, you are a cheater!'

'Hey, Latski!' cried one player.

'That's a terrible accusation,' said another.

'How do you know he's cheating?' asked the third.

'Because he just discarded a seven!' cried Latski. 'The hand I dealt him was a pair of fours, a six, jack, and nine!'

⌒

Michael Devlin, walking down Third Avenue, was jumped by two husky thugs. Devlin fought like a tiger but to no avail, alas; the thugs beat him up – smashed his glasses, broke his nose, and pinned him to the ground. They tore his wallet out of his pocket, but it contained only three dollar bills. They turned his pockets inside out – but they only contained seventeen cents.

The thugs gazed at each other in amazement. 'Hey, man,' one called to Devlin, 'you some kind of nut? You put up a fight like that for a lousy three bucks?!'

'I thought you were after the two hundred in my socks!'

⌒

'Canvasback' Carlin, the pugilist with seventeen straight defeats, took a terrific rain of blows and fell to the mat, dazed.

The referee began to semaphore his arm, counting 'One . . . two . . .'

Carlin wobbled up blearily.

'. . . three . . . four . . .'

Carlin started to get to one knee, when his manager shouted, 'No, no! Stay down! Until eight!'

Carlin blinked. 'Uh – wha' time is it now?'

After sixteen dreadful days adrift on a raft in the Atlantic, ship-wrecked, without food or drink or shelter from the rains, Stanislaw Karpazik said to Fletcher and Cohn, 'Let's pray to God. It's our only chance. Let's pray like *crazy*!'

The three men prayed with uncommon fervour. And lo! – from the sky there appeared a luminous angel. 'Dispel your fears, O men of faith,' said the angel. 'Your Maker has heard your plea and has sent me with His authority to grant each of you one wish!'

'Thank God, thank God!' cried Harry Cohen. 'I wish – please – to be whisked to the finest restaurant in New York!'

The angel nodded, and Mr Cohen vanished into the clouds.

'And I,' gasped Morton Fletcher, 'pray God, I – want to be in the Tour d'Argent in Paris!'

The angel nodded and Mr Fletcher was instantly swept upwards and out of sight.

'And your wish?' the angel asked Karpazik.

'I'm *lonely*. I wish those two were back here!'

See also **Chelm, Nebechs, Shaggy Dogs, Shlemiels**

Education

Education   The ability to describe a bathing beauty
                without using your hands.

        The ability to give directions without taking your
                hands out of your pockets.

The path from cocky ignorance to miserable
uncertainty.

That which reveals to the wise, and conceals from
the stupid, the vast limits of their knowledge.

L. R.

What you must acquire without interference from your schooling.

MARK TWAIN

What remains after you have forgotten all you have been taught.

LORD HALIFAX

On the desk of a kindergarten teacher

THINK SMALL

Mrs Flugelman hurried to the door of her son's room. 'Bernie!
Bernie! It's late. Get up!'

Her son sleepily grumbled, 'I don' wanna get up.'

Mrs Flugelman flung the door open. 'Bernie! You *have* to get up
– wash, dress, eat, go to school!'

Bernie said, 'I don' wanna go to school.'

'Bernie!' His mother recoiled in horror. 'What's gotten into you?
All of a sudden you don't want to go to *school*?!'

'I hate school!' said Bernie. 'The teachers hate me. The kids call
me "Four-eyes". They make fun of the way I talk! They throw spit-
balls at me! They put nails on my chair. They – '

'Bernie, stop that at once! You – must – go – to – school!'

'Why?'

'For two reasons: first, you're forty-six years old – '

'Oh, ma . . .'

' – And second, you're the principal!'

MAXIE: Papa, will you buy me – to help in all my schoolwork – an
encyclopedia?

FATHER: Are you crazy? You can walk to school, like all the other
kids do.

On college bulletin board

Learn from the past:
DON'T TAKE HISTORY 4

Caterina Delfaco brought several of her college chums home for the weekend. With considerable intensity they discussed Darwin and the revisionists' criticism of the theory of evolution.

To all of this, Caterina's old-fashioned grandmother, born and raised in Sicily, said, 'Younga girls, justa ready to live – why you worry about sucha thing?'

'It's a very complex subject, gramma.'

'Isa *simple*!' Gramma scoffed. 'In old country, we know answer. Listen: ifa *bambino* look like papa, thassa heredity. But ifa he look like *vicino* – how you say, *vicino*, Caterina?'

'"Neighbour," gramma.'

'If bambino look like neighbour, thassa . . .'

'Environment,' sighed Caterina.

You must know a great deal about a subject to know how little is known about it.

L. R.

From St Andrew's University brochure

> Apart from an isolated incident of violence in 1470,
> when the Dean of the Faculty of Arts was shot at
> with bows and arrows, and if one glosses over the
> Jacobite demonstrations of 1715, the university has
> been singularly free of student unrest.

R. O. White, president of the Altoona Bank, went back to college for his class reunion. He dropped in on his old economics professor. And as they were chatting, the professor said, 'Here's something that will interest you – this year's final exam.'

White scanned the exam, then said, 'I could swear these are the identical questions you asked my class twenty years ago!'

'Quite so,' said the professor with a smile.

'But if you always ask the same questions, don't you think the students will get wise?'

'They do.'

'Don't they pass the questions on to next year's class?'

'Sure.'

'Then doesn't everyone get an A on every exam?'

'Not at all,' said the professor. 'In economics, the questions stay the same, year after year – but we keep changing the answers.'

ᔆ

A maiden at college, Miss Breeze,
Weighed down by B.A.'s and Ph.D.'s.
Collapsed from the strain.
Said her doctor, 'It's plain,
You are killing yourself – by degrees.'

ᔆ

Sister Elizabeth moved among the desks, chatting with each of the new students in the St Ignatius Sunday School class. 'And what's your name, lass?'

'Jennifer McGonigle.'

'An' do you read Gaelic?'

Jennifer knit her brow. 'Sister, Oy only been here five minutes.'

ᔆ

PROFESSOR: Miss Gomez, can you tell the class the name of the philosopher who wrote *The Critique of Pure Reason*?

MISS GOMEZ: (*blushing*): I can't.

PROFESSOR: Good! That's the first correct answer you've given all semester.*

ᔆ

Mr McNulty and his grandson, Stephen, age ten, were taking a walk. 'Grampa,' said Stephen, 'what's the largest ocean on the globe?'

'Eh – oh my. That's a poser, it is.' said Mr McNulty.

A little later, Stephen asked, 'How far is it from Dublin to Tanzania?'

Mr McNulty scratched his head. 'Faith! – and it's very far, is all I know.'

*The *Critique* was, of course, written by I(mmanuel) Kant.

And a little later the boy asked, 'Why is the sky blue?'

Mr McNulty frowned, 'Begorra, if I – ' then, observing the expression on little Stephen's face, he quickly added, 'Don't be gettin' discouraged, lad. Ask me more, more. How ilse can a young 'un be expectin' to *learn* anythin'?!'

See also **The English, The English Language**

Embarrassing Moments

The young man went into the airline ticket office and scanned the three women behind the counters. One was an attractive brunette, one a pleasant, plain girl, and the third a ravishing redhead with an ample bosom. The young man stepped to her station. 'What flights do you have to Pittsburgh?'

As she leaned over the schedule, her uniform revealed a creamy expanse; the young man's eyes popped.

'Pittsburgh – Pittsburgh...' The buxom beauty looked up. 'Next flight at three fifteen.'

'Okay. I'll take a picket to – ' He stopped, crimson. 'Oh, God!'

The newly-weds were having their new apartment painted. The new wife, coming out of the shower and slipping into a bathrobe, suddenly noticed a large handprint on a freshly painted wall of the bedroom. 'Painter!' she called down the stairs. 'Painter! Would you please come up here?'

The painter came up the stairs.

'You won't *believe* this!' said the bride. 'Would you like to see where my husband put his hand in the dark last night?'

The painter cleared his throat. 'I sure would, lady. But first I've got to finish the downstairs closet.'

On a very crowded bus in the Bronx, Mrs Frenkel kept groping in her huge, zippered handbag for her change purse.

'Lady,' said the man next to her, 'I'll pay your fare.'

'No, thank you, I can afford!' said Mrs Frenkel – and groped and fumbled some more.

'Lady, I will *gladly* pay – '

'No, no. I'll get mine purse open – '

'Lady, till you get it open, you already unzipped my pants three times!'

A senator, who prided himself on having a phenomenal memory, was pumping hands in the receiving line during his campaign for re-election. A modest little man approached him, saying, 'Senator, you don't remember me, but back in the seventies I made your shirts – '

'Major Shurtz,' the senator boomed. 'I'd recognize you anywhere!'

TRUE STORY

A pretty girl, suffering from hay fever, leaving for a posh dinner party, decided she needed two handkerchiefs for the evening – and stuck the extra one into her bodice.

At the dinner, having used up one handkerchief, she reached into her bosom for the fresh one. She rummaged around without success – and suddenly became aware that the conversation had stopped and all the guests were watching her. 'Excuse me!' she exclaimed. 'But I *know* I had two when I arrived.'

See also **Can You Believe It?, Dummies, Shlemiels, Snafus, True Tales**

The English

THE ENGLISH, THE JEWS – AND OTHERS

Englishmen prize privacy; Jews prize intimacy.

The English dislike displaying their feelings; Jews think feelings are meant to be verbalized.

Englishmen understate the serious ('The riot was a bit of a mess') and overstate the trivial ('What a *frightfully* amusing hat!');

Jews inflate what is important ('That will blacken his name for all time!') and pooh-pooh what is not cataclysmic ('Stroke-shmoke, he can still wink with one eye!').

The English repress uneasiness; Jews feed it banquets of nourishment.

An Englishman treats a disaster as unfortunate; a Jew thinks a hangnail an injustice.

The English are embarrassed by confidences; Jews are let down by 'coldness.' . . .

Where Egypt wails, England blinks. Where Hindu women tear their hair, English women study their nails.

An Italian explodes invective; an Englishman sniffs, 'Really?'

When the Russians thunder '*Averyone* knows . . .', the English demur 'But I should think that . . .'

Where Americans cry, 'It's terrific!' Englishmen concede, 'Rather impressive.'

And where Englishmen murmur 'What a pity,' Jews cry 'What a disaster!'

Jews may strike Anglo-Saxons as verbose and melodramatic because Jews are early taught to feel an *obligation* to respond to the misfortunes of others with visible, audible sympathy – so that no one can possibly fail to recognize the depth and sensitivity of one's compassion.

To Jews, emotions are not meant to be nursed in private: they are meant to be dramatized and displayed – so that they can be *shared*. . . .

The English think a 'stiff upper lip' is a sign of courage; Mediterranean people judge a 'stiff upper lip' to be *inappropriate* (why should suffering cast doubt on courage?) – since eyes filled with tears, and eloquent expressions of consolation, can give so much comfort to those, stricken by fate, who have been raised, too, to expect men to be *simpático*, to act decently, to be *sympatish* conveyors of 'feeling-with.'

I have come to the conclusion that Americans treat 'neurotic' as a synonym for 'nuts'; that Englishmen think 'neurotic' an adjective applicable to foreigners; and that Jews consider 'neurotic' a synonym for 'human'.

from the introduction to my
Treasury of Jewish Quotations

Scene: English Speaking Union Headquarters, London

'Calderwood? Are you, by chance, related to the Wiltshire Calderwoods?' asked Lord Parkenhurst.

'I'm afraid not,' said the American.

'Ah, then the Calderwoods of Burford Manor?'

'Nope. Sorry, sir.... You Englishmen are so conscious of ancestry...'

'But of course,' sniffed Lord Parkenhurst. 'I, for example, can trace my forebears all the way back to Queen Anne.'

'Well,' sighed the American, 'I have Irish, Italian, French and Portuguese blood.'

'By Jove!' exclaimed Lord Parkenhurst. 'How sporting of your mother.'

Sign in Midlands hotel garden:

Ladies and gentlemen will not, and others must not, pick the flowers in this garden.

The English Language

THE ORDEAL OF MR PARKHILL

Mr Parkhill did not see how he could, in conscience, promote Mr Kaplan to Miss Higby's grade (only last week Mr Kaplan had referred to the codifier of the laws of gravity as 'Isaac Newman'), and he knew that he could not bring himself to advise Mr Kaplan, as he was often tempted, to transfer to some other night school where he might perhaps be happier. The undeniable fact was that there was no other night school in which Hyman Kaplan could possibly be happier. Mr Parkhill might be happier; Miss Higby might be happier; a dozen members of the beginners' grade would surely be happier. But Mr Kaplan? That intrepid scholar displayed the strongest conceivable affection, an affection bordering on the lyrical, for his alma mater.

That was another thing. Strictly speaking, of course, the ANPSA could not possibly be the alma mater of someone who had never graduated from it; but Mr Kaplan had a way of acting as if it were.

That was yet another of the baffling characteristics that made Mr Kaplan so difficult to contend with: his cavalier attitude to reality, which he seemed to think he could alter to suit himself. How else could one describe a man who identified the immortal Strauss waltz as 'the Blue Daniel'? Or who, in recounting the tale of the cloak spread in the mud before Queen Elizabeth, insisted on crediting the gallantry to 'Sir Walter Reilly'? Or who identified our first First Lady as 'Mother Washington'? True, George Washington was the father of our country, but that did not make Martha the *mother*. It was all terribly frustrating.

Every way Mr Parkhill turned, he seemed to sink deeper and deeper into the Kaplan morass. If Mr Kaplan could not be promoted, much less graduated, what *could* be done about him? Sometimes it looked to Mr Parkhill as if Mr Kaplan was deliberately trying to stay in the beginners' grade for the rest of his (i.e., Mr Parkhill's) life . . .

What could be done about Hyman Kaplan? The man simply refused to learn. No, Mr Parkhill promptly corrected himself: it was not that Mr Kaplan refused to learn; what Mr Kaplan refused to do was *conform*. That was an entirely different matter. Mr Parkhill could get Mr Kaplan to understand a rule – of grammar or spelling or punctuation; what he did not seem able to do was get Mr Kaplan to *agree* with it. Somewhere, somehow, Hyman Kaplan had gotten it into his head that to bend the knee to custom was a hairsbreadth from bending the neck to slavery. (To Mr Kaplan, the plural of 'pie' was 'pious'.)

Nor was that all which impeded Mr Kaplan's progress. The laws of English, after all, have developed century after century, like the common law; and like the common law, they gain in authority precisely from the fact that men go on observing them down the countless years. But Mr Kaplan was not in the slightest impressed by precedent. He seemed to take the position that each rule of grammar, each canon of syntax, each convention of usage, no matter how ancient or how formidable, had to prove its case anew – to him. He seemed to make the whole English language start from scratch. (The plural of 'sandwich', he had once declaimed, is 'delicatessen'.)

And there was another perplexity. Whereas all the other students came to school in order to be instructed, Mr Kaplan seemed to come in order to be consulted. It had taken a good deal of persuasion on Mr Parkhill's part, for instance, to convince Mr Kaplan that there simply is no feminine form of 'ghost'. If the feminine of 'host' is 'hostess', Mr Kaplan had observed, then surely the feminine of 'ghost' should be 'ghostess'.

It was most trying. Not that Mr Kaplan was an obstreperous student. On the contrary. Not one of Mr Parkhill's abecedarians had ever been more eager, more enthusiastic, more athirst and aflame for knowledge. The trouble was that Mr Kaplan was so eager, so enthusiastic, so athirst and aflame that he managed to convert the classroom into a courtroom – a courtroom, moreover, in which the entire English language found itself put on the stand as defendant.

How else could one describe the extraordinary process by which Mr Kaplan had come to the conclusion that if a pronoun is a word used instead of a noun, a proverb is a pronoun used in place of a verb? It was preposterous, of course; yet when Mr Parkhill had challenged Mr Kaplan to give the class *one single example* of a pronoun used in place of a verb, Mr Kaplan, transported by that elation which possessed him *in statu pupillari*, beamed, 'I'll give *t'ree* exemples. Soppoze you are on vacation, an' sombody esks: "Who vants to go for a svim?" T'ree pipple enswer: "I!" "Me!" "You!" All pronouns. No voibs.' (Mr Olansky had almost had a stroke that night.)

Surely a student could not be permitted to go on changing the tongue of Keats and Swift and Trollope to suit himself. But if a pupil refused to accept authority, the testimony of experts, the awesome weight of precedent, to what higher court could his preceptor possibly appeal? Ay, there was the rub. Mr Kaplan believed that modern cities consist of streets, boulevards, and revenues. He gave the principal parts of the verb 'to fail' as 'fail ... failed ... bankrupt'. Once he had stunned the beginners' grade of the American Night Preparatory School for Adults by announcing that the opposite of 'inhale' is – 'dead'. And once he drove poor Miss Mitnick, who was always right but never victorious, to tears – when he declared that whenever he was on vacation, 'I gat op six o'clock in the morning no matter what time it is.' And the irrepressible scholar had given the positive, comparative, and superlative forms of 'good' as 'good ... better ... high cless!' and of 'bad' as nothing less than 'bad ... worse ... rotten!' There was no end to Mr Kaplan's inventive embellishments of the English tongue.

Mind you, Mr Parkhill reminded himself, Mr Kaplan did not deny that English had rules – good rules, sensible rules. What he would not accept, apparently, was that the rules applied to *him*. Mr Kaplan had a way of getting Mr Parkhill to submit each rule to the test of reason, and Mr Parkhill was beginning to face the awful suspicion that he was no match for Mr Kaplan, who had a way of operating with rules of reason entirely his own. Only a man with rules of reason entirely his own would dare to give the opposite of 'height' as 'lowth' or the plural of 'blouse' as 'blice' or the plural of 'woman' as 'married'.

There was no longer any doubt in Mr Parkhill's mind that Mr Kaplan did inhabit a universe all his own. That would explain how Mr Kaplan had come to define 'diameter' as a machine that counts dimes, and once dubbed the waterway that connects the Atlantic and Pacific 'the Panama Kennel'. Mr Kaplan expressed considerable admiration for the great Roman ruler he called 'Julius Scissor'.

Mr Parkhill passed his hand across his brow. He wondered if it might not be best to think of Mr Kaplan not as a pupil but as some sort of cosmic force, beyond human influence, a reckless, independent star that roared through the heavens in its own unconstrained and unpredictable orbit. Mr Kaplan was *sui generis*. Perhaps that was why he so often responded with delight, rather than despair, when Mr Parkhill corrected him. It had taken Mr Parkhill a long time to discover that Mr Kaplan's smile signified not agreement but consolation.

One night Mr Kaplan had delivered a rhapsodic speech on a topic that he had announced as 'Amazink Stories Abot Names in US'. New York, he had cheerfully confided to his comrades, was originally called 'New Hamsterdam'. Montana was so named because it was 'full of montains', and Ohio, he averred, 'sonds like a Indian yawnink'. An Indian yawning... And once he had given the opposite of 'dismay' as 'next June'.

Sometimes Mr Parkhill thought Mr Kaplan would never find peace until he had invented a language all his own.

adapted from my
O K*A*P*L*A*N! MY K*A*P*L*A*N!

ON ENGLISH
One fowl is a goose, but two are called geese
Yet the plural of mouse should never be meese,

If I speak of a foot and you show me your feet,
And I give you a boot, would a pair be called beet?
If one is a tooth and the whole set are teeth,
Why should not the plural of booth be called beeth?

THE TWENTY-FIVE BASIC RULES OF
ENGLISH SPELLING AND GRAMMAR

1. Correct spelling is a Must.
2. 'Just between you and I' is a Mustn't. It's as much of a mustn't as 'They telephoned she'.
3. Be sure to never split an infinitive.
4. Don't dangle with participles: 'Running for the bus, a taxi hit my uncle.'
5. The difference between 'teach' and 'learn' should learn you to pay attention. Teachers don't have to pay attention, so they don't learn; they just teach.
6. When studying grammar, a spiral notebook of well-lined pages are useful. (This shows that subjects and verbs are enemies.)
7. Don't never use no double negative. Triple negative are even worst.
8. Always make a pronoun agree with their referent.
9. Beware of the 'them-those' trap. For instance, don't write, 'Them apples are rotten' if they are not.
10. Many people *love* to use commas, which are not necessary. For instance, 'She ate, the fool' is a comment. 'She ate the fool' is correct, if she is a cannibal.
11. One of the trickiest points in punctuation is to use apostrophe's correctly. They are as sensitive as measle's.
12. Never use 'real' when you mean ' very'. Therefore: 'She is real stupid' shows that you are very stupid. (This point is real important.)
13. Adjectives are not adverbs. Write careful. (I know that's hardly.)
14. Question marks can be dynamite. Use them carefully. 'You sure are pretty?' means you are not sure I am pretty. That is an insult.
15. Many a student is undone by 'who' and 'whom'. Remember

George Ade's remark: '"Whom are you?" she asked, for she had gone to night school.'

16. Avoid the excessive use of exclamation points!!!! It is silly to write, 'Yesterday, I woke up!!!' because that suggests that today you did not, which is probably true.

17. When you want to say something that indicates anyone, or all of us, the pronoun 'one' is better than 'he' or 'she'. Fats Waller put it neatly: 'One never knows, do one?'

18. Observe the difference between 'don't' and 'doesn't'. It's shocking to hear so many high-school graduates say 'He don't care.' What they mean, of course, is 'I don't care.' Their grades proved it.

19. Never write 'heighth' or 'weighth'. They just are not righth.

20. If you write 'Who's hand is stroking my thigh?' you'll never know who's pulling whose leg. Such information can be valuable.

21. 'Irregardless' is not in the dictionary. 'Hopefully' is – and I hope to God you never use it.

22. Don't use 'neither' when you mean 'either'. Either use 'neither' correctly or don't use it all all. And don't use 'either' if you mean 'ether' neither.

23. Guard against absurd and unnecessary repetitions. This here rule is especially important for new beginners.

24. A real booby trap to avoid is 'when' – especially when a sentence like 'I do not deny I wasn't afraid' occurs when you mean 'I won't deny I *was* afraid.' Most writers are, so they master syntax, which is the only tax that doesn't cost money.

25. Don't forget the crucial difference between 'lie' and 'lay'.
   a. The former takes no object ('I lie in bed') but the latter must ('Lay that pistol down, mother').
   b. 'To lie' means to express something not true; 'to lay' means expressing something more urgent.

Okay? Now, memorize these laws, plus one more: be sure to reread anything you write to make sure you don't accidentally any words out.

L. R. PLUS PREDECESSORS

Casey Stengel, master mangler of our tongue, was asked how it felt to be eighty years old. 'Let me just put it this way,' said Casey.

'You have to remember: a lot of people my age are dead at the present time.'

‿

From a brochure of a Tokyo car rental agency

When a passenger of foot heave in sight, tootle the horn.
Trumpet at him melodiously first,
but if he still obstacles your passage
then tootle him with vigour.

thanks to DONALD CARROLL

‿

Sign in men's WC, basement, British Museum

PLEASE OBSERVE:
THESE FACILITIES ARE INTENDED
FOR CASUAL ABLUTIONS ONLY

‿

On a 'closed' window in a Brighton bank:

SERVICE SUSPENDED
WHILST CASHIER IS ENGAGED
ON ANCILLARY TILL ENTRIES

‿

On London lamp-posts to which wire-mesh trash cans are attached

ANY PERSON NOT PUTTING LITTER INTO
THIS BASKET WILL BE LIABLE TO A FINE OF £5

(To this, H. W. Fowler railed: 'Those who have no litter to put into the basket must, it seems, rush to find some.')

‿

My wife, phoning Chicago from London: 'Is this the Overseas operator?'
A pitying voice replied, 'This is *one* of them, luv.'

‿

On Savile Row, I studied myself in the mirror and remarked, 'Isn't the jacket too large?'

The proprietor cleared his throat: 'If you will but permit the garment to assume its natural aplomb . . .'

To the *London Observer*

> Gentlemen:
>
>   I was impressed by your article headed "Escapees".   I thought it, was written by a deep thinkee.   But 'are you trend followees or trend settees?   Should you change your name to the Observee?   That might please the most forward-looking of your readees.
>
> Roy Herbert

See also **Accents, Bloopers, Radio and TV, Boo-boos, Famous People (as seen by Children), Freudian Slips, Goldwyniana, Graffiti, Headlines That Haunt Me, Malaprops, News Items That Haunt Me**

Epitaphs

Epitaphs   A monumental liar.

An inscription which hopes that virtues acquired by death will have a retroactive effect.

AMBROSE BIERCE

        Lying on behalf of those lying in state.

The revelation of such virtues that we would be well advised to resurrect the dead and bury the living.

L. R.

On a Tombstone in Dublin

> Beneath this lavish stone lies
> ALOYSIUS XAVIER SMILEY
> Buried one beautiful day in May

He lived the lovely life of Reilly –
Whenever Reilly was away.

∽

Herewith, epitaphs selected by a handful of celebrities for their own tombstones:

Clive Brook: Excuse me for not rising.

H. G. Wells: I *told* you so, dammit!

Dorothy Parker: Excuse my dust.

Warner Baxter: Did you hear about my operation?

Milton Berle: This one's on me.

Robert Benchley: All of this is over my head.

Author of mysteries: I'm involved in a plot.

L. R.:   This is much too deep for me.

A hypochondriac: I kept *telling* you I was sick!

Nunnally Johnson:

    I *thought* there was a funny taste about that last one.

Eulogies

Even the widow could not deny that her late husband, Norm, had been greatly disliked in the community. He had not one good friend; critics he had by the score. The Widow Schwartzberg asked Rabbi Nagel, 'Doesn't even a man like Norman – a model husband he was not – deserve some kind words after he *dies*?'

'You're right, Mrs Schwartzberg,' said the rabbi. 'I'll give your Norman a eulogy – a eulogy no one will ever forget.'

A large audience came to hear how Rabbi Nagel would frame a

funeral oration for Norman Schwartzberg. Here is what Rabbi Nagel declaimed:

> We are here to say goodbye to Norman Schwartz-berg. Frankly, he was not an admirable man. He never contributed to charity, he left many debts, his word was not as good as his bond, he drank too much, he carried on in ways to bring pain and sorrow to his faithful wife. . . . But one thing I can tell all of you, with profound conviction: compared to his brother Cooky, Norman was an absolute saint!

See also **Epitaphs**

Evidence

An English spinster, disliked in the village because of her superior ways and bluenose judgments, loudly accused Rufus Andrews of having reverted to his old heavy-drinking habits. 'I observed his wheelbarrow outside the local pub at eleven o'clock last night!'

That night, Rufus Andrews placed his wheelbarrow outside the spinster's door. It was still there next morning. . . .

It was a smashing success of a cocktail party the Fullertons threw, so much so that after an hour Mrs Halley tugged at her husband's sleeve and declared, 'Harvey, don't you think you – ought to stop drinking? . . . Why, your whole face is beginning to look blurred!'

The first mate, having received a cable that he was now the father of a fine, eight-pound boy, went on a glorious binge. The next morning, as he took the helm, he read in the ship's log: 'First mate Jennison was drunk last night.'

When the captain came into the cabin, Jennison said, 'Sir, I wish you would remove that entry in the log. I've never, never in my life been drunk before. Not on duty or off. But you see . . . last night, I received this cable!' He showed the captain the cable.

The captain read it. 'Congratulations, Jennison. But the entry stays in the log. After all, you *were* drunk.'

'Yes, sir, but – '

'There are no ifs, ands, or buts. Facts are facts!'

The next morning, the captain found this entry in the ship's log: 'The captain was sober last night.'

See also **Appearances, Can You Believe It, Courts, Hanky-panky, News Items That Haunt Me**

Faith

Faith can move mountains, but not furniture.

Homer Morton went off alone one day to scale the sheerest face of Mount Hood. He dug his crampon on to a ledge, which gave way, and Homer fell 150 feet – managing, by a miracle, to grab a branch from a gnarled tree that was growing in a crevice. He dangled there helplessly, swinging back and forth, calling, 'Help! Oh, God! Help!'

At last an immense, orotund voice far above intoned, 'My son, did you call?'

'Oh, yes, yes!' cried Homer. 'Please!'

'Do you at this moment have full true trust in Me?'

'Yes! Oh, Lord, yes!'

'Will you obey Me – without reservation?'

'Oh, yes, Lord!'

'Then, my son, let go of that branch . . .'

'*What?!*'

'I said, "Let . . . go . . . of . . . that . . . branch."'

A pause; then Morton said, 'Excuse me, Sir, but – is there anyone else up there?!'

'Fortunately we're insured against Acts of God,' said the

Reverend Martin after lightning struck, sending rafters crashing down on the church altar.

⌒

Canon Kilnarnock was travelling to London. The train stopped at Cambridge. A heavyset man of about forty entered the compartment. The two nodded to each other.

Canon Kilnarnock returned to his breviary. The large man sat down and opened a copy of a book whose bold title was visible to the canon:

Why I Am Not a Christian
by
Bertrand Russell

The canon sighed.

The train started, then stopped. A conductor, walking along the platform, called, 'Ten-minute delay. . . . Ten-minute delay.'

'Oh, dear, oh, dear,' said the canon. He glanced at his watch. 'I may miss my connection.'

'Let us pray you do not,' smiled the man from Cambridge, then winked.

'Ay. Pulling my leg a wee bit are ye?'

'I daresay,' the man chuckled.

'Ye nae believe in prayer?'

'No, I do not.'

'May I ask, what thin is y'r faith?'

'I,' said the man, 'am an atheist. . . . Does that offend you?'

The canon shrugged. 'Have y' thin read much o' the Good Book?'

'Not a line since I was sixteen.'

'Do y' know the arguments for faith by Saint Thomas Aquinas?' The man smiled. 'No.'

'Have ye perhaps read Saint Augustine?'

'I never felt the need to.'

'P'haps thin, Cardinal Newman? . . . E'en Malcolm Muggeridge?'

'No, no. They all seem to be gas bags.'

The canon studied the big man thoughtfully. 'Dare I be frank, sir, to a total stranger?'

'Of *course* you may, sir. I rather enjoy a healthy difference of opinion.'

'Well thin, sir. Ay have news f'r ye. Y're not an atheist. No, no. Y're an ignoramus.'

See also **God, Heaven, Reason**

Famous People (as Seen by Children)

Radium was discovered by Madman Curry.

The most famous Italian composer was Libretto.

Isaac Newman passed the law of gravity.

Beethoven had ten children; he practised on a spinster in his attic.

The biggest inventor (besides Thomas Edison) is Pat Pending.

The man who fought the windmills of Spain was Don Coyote.

Popular authors can win the Pullet Surprise.

The Gorgons looked like women, but more horrible.

Ben and Dick Arnold were terrible traitors.

See also **Cynics' Dictionary**

Fan Mail

Every writer learns, sooner or later, that a certain number of those who admire his work, and write in to tell him so, are oddballs. Others are not so much odd as nuts.

I don't know why people think that a writer is a sage, a seer, a psychiatrist – and an expert on bearded irises – all rolled into one; but readers do, they certainly do. I suppose it's because they attribute magic to print, and confuse a skill (writing) with a state (wisdom). Whatever the reason, I have received some of the most extraordinary, flabbergasting, cockamamy requests you can imagine from earnest letter-writing fans. My prose seems to exert a special magnetic effect upon epileptic masseuses and nearsighted bowlers.

Now, I have never mastered the art of solemn flippancy achieved by the late H. L. Mencken, whose hate mail was steeped in vituperative juices. Mencken answered all overwrought rages with a postcard on which was printed, briefly and to the point:

```
          Dear Sir or Madam:
          You may be right.
                    Yours,
                    H.L. Mencken
```

This answer often drove his irate correspondents up the wall.

I could never match such cold-blooded, definitive irony. I always answer letters gravely, even when they deserve scorn. This compulsive kindliness is both disgusting and cowardly. Whenever I go over my correspondence at the end of the year, I am stricken with shame. So, like any craven recreant, I try to restore my self-esteem by composing in my mind those searing, soul-satisfying replies I *should* have sent. Here, in my annual rite of purgation, are excerpts from some of the letters I received from readers last year, plus the answers I wish I had had the gumption to send back.

Who wrote 'The Battle Hymn of the Republic'?

I did.

I heard someone say that you once won the Noble Prize. Is that true?

Yes. I won the Noble Prize in 1971 for my invention of an index to Webster's Dictionary.

The Noble Foundation medal is inscribed:

TO A NOBLE FELLOW
FROM
MORRIS R. NOBLE

Morris R. Noble, who died of prolonged inhaling, was an immigrant from Bialystock who founded the Hug-Tite Girdle Corporation. It was his lifelong interest in girdles that made him set up a foundation.

Do you believe in interracial marriage?

Absolutely not. Intermarriage between the male and female races is the sole cause of humanity's problems.

. . . the Secret Meaning of Isaiah 8:14 makes it ABSOLUTELY PLAIN the world will END August 3 at 10:30 P.M.!!! What do you say to that?

Isaiah man like you is crocked.

In one of your books you say that you clip newspapers and magazines all the time for your files. I would like to know – what is your favouritemost clipping?

This one, from a small-town paper in Iowa:

> The baseball game between the Rockets and the Huskers was held in Mr Simpson's cow pasture, and ended in the third inning, with the score tied 1–1, when a runner slid into what he thought was second base.

Who was the first man in history to cross the United States on roller skates? It is my ambition to do something like that.

He was crazy. So are you.

I heard a TV discussion which mentioned the fact that Einstein proved that space is curved. This idea threw me for a loop. Can you explain 'Space is curved'?

Easily. You know what 'space' is. You know what 'curved' means. Now: the whole concept depends on what Einstein meant by 'is'.

Who was the first police commissioner of Kalamazoo, Michigan?

I was.

Do you know a cure for hiccups?

Yes.

We just bought a French poodle for our daughter, who wants to call him Amen-hotep. Can you give us an idea about what to do? We think Amen-hotep is a peculiar name for a poodle.

So do I. Amen-hotep was not French: he was an Egyptian and a gambler, addicted to playing pharaoh.

Tell your daughter she must learn to respect other people's hangups. A poodle named Amen-hotep is likely to think he is a mummy and may spend all his time lying on the floor with his paws folded across his chest. Dogs who lie on their back all day are no fun to throw sticks at.

My husband and I often read you, and he gets very angry with me because I do not agree with him. Whom do you think is right?

If he likes my work, him is right. If he doesn't, youm is.

My wife is a wiz at Brain-teasers and gave me one I can't figure out. It is driving me nuts:

'Horace is 2 years younger than his sister, Mame, and is losing his teeth. Mame is 4 years older than the cheerleader of their school in Great Neck. The janitor, who is always whistling, night and day, is 72. The total age of these four people is 183. What's the principle's name?'

My wife says the answer is easily apparent!

I am surprised you find this brain-teaser difficult. The answer is a cinch:
1. 'Night and Day' was written by Cole Porter, which is a perfect name for a janitor.
2. The difference between 'principle' and principal' is seven.
3. If Horace is losing his teeth while two years younger than his sister, put the blame on Mame.
4. If the janitor is seventy-two, he should quit and collect Social Security.

5. The principal's name is not Apparent. It is Theodore Feld-
    man, the most popular name for high school principals in
    Great Neck.

P.S. If I had a wife like yours, I would fill my back yard with quick-
    sand.

                                    from my *The Power of Positive Nonsense*

Which politician do you most (and least) admire?

The politician I most admire is the English bucko who proclaimed, 'I promise you that if I am elected, I will be neither partial
nor impartial.'

The politician I most despise is the flimflammer who told the
voters in Florida, in a campaign against Senator Claude Pepper:
'Did you know that my opponent once *matriculated* at college?
That he openly practices *monogamy?* That his sister works in New
York as a well-known *thespian!*'

Poor Pepper was clobbered at the polls.

In your opinion who was the greatest shortstop of all times?

In my opinion, I was the greatest shortstop of all time. The only
shortstop who was shorter was 'Pee-Wee' Pincus, who played for
the New Haven Nudnicks. 'Pee-Wee' was so short that even with
cleats on his shoes he could walk under the tables down at Mory's.

My biology teacher told us that grasshoppers make their buzzing sounds
by rubbing their back legs together. Is this true?

This is one of the most ridiculous prejudices law-abiding grasshoppers have to put up with. Grasshoppers make those buzzing
noises not by rubbing their back legs together but by blowing on
tiny kazoos which they conceal under their wings. The male
makes the 'zzz' sound and the female makes the 'bzz' sound.

Sometimes a grasshopper will produce both a 'zzz' and a 'bzz'
sound simultaneously, like this: 'ZzzBzzzzz'. That means you are
listening to a grasshopper who has an identity crisis.

In English novels they are always giving someone's weight not in pounds
but in 'stones'. How can I find out how many pounds are in a stone?

Weigh the stone, dummy.

Which one man or woman do you think has done the most for the human race?

Whitcomb L. Judson. He invented the zipper.

What is the quickest way how someone gets to be a 'pro' writer?

The quickest way how someone gets to be a 'pro' writer is to compose petitions in support of causes, like:

DISARM TODAY!

or

YANKEE, GET LOST!

That will put you in the *pro* ranks at once.

If you want to be a con writer, on the other hand, compose patriotic petitions *against* things, like:

BOYCOTT BEETS FROM BURUNDI

or

STAMP OUT DANGLING PARTICIPLES

Who discovered the Sea of Cortez?

I did.

Did you ever know Aimee Semple McPherson?

No. But I did enjoy her evangelical shenanigans. What I most admire is her faith: she was buried with a telephone beside her.

How did animals ever get the names we call them by?

One of the tidier things man has done is to give names to things: birds, beasts, insects, fishes. This was not easy. An ichthyologist, for instance, can't just take a pencil and clipboard and dive down to a blunt-nosed flounder, say, and ask: 'Excuse me, fish: I am taking a poll for the US Census Bureau. What is your name, please?'

The men in charge of fish-naming *did* try this system at first, but they got fouled up something terrible because every fish gave the same answer: 'Glp.'

This led the ichthyologist, who have an unshakable faith in data, to conclude that *all* fish are named 'Glp'. But when they fed this into a computer and asked for its opinion, quick as a flash came the answer: 'No!' When a computer answers 'No!' instead of just flipping its discs, you can be sure something important has happened in the world of science.

The same thing happened to the zoologists, who were assigned to name animals. *Every single specimen of a species interviewed gave the same name.* Every dog, for instance, said his name was 'Bark', every cat, 'Meow', every cow, 'Moo', and so on.

For a long time, during the Idiopathic Era, people went around calling every dog 'Bark' and no one minded, but when men began to move out to the suburbs and called their dogs in from the street to give them their vitamin-enriched chopped liver, any one man's call of 'Here, Bark! Here, Bark, Bark, Bark!' brought every dog in the neighbourhood to his door. They came like lemmings, and many died of overeating.

Things couldn't go on this way, so dogologists decided to name each *breed*, once and for all. They gave many a dog a bad name, like 'Schnauzer'. Anyone knows that if you call a sensitive dog a Schnauzer, he will develop post-nasal drip.

୧

Is it true that in Bali, servants fall into a trance the minute you order them to do something?

Yes. The Balinese have such a horror of being told to do something that they fall into a coma.

You will no doubt ask, 'Then how can you get a servant to do anything – like, say, getting your wife's hat out of the car?'

'This way:

YOU: Bongo, I recall that our car has one seat in front and another in back, has it not?

BONGO: I share that recollection, master.

YOU: And is it not true that when my wife, your lovely mistress, left this morning, she was wearing a hat?

BONGO: I did observe that myself.

YOU: (*chuckling merrily*) I remember certain occasions when she returned *without* her hat. Ha, ha, ha. Can you remember similar events?

BONGO: Ha, ha, ha, yes, many.

YOU: Then, dear Bongo, perhaps you could drift out to the car and observe whether the hat of the mistress is indeed on that back seat we just discussed?

BONGO: An excellent suggestion, master.

YOU: And if you *do* observe the hat of the mistress there, would you be so kind as to bring it into the house where, I assure you, both it and your admirable services will be hugely appreciated?

Baliphiles tell me that if you talk this way, the chances are even-Stephen that Bongo will not fall into a trance.

Fate

THE ACCURSED EMERALD

To the great charity ball of the season, the buxom dowager wore a huge emerald pendant. And in the ladies' powder room at the Hotel Pierre, all the women crowded around her to get a closer look at the glistening gem. The dowager boasted, 'This happens to be the third largest emerald in the whole world. The largest is the Queen of England's. Then comes the Onassis. Then comes this one, which is called the Lefkowitz.'

'What a jewel!'

'How lucky you are!'

'Wait, nothing in life is that easy,' said the dowager. 'Unfortunately, the wearer of the fabulous Lefkowitz emerald must bear with the famous Lefkowitz curse.'

The ladies were silent for but a second. 'And what is the Lefkowitz curse?'

The dowager sighed, 'Lefkowitz.'

Message in fortune cookie: You will make fortune on next investment.

Message in next fortune cookie: Disregard previous message.

Flashers

Old Mr Cardohy, in room 109 of the old people's home, was as mischievous as he was spry – and bored. One day, reading about the wave of 'streakers' around the country, he decided, on a sudden impulse, to undress and, during dinner, run through the dining room.

The room was indeed packed when naked Mr Cardohy appeared in the doorway, yelled 'Eureka!', ran around the tables and out.

The gaping silence was broken by old man Strudnick, a tailor: 'Whatever that nut was wearing, folks, he should never wear it again until he has it *pressed*, for God's sake!'

See also **Appearances, Clothes**

Freudian Slips

These items actually appeared in print: none was invented by this delighted compiler.

L. R.

Upon arriving at the Honolulu airport, two men were given coveted lays by Hawaiian maidens.

The rapists tell us . . .*

The President, who has been sick for several days, is now in bed with a coed.

They were married and lived happily even after.

There are millions of desirable women who are unattacked, and hungry for love.

*Therapists.

Mr and Mrs Fechner returned yesterday from Hawaii, where they spent two weeks of unallowed pleasure.

The head of the investment firm would not say whether, in his own private holdings, he was more interested in stocks or blonds.

A seven-pound baby boy arrived last night to frighten the lives of Mr and Mrs Sherman Caswell.

Before the verdict was rendered this morning, 'Miss Mexico' told interviewers that if the court freed her, she would become a nut.

Mrs and Mr Seligman have lied most of their married life in Hartford.

Overcome by gas while taking a bath, she owes her life to the watchfulness of the janitor.

The prosecutors, representing the State, asked prospective jurors if they would inflict the death penalty 'if the evidence warranted it.' Those who said they were opposed to capital punishment under any circumstances were executed.

The Red Cross paid for emergency care and later found a free bed for him in an institution specializing in the treatment of artcritics.

The protesting students insisted that before they were arrested they only intended to show their opposition to the speaker by pissing.

Telegram to wife

HAVING WONDERFUL TIME. WISH YOU WERE HER.

On bill from lawyer, typed by his secretary: Bull rendered: $500.

BEAUTY QUEEN UNVEILS BUST
AT DEDICATION CEREMONY

News column: James Melville, the district attorney, then forcefully addressed the jury and gummed up the case.

Society column: Their annual ball was held last night at the Hilton Hotel. Seldom have we seen such a glittering display of beaux and bellies.

Social notes: He is visiting our town with his bitter half.

In department store: Bath towels for your whole damp family.

Mr and Mrs Oliver Sloane request the pleasure of your presents at the marriage of their daughter . . .

If we would only send young American tenors to stud abroad, they would return immensely improved.

VOTE FOR
JORDAN BARNES
Your fiend in City Hall

The report was signed by five faulty members of the university.

She went into the hospital after being bitten by a spider in a bathing suit.

Mr Okum lives with his wife, his high-school sweetheart, and three sons.

When his wife called from London, Mr Favish said, 'It was wonderful to hear her voice and realize she was over three thousand miles away.'

He collapsed on the sidewalk and died without medical assistance.

Service magazine for home furnishings: Mr Frenkel won the national bedding award from the National Association. Mr Frenkel has ten children.

His friends could give no reason why he should have committed suicide. He is single.

The chief is inclined to believe that a crossed wife might be the cause of the fire.

The bride and her mother were in the deceiving line.

The All-Girl orchestra was rather weak in the bras section.

Mrs Williams of the Home Garden Club gave a short talk on how to keep ants out of your blooming pants.

Wanted:
Job as janitor. Long experience.
Expert moper.

See also **Bloopers, Radio and TV, Boo-boos, Headlines That Haunt Me, How's That Again?, Malaprops, News Items That Haunt Me, Typos**

Freudian Tales

Tilly Schechtman was unmarried. She had never been married. She had never been proposed to. She had never even been – betrayed. And, alas, Tilly was thirty-three years old – plain, not graceful, plump – and by now boy-shy and man-scared. Her parents grieved sorely over Tilly's sad, sad plight.

One day, Mrs Schechtman said to Tilly, 'I have been thinking and thinking, and I think I have a good idea. To end this sitting around, night after night, hoping *maybe* some nice man just will come . . . from where, Tilly? From the clouds? From a star? A white knight, I suppose, on a pony – '

'Mama. . . .'

'Tilly, it's a whole lot smarter you should put an ad in the newspaper!'

'Mama!' gasped the spinster. 'Are you joking?'

'I'm not joking.'

'But the *shame* – '

'What shame? You don't give your *name*, Tilly. You write it like this.' She handed her daughter a paper, on which she had carefully printed:

A CHARMING JEWISH GIRL, FROM FINE FAMILY,
EDUCATED, GOOD COOK, BIG READER, AGE 28, WOULD
LIKE TO MEET KIND, INTELLIGENT, REFINED JEWISH
GENTLEMAN. OBJECT: FRIENDSHIP FIRST. CONCERTS,
PLAYS, WALKS IN PARK, LECTURES, MUSEUMS . . .
THEN MAYBE MARRIAGE

—BOX 462.

Tilly stammered and gulped protestations, but her mother insisted, 'What can you *lose*, Tilly? And just think of what could happen! Who knows? A good man – a teacher. With your intelligence, all the books you have read, the music you know . . .'

And so the advertisement appeared. And each morning the girl known as 'Box 462' hastened down three flights of stairs to meet the postman. . . .

On the fifth day she came running up and burst into the apartment: 'Mama! An answer! Forwarded from the paper!' With flushed cheeks, Tilly ripped open the envelope, devoured the contents – sank into a chair as if in a state of shock, and burst into tears.

'Tilly!' cried Mrs Schechtman, 'Tilly! Tell mama! What's *wrong?*'

In a strangling voice, Tilly said, 'It's from papa.'

See also **Just Jokes**

Gambling

Two friends, Nora and Cindy, recently divorced, decided to celebrate their freedom with a weekend of gambling in Las Vegas. In the Scheherazade Casino, they walked past the slot machines, the blackjack tables, the dice wells – to the roulette tables. 'All my *life* I've wanted to play roulette,' said Nora. 'How do I decide which number to choose?'

'It's all luck,' said Cindy. 'Look, my address is Eighteen eighteen Eighteenth Street. So I'll – ' she placed a chip on number eighteen. 'Maybe it's my lucky number.'

Nora said, 'I don't have a lucky number . . .'

'Your age,' said Cindy. 'Why not put a chip on your age?'

Nora placed a hundred dollars' worth of chips on number thirty-four.

'Bets closed!' The croupier spun the wheel, then tossed the little ball into the whirling circle. The ball bounced and clacked and Cindy's eyes were wide as saucers. The ball nestled into its cradle. 'Number forty-two,' intoned the croupier.

'Too bad, dear,' said Cindy, turning to Nora.

Nora lay on the floor. She had fainted.

⌒

On a slot machine

Warning: This Machine is Coiniverous!

⌒

Scene: Atlantic City Rooming House

BOY: Golly, Pop, all the other boys in my class play ball in the schoolyard every day – and hang out together – and go swimming –

POP: Shut up, Alfred. Deal.

⌒

Gambling: The only certain way of getting nothing for something.

WILSON MIZNER

BAER: Did you know there's an absolutely foolproof way to come home from Vegas or Atlantic City with a small fortune?

ASPIS: Really? What's that?

BAER: Go there with a large fortune.

See also **Ingenuity, Stratagems**

The Gay Set

Bisexual: A man who likes girls as well as the next fellow.

'Mrs Brett, is it true that your grandson is a practising homo-sexual?'

Mrs Brett sighed sadly, 'Yeah.'

'So where is his office?'

'Hello, mother.'

'Hel-*lo*, Sherman. How is my darling, my favourite son?'

'Fine, mama. Great.'

'Thank God. You're eating well—?'

'Mama, listen, I'm married!'

'*Married?* Sherman? *Mazel tov* and you should be happy for a hundred and twenty years—'

'Mama, wait. Listen . . . I didn't marry a Jew . . .'

'So? I know some wonderful gentiles.'

'But, mama. I hope you're not prejudiced – against blacks.'

'Me? Prejudiced? Don't be silly. "Grow with the times," that's what I always say. You have to grow with the times! . . . So what's her name?'

'Mama, that's another thing. Brace yourself. "Her" name is – Peter.'

Silence '"Peter?!"'

'Yes, mama.'

'That's not a nickname, for like Patricia?'

'No, mama. Peter is a boy. We really love each other. . . . We're trying to find a place to live. There's so much prejudice against blacks. . . . We want to start a home – '

'Until you find a place, Sherman darling, you and Peter can come and stay with us!'

'Oh, mama, you're wonderful. . . . But how can we stay with you? Your apartment only has one bedroom . . .'

'So? You and Peter can't sleep in one bedroom?!'

'Sure, mama—but where will you and papa sleep?'

'That worries you? Put it out of your *mind*, Sherman. Your papa will sleep on the couch in the living room. Many is the night he slept there, when I had the flu, when my back was in traction – '

'Oh, wonderful. But, mama, if Peter and I share the bedroom and papa takes the sofa – where will *you* sleep?'

'Ah, Sherman, my own little Sherman – don't you know yet that about your mother, who loves you more than life itself, you never, *never* have to worry?'

'But you can't sleep on the floor – '

'Who sleeps on a floor? Don't *worry*, Sherman. I will never cause you trouble or discomfort. I will never stand in the way of your happiness. I – '

'Mama, stop beating around the bush. *Where* will you sleep?'

'Who'll sleep? Relax, Sherman. The minute I'm hanging up to finish this wonderful heart-to-heart talk between a mother and her son, I'm going to jump out of the window.'

Scene: The Palm Court, Plaza Hotel

Mrs William Forsythe was having tea with her twenty-three-year-old son, the handsome – indeed, the very handsome – Reginald. The teacup trembled in Mrs Forsythe's hand when Reginald said, 'But I *love* him, mother. And Marvin loves me. We want to get mar – '

'*Please!*' said Mrs Forsythe, 'can you imagine what people will *say?*'

'We don't care,' said Reginald. 'But I do, very much, want *your* blessing!'

'No, Reggie. Never!'

'Are you so old-fashioned, mother? So afraid of convention? Give me one reason, other than – '

Mrs Forsythe looked her son straight in the eye. 'He's *Jewish!*'

God

A brilliant young student came to the old, learned rabbi and defiantly exclaimed. 'I must tell you the truth: I have become an atheist! I no longer believe in God.'

'And how long,' asked the elder, 'have you been studying Talmud?'

'Five years.'

'Only five years,' exclaimed the rabbi, 'and you have the *nerve* to call yourself an atheist?!'

Don't blame God: He's only human.

L. R.

If triangles had a god, he would have three sides.

VOLTAIRE

Man is surely crazy; he can't make a worm, but he makes gods by the dozen.

God: the most popular scapegoat for our sins.

MARK TWAIN

God will forgive me: it is his *métier*.

HEINRICH HEINE

God said, 'Let us make man in our image,' and Man said, 'Let us make God in our image.'

DOUGLAS JERROLD

YIDDISH SAYINGS

What the Lord does is certainly best – probably.

Dear God: You help total *strangers* – so why not me?

Dear God: I am a believing Jew and know that You will provide: but please tell me: why You don't provide *until* You provide?!

If God lived on earth, men would knock out all His windows.

God is not everything that exists; God is everything that does not exist.

REMY DE GOURMONT

Rabbi Beckman, the young, new rabbi in a Connecticut temple, greatly loved to play golf.

One sunny Saturday morning, after services, Rabbi Beckman felt so powerful a craving to play a few holes, that he begged God to forgive him for breaking the Sabbath, tossed his golf bag into the back of the car, and sped off to a course where he was certain no one would recognize him. With an apology to his Maker, the Rabbi teed off. . . .

Up in heaven, Moses suddenly bolted upright. 'Lord! Lord!' he cried. 'Do my eyes deceive me? There, Holy One – do You *see?*'

'Y-yes,' said the Lord.

'That's Rabbi Sylvan Beckman!' said Moses. 'Playing golf on Your Holy Sabbath!'

'Dear me,' sighed the Lord.

'Such a transgression!' said Moses. 'How will You punish him?'

'We must teach him a lesson.' God cupped His hands over His mouth and – just as Rabbi Beckman teed off for the second hole, the Almighty, King of the Universe, let out His breath in a mighty, cosmic *'Whoooosh!'*

The powerful sound caught the rabbi's golf ball in midair, lifted it two hundred yards, flipped it around a tree, over a stream, and into the cup – for a remarkable hole in one!

Moses stared at God. *'That* You call a punishment, Lord?'

The Lord winked. 'Whom can he *tell?'*

☙

'But how can you be so positive that God does not exist?' asked the priest.

The atheist huffed: 'A man has to believe in *some*thing!'

☙

Mr Somekh, aged seventy-four, was taking his first trip by air. He was given a seat next to a swarthy Arab wearing the traditional kaffiyeh (head-dress) and djellabah (robe). The Arab stared at the old man, buckled his seatbelt, and deliberately spat on Mr Somekh's shoes. . . .

The plane took off, levelled off. . . . The Arab put his head back and dozed off. . . .

Soon the aircraft ran into a storm: tremendous bouncings up and around, and fierce, sudden droppings down. Poor Mr Somekh grabbed for the airsickness bag stuffed in the pocket ahead – but alas, alas; it was too late. All over the sleeping Arab's white robe, Mr Somekh threw up. . . .

The old man fearfully closed his eyes and gave a prayer to the Lord, 'Help me, Your pious servant. Give me an idea. When this crazy man awakens and sees his robe, he'll pull out that dagger and stab me in the heart! O Lord, Lord, *never* did I need Your help so badly!' With pounding heart Mr Somekh waited for his seat-mate to awaken. . . .

And when the Arab yawned and opened his eyes, Mr Somekh, suddenly hearing a divine whisper in his ears, leaned forward and politely smiled, 'So, Mister from Arabia – are you feeling better now?'

~

> God's plan got off to a happy beginning
> But Adam ruined it by sinning!
> I hope the whole story
> Will end in God's glory,
> But right now the wrong side is winning.

~

Three rowboats moved along the totally flooded streets, and the water was still rising as the torrent from heaven raged unabated. The rescuers spied a strange figure on the roof of a small building: a tall, bearded man, wearing a wide, flat black hat, his arms crossed.

'Come down!' shouted the rowers. 'Get into the boat!'

The tall figure gestured calmly. 'Save others. Do not worry about me. I am Rabbi Gershon Rosenbloom. The *Lord* will save me!'

An hour later, another boat – this one with an outboard motor – approached. 'Hey! You on the roof! Come down! The waters are still rising!'

The rabbi, standing cross-armed despite water up to his waist, called out, 'Go *on*! Save others. I am a rabbi. I have complete faith in my Lord!'

And an hour after that, the rains still pouring down, a helicop-ter, searching for survivors of the flood, hovered above the rabbi on the roof, lowered its ladder, the pilot's voice bellowing out of a bullhorn: 'Grab that ladder, man! The water's up to your *chin!* This is your last – '

'Fear not!' sang the rabbi. 'I am a man of God! And – He – will – *glub, glub, kmpf...*' And Rabbi Gershon Rosenbloom, that good and faithful servant of the Lord, sank beneath the rising waters.

Being a soul of the utmost virtue, without stain throughout his life, the rabbi, within an instant after drowning, found himself among the Heavenly Throng, gazing at the effulgent radiance of God Himself

'Oh, Lord!' cried the rabbi, 'How *could* You? I had absolute faith in You, and You let me drown! How could You let me down – '

'"Let you *down*?"' bridled the Lord. 'I sent two boats and a helicopter to take you off that roof, you idiot!'

A most pious old Jew prayed in the synagogue thrice every day of his adult life. His worldly business partner had not once set foot therein. And in his seventieth year the old Jew addressed the Lord thus: 'Oh, God, Blessed be Thy Name, have I not every day since my *Bar Mitzva* celebrated Your Glory? Have I ever made a move, named a child, taken a trip, without consulting You first? Is there a more devout, humble, observing soul in all Your fold?... And now I'm old, I can't sleep, I'm poor.... But my partner! That no-good! Not *once* has he ever made a prayer! Not a penny has he given to the synagogue! He drinks, he gambles, he runs around with loose women – and he's worth a *fortune!*... Dear God, King of All the Universe, I am not asking You to punish him, but please tell me: why, why, *why* have You treated me this way?'

The synagogue rumbled as The Voice intoned: 'Because all you do, day after day, is *nag, nag, nag* me!'

See also **Clergy, Faith, Heaven, Religion**

Goldwyniana

Note: Samuel Goldwyn (né Shmuel Gelbfisz) was a superb maker of movies, an incomparable judge of stories, and a master of creative malapropism. The following transformations of English are not limited to Mr Goldwyn's observations; but they all qualify for inclusion in that category of startling and instructive solecisms

with which the ex-glove salesman so generously endowed us.
   Items which are indubitably the product of Mr Goldwyn are
identified by his initials.

Acting
Tell them to put more life in their dying.

Tell them to stand closer apart.

Aplomb: I don't care about that; it rolls off my back like a duck.

Argument: You fail to overlook the crucial point!

Autobiography: How would you like to write my autobiography?

Business: If I was in this business only for the business, I wouldn't
   be in this business.

Decorum: For your information, just answer me one question!

Decision
True, I've been a long time making up my mind about buying your
book. But now I'm giving you a definite answer. I won't say yes
and I won't say no – but I'm giving you a *definite* maybe.

S. G.

Emphasis: I'll give it to you in two words: im possible.

S. G.

Floods: The damage is so great they'll have to evaporate three
   cities.

Impossibilities: It's absolutely impossible – but it has possibilities.

Lesbians
'Mr Goldwyn, I don't think you'd want to make that story: it's
about two Lesbians!'
   'So? We can change them to Americans.'

Memory: Put it out of your mind. In no time, it will be a forgotten
   memory.

Movie business: You'll get along fine in this business as long as you don't bite the hand that lays the golden eggs.

Movies
The wide screen will make bad films twice as bad.

S. G.

Go see that turkey for yourself, and see for yourself why you shouldn't see it.

That movie? Terrible! Don't fail to miss it if you can!

They didn't *release* that movie; it escaped.

Columbia would be smart to take that film and cut it up into guitar picks.

IRVING CAESAR

Oral contract: An oral contract isn't worth the paper it's written on.

S. G.

Pride: I don't pay any attention to him. I don't even ignore him.

Producers: Producers shouldn't get ulcers; they should *give* them.

S. G.

Rejection: Gentlemen, I have made up my mind. Include me out.

S. G.

Scenery: I love true nature, where the hand of man never set foot.

Sculpture: My wife's hands are so beautiful, I'm having a bust made of them.

S. G.

Singers: Can she *sing?* She's practically a Florence Nightingale.

Stars: Give me a couple of years and I'll make that actress an overnight success.

Stories for the silver screen
That story is wonderful. It's magnificent. It's *prolific*.

S. G.

What do you mean the story is too caustic? Who cares about
expense?

S. G.

Travel: When I travel, I always like a nice hotel suite, where I can
put up with my wife.

S. G.

Writers
'We just have to get fresh talent around here,' complained Mr.
Goldwyn. 'Take our writers. They're getting old. They're stale.
We should hire some young, talented unknowns!'
  'Wonderful,' said his story editor. 'I know one.'
  'What's his name?'
  'Raymond Jesperson.'
  'I never even heard of him. Can't you think of anyone else?'

I'm overpaying [Ben] Hecht something terrible – but he's worth it.

S. G.

Goldwyn to L. B. Mayer: 'We're both in real trouble!'
  'Why?'
  'Because you have Gable under contract, and I want him.'

'Mr Goldwyn, I just became the father of a boy!'
  'Wonderful. What are you going to call him?'
  'Ronald.'
  '*Ronald?*' echoed Goldwyn. 'What kind of name is that? Today
every Tom, Dick, and Harry is named Ronald.'

At Arthur Mayer's place in Connecticut, Mr Goldwyn saw a
curious metal object on a pedestal in the centre of the garden.
'What's that?' he asked.
  'It's a sundial, Sam,' said Mayer.

'A *sun*dial? What does it do?'

'The vertical part casts a shadow, and the place that shadow falls on...' Mayer carefully explained how a sundial marks off time.

'My!' chuck-chucked Goldwyn. 'What won't they think up next!'

Mr and Mrs Goldwyn were about to sail to Hawaii on a vacation. A group of relatives, friends and employees came to the dock to see them off. As the ship started to slip away, Goldwyn put his hands to his mouth and sang out: '*Bon voyage!*'

Goldwyn had got into a severe wrangle with Walter Wanger about a female star Goldwyn wanted and Wanger had under contract. The negotiations between the lawyers got nowhere. Wanger telephoned Goldwyn. 'Look, Sam. We're getting nowhere. Why not submit the whole mess to arbitration?'

'Fine! Great!' said Goldwyn. 'I agree – just so it's understood I get her.'

At a large dinner in his home, Goldwyn declared, 'Listen, during all the ins and outs of my career, no matter what – no one in Hollywood ever had to sue me!'

'Hold it, Sam,' said one guest. 'Why, at this table alone I – Willie – Joe – and Ben have taken you to court!'

'I meant, present company excepted.'

See also **Bloopers, Radio and TV, Boo-boos, Cynics' Dictionary, Malaprops, Typos**

Graffiti

In men's room of an expensive restaurant that serves mediocre food:

DUNCAN HINES WEPT HERE

On menu of diner: All meats declared A-1

On the mirror above the washbasin in a men's room

THINK!

Under this, a wag had printed an arrow, pointing downward and this word:

THOAP

In college dorm   A little coitus
                           Never hoitus.

On medical building   Neuroses are red,
                           Depression is blue,
                           I'm schizophrenic
                           How about you?

Chalked on wall   GET OUT OF ANGOLA!
                     And below in another hand:
                        What's Her Last Name?

On bulletin board in mathematics building of a college in New England: I love the girls – but, oh, Euclid!

On college wall: Just because you're paranoid, don't think they don't hate you.

On church bulletin board: If Jesus was a Jew, how come he has a Puerto Rican name?

On college wall   *God*
                                      is
                                    Dead!
                                 – Nietzsche

and underneath: No. Nietzsche
                                   is Dead.
                                   – God

See also **Advertisements, Boo-boos, Freudian Slips, Headlines That Haunt Me, Malaprops, Signs, Typos**

Groucho

A MEMOIR

One day, years ago, when I was committing movies, my phone rang in Beverly Hills. I shall give you as much of the conversation as I can retrieve from a memory bank whose circuits were blown ga-ga:

ROSTEN: Hello.

VOICE: Do I have the honour of addressing the world-famed proctologist, Marmaduke Montague?

ROSTEN: You have the wrong number.

VOICE: Then why did you answer?! You impostor! ... For *years* I've been calling this number and getting Professor Marmaduke Montague. *What have you done with his body?* I'm going to call the police! *What* I'll call them is none of your business. What number *is* this, anyway?

ROSTEN: (indignantly) This is Crestview-eight, two, nine –

VOICE: Aha! So you admit it! Why, if you were a man you'd come over and knock all my teeth out.

ROSTEN: I –

VOICE: If you were *half* a man, you'd knock half my teeth out.

ROSTEN: Who –

VOICE: And if you were a woman we could dance away the night in wild – *don't hang up!* You're a pretty dull conversationalist, Leo, if I have to say so myself. All *you* do is grunt, gripe, and sputter. That, by the bye, is a perfect name for an outboard motor. ... This is Groucho – as if you cared, running around with all those other starlets. I'm not that kind of girl. I'm not that kind of boy either. ... Are you free for lunch? Fine. The Derby. I'll have a rose clenched between my teeth.

∽

In the ten years I spent in Hollywood, I was the patsy for a dozen phone calls of the same maniacal order. They were not as easy to spot as you may think, for they came at all sorts of hours, at reasonable intervals, and used a crafty assortment of voices. Every call began with an entirely plausible greeting:

'Hello. My name is Iphigene Wimbledon. Is this Leo Rosten?'

Or, ''ollo? Here iss Pierre Jouvert, *directeur* of Eiffel Tours . . .'

Or, 'My name is Hollister, Floyd Hollister, of Sloat, Bankhead, and Dooley, appointed by the Probate Court to act as executors of the estate of Elmo Rosten, the oil billionaire from Waco, Texas.'

Once I had been suckered, the Master hauled off and let me have it. Iphigene Wimbledon offered to sell my son ('A kid like that could net you ten-twelve thousand in today's market'). Pierre Jouvert read me a pornographic ode to the Catacombs ('You can get the entire set, bound in caterpillar cloth, for only – '). And the putative Floyd Hollister was trying to locate any relative of Elmo Rosten, especially Sister Teresa Ginsberg ('whose will left her collection of *mezuzas* to the Knights of Chocolate Malta').

At one time or another, during my decade in Hollywood, I was denounced for housing the leader of a white-slave ring, begged by a dentist from Pomona to let him fit me with stainless-steel bicuspids *entirely free* ('It's my only way of getting known in this dental institution'), and warned by a fire inspector not to have my roof sprayed with Mom's Fire Retardant 'which is *actually a mouthwash*' when 'a coat of buttermilk will do the job at less than half the cost.'

It was quite a life.

⌒

At one lunch a gushy dowager leaned over between us and cooed, '*Do* forgive me for intruding, but – are you Groucho Marx?'

'No,' iced my host, 'are you?'

⌒

He was a wizard of reason run amok. He perfected the logic of lunacy. He also mocked the lunacy of logic. Consider his resignation from a certain club:

> I do not wish to belong to the kind of club that
> accepts people like me as members.

⌒

Shortly after he settled in Los Angeles, he was being driven

around by a friend. As they took a long curve on Sunset Boulevard, the sparkling Pacific opened below them. On the beautiful
sands stretched a row of cabanas with pretty striped awnings.
'That's the C—— Beach Club,' said his friend.

'Nifty,' said Groucho. 'That would be a good club for me and
my family.'

The friend cleared his throat. 'Um – forget it ... They don't
admit Jews.'

To which Groucho, whose wife was gentile, replied, 'My son is
half-Jewish. Do you think they'd let him go into the water up to
his knees?'

When a bank sent him an effusive form letter, after he had opened
an account, a letter that ended with the obligatory sentiment: 'If
we can ever be of any assistance, do not hesitate to call on us,'
Marx called on them pronto:

```
Gentlemen:
     The best assistance you can give me is
to steal some money from the account of one
of your richer clients and credit it to
mine.
                              Groucho Marx
```

When *Variety*, the bible of show biz, editorialized that the Marx
Brothers could earn twenty thousand dollars a week if they would
only work together again, Marx wrote the editor:

```
Dear Sir:
     Apparently you are under the impression
that the only thing that matters in this
world is money.    That is quite true.
                              Groucho Marx
```

Marx was once dragooned into serving as manager of the movie
Comedians in their annual charity match against the Actors. He
told Jack Benny to lead off. 'All right, Benny. Get up there and hit
a home run.'

Benny struck out.

Marx resigned. 'I can't manage a team that won't follow instructions.'

❧

A pretty actress tried to flatter him by cooing, 'You're a man after my own heart.'
'That's not all I'm after,' leered Groucho.

A FAN: It's a real pleasure for me to meet Groucho Marx.
GROUCHO (*sneering*): I've known him for years, and I can tell you it's not much of a pleasure.

❧

On a radio show

GROUCHO: Is it true that all you professional wrestlers fake most of your matches?
WRESTLER: That's a darn dirty rumour!
GROUCHO: How many dirty rumours have you wrestled lately?

❧

They came back on a small English ship. I think it was a base Cunard.

GROUCHO MARX

He had a need to puncture decorum. During World War II, he was at an Army training camp to entertain the soldiers. In the quarters of the commanding general, the phone rang. Groucho picked it up, crooning, 'World War *Two*-oo.'

❧

Groucho's friends, praising a local psychic's powers of divination, begged Groucho to attend a séance. Groucho sat quiet and respectful, as the swami stared into a crystal ball, called up departed souls from the Beyond, and answered questions from his paying guests – question after question – in an eerie monotone. After a prolonged spell of omniscience, the sorcerer intoned, 'My medium ... is growing tired.... There is time for ... one more question.'
Groucho asked it. 'What's the capital of North Dakota?'

At a Bel Air party, Groucho proposed this toast to the hostess. 'Madam, I drink to your beauty, your charm, your wit – and I hope this gives you some idea of the lengths I will go to get a drink around here.'

Groucho's calculated derangement, abetted by that rasp of a voice, that black smear of moustache, that roué's lope, those waggling eyebrows, that one wall-eye, that stare of contempt – expressed what the rest of us simply have not the wit, much less the audacity, to utter. When a woman said, 'I made a stew last night,' Groucho leered, 'Anyone I know?'

To a hostess, upon leaving her party, he said, 'Don't think this hasn't been an unusually dull evening, because it has.'

Once, leaving his house after dinner, I paused to say, 'I'd like to say goodbye to your wife.'

Said Groucho, 'Who wouldn't?'

A tipsy tourist once placed his arm around Marx's shoulders and cackled, 'Groucho, you son-of-a-gun, I bet you don't remember me!'

Marx fixed the oaf with a baleful eye. 'Sir, I never forget a face – but in your case I'll be glad to make an exception.'

His correspondence with me was sprinkled with such corkers as:

Home is where you hang your head.

Writing to you is like corresponding with an aching void.

You don't have to have relatives in St Louis to be miserable.

Of all his sideswipes, the one I most admire is this:

Dear Junior:

    Excuse me for not answering your letter sooner. I have not been answering so many letters lately that I couldn't get round to not answering yours in time.

He once offered to write a blurb for one of my books:

> From the moment I picked this book up until the
> moment I put it down, I could not stop laughing.
> Some day I hope to read it.

On 'You Bet Your Life', his celebrated television show, a nurse
from Australia, when asked, 'Where are you from?' replied. 'I
flew here by plane.'

Groucho nodded. 'A girl would be a fool to try it any other way.'

When a Japanese lad said he was twenty-one, Groucho asked,
'Is that in years or in yen?'

'You don't count age in yen,' said the young man.

'No? I have a yen to be thirty again.'

One of the contestants turned out to be from cornhusker
country. Let's call him Floyd.

GROUCHO: How did you meet your wife?

FLOYD: Well, I drive a truck –

GROUCHO: You ran over her?

FLOYD: No. She was in the barn –

GROUCHO: You drove your truck into a *barn*?

FLOYD: No, no, Groucho. Her family had been missing some chickens –

GROUCHO: (*incredulously*) They were lonely for *chickens*?

FLOYD: No. They had been *missing* them, so they turned on a light
in the barnyard, and I'm driving up to get some turkeys, and
her father hollers, 'The turkeys are in the barn – '

GROUCHO: (*horrified*) You married a *turkey*?

FLOYD: No, *no*. As I go to the barn, a big skunk starts for the
chicken-house, and a girl yells, 'Get that skunk, too' – and we
both smelled so bad – no one else would come close to us –

GROUCHO: That's the most romantic story I ever heard.

One night Groucho was interviewing a beautiful model. 'You
must have all sorts of exciting experiences.'

'N-no,' she said. 'It's just routine.'

Groucho gaped. 'What are you modelling: *clay*?'

He was driving back from a casual trip to Tijuana, Mexico. On the California side of the border, the US immigration officials asked each driver a few questions. When Groucho's car stopped, the fed touched the brim of his hat and said, 'Are you an American citizen?'

'Certainly,' said Groucho.

'And where were you born?'

'New York.'

'What's your occupation?'

Groucho leaned out of the window to whisper. 'Smuggler.'

And once, emerging from the preview of a Doris Day movie, in which that wide-eyed, wholesome, all-American maiden spent an hour and a half resisting the blandishments of Cary Grant, someone asked Groucho, 'Do you know Doris Day?'

The mordant crow said, 'Shucks, I knew her before she was a virgin.'

At a testimonial dinner to S. J. Perelman:

This is a man who has not let success go to his head – a man who is humble and unspoiled. He is as unassuming, as comfortable to be with as an old glove – and just about as interesting.

GROUCHO: How old are you, ma'am?

CONTESTANT: I'm – approaching forty.

GROUCHO: From which direction?

One night he was driving me to a meeting. I suddenly remembered it was my father's birthday. 'Can you stop at a Western Union office?' I asked. 'I want to wire my father.'

'What's wrong?' asked Groucho. 'Can't he stand by himself?'

Groucho's old friend, Goodman Ace, was staying with Marx in Beverly Hills. At breakfast, Ace said to Groucho, 'This orange juice is delicious.' Turning to the maid, he said, 'Could I have another glass, please?'

'Wait a minute, Ace,' said Groucho. 'Do you think oranges grow on trees?'

See also **Chutzpa, Cynics' Dictionary, Goldwyniana, Put-downs, Retorts, Repartee, Sarcasm, Waiters, Wit, Wordplay**

Hanky-panky

Scene: London Club

'I say, Rippleworth,' said Lord Bunleigh, 'did you know that Lady Cynthia Paget always wears black garters?'

''Pon my word!' exclaimed Rippleworth. 'Why?'

Lord Bunleigh stared into his glass thoughtfully. 'In memory, I suppose, of all the fine chaps who have passed beyond.'

Sign in go-go bar:

4 Gorgeous Dance Girls
3 Costumes

Eamonn McCone came home early, to his cottage in Galway – and there, to his total discombobulation, he beheld his wife, Erin, under the sheets with his best friend, Patrick O'Flynn.

'Erin!' cried Eamonn. 'Me own wife! Me own true love! How kin ye be doin' such a terrible thing?! And you, Patrick, as close t' me as me own brother – by all that's holy, O'Flynn, can't ye even stop while I'm *talking*?!'

∽

'Oh, Seymour, will you love me always?'

'Absolutely, sweetheart. Which way would you like me to try first?'

HENNY YOUNGMAN

∽

Charlotte Devere, an attractive widow, was depressed by the life in the suburb into which she had recently moved. One day she hastened to her neighbour's house. 'Leora,' she said, with some embarrassment, 'you're the only one I can ask. Would you give me some – confidential advice?'

'Gladly.'

Charlotte blushed. 'How – how do you go about having an affair in this town?'

'Well, I,' beamed Leora, 'always start with "The Star-Spangled Banner."'

∽

At Sonny Kotcher's Gym, two men in the exercise class were undressing. One man started unhooking his – girdle.

The other goggled, 'Hey, Morrie, since when do you wear a girdle?'

Morrie grimaced. 'Since my wife found it in my glove compartment.'

∽

Into the phone, Dexter said, 'Hello?'

'Hu-llo,' answered a very deep voice.

Dexter hesitated, then said, 'I'm – trying to reach my home. God, I hope I have the wrong number!'

∽

Marcel Duschanel, suddenly widowed at fifty-two, went to the south of France to escape from his sorrows and try to gain a new lease on life. He took a suite at the Hotel Carousel overlooking the grand pool, and he sat in the sun and observed the divings and splashings and merriment, the flirtings and snugglings, the court-ships and kisses of the beautiful young people around the pool.

One man in particular stood out amidst the crowd of sun wor-shippers and macho males. He stood out not only because he was entirely grey-haired, pale, his cheeks lined, but because he was never without two or three beautiful maidens at his side, or at his table near the pool, or at his regular table in the Palm d'Or Restaurant. And every night, the hotel gossips reminded Marcel Duschanel that the man was off dancing at some nightclub, or dashing off to Monaco to gamble, or carousing until the early, early hours.

For several weeks, Marcel Duschanel enviously observed this phenomenal old-timer. One night, soon after dinner, Duschanel found himself in the men's room, when in came the grey-haired man. He headed straight for the mirror, carefully combing, brushing, patting his grey hair.

'M'sieur!' Duschanel exclaimed. 'What a piece of good fortune. I have been so hoping we might perhaps meet...'

'Ah?'

'You see, we are in the same hotel – and I have been filled with admiration for the way you live, your *joie de vivre*, your many girl-friends...'

The man smiled.

'A thousand pardons, m'sieur – but I trust you will not take offence if I ask you a question: how old *are* you?'

The *roué* shrugged. 'Twenty-nine.'

Ray Tucker was so tired that he quit work at three and drove home from his office. He parked his car next to his wife's and went into the house. On the living-room couch he beheld his wife in the arms of another man.

'What in hell is going on here?' Tucker shouted. 'Lana – darling – who *is* this guy?'

Said Lana. 'That's a perfectly fair question, dear.' She turned to the man. 'What's your name, sweetheart?'

Mistress: What goes between a mister and a mattress.

JOE E. LEWIS

The judge studied the tall, muscular woman, then frowned at the small, thin man, then turned back to the woman. 'Madam,' he cleared his throat, ' – am I to understand you are accusing this man of – *rape?*'

'Absolutely,' huffed the Amazon.

'Was he – holding a gun at the time?'

'Nope.'

'Did he tie you up?'

'Nope.'

'Well, madam, you are at least six feet tall and weigh at least a hundred and eighty pounds, whereas this man is not much over five feet – I wonder how in the absence of a weapon, rape could –'

'I stooped a bit.'

The two women were sharing confidences over their tea. 'I don't know what to do about my husband any more,' said Louise. 'Do you know that he never comes home until long, long past midnight?!'

'Oh, dear. My husband used to be like that – but no more. Never!'

'What changed him?'

Her friend smiled. 'What changed him, my dear, is that every time he stealthily opened the door, at one or two or three in the morning, I would sweetly call out, "Is that you, Everett?"'

'That was all there was to it?'

'Uh-huh.'

'But why would *that* stop him?'

'Because his name is Herbie.'

Chittingham accosted Farnsworth in the club lobby. 'I say, Farnsworth. Have you recently had a – bit of a fling with my wife?'

Farnsworth cleared his throat. 'Well, old boy, since you are so straightforward about it – I must say, yes, I have.'

'Well now, Farnsworth, I – do – not – much – like – that!'

Farnsworth nodded. 'Can't blame you, old boy, I didn't like it much, either.'

'Nelly,' said Jacqueline, 'we've been friends for so long, and gone through so much together –'

'What are you trying to say, Jackie?'

'Look, if this is out of line . . .'

'Nothing you ask me can be out of line.'

'All right.' Jacqueline took a long deep breath. 'Nelly – are you cheating on your husband?'

Nelly shrugged. 'Who else?'

See also **Sex, Typos**

Headlines That Haunt Me

MASSIVE ORGAN DRAWS CROWD

Lucky Girl Sees Friends Die

FATHER OF NINE FINED $100 FOR FAILING TO STOP

DEAD POLICEMAN ON FORCE 23 YEARS

26-YEAR FRIENDSHIP ENDS AT ALTAR

MIXED MARRIAGE CONDUCTED BY RABBIT

MAN FOUND DEAD IN CEMETERY

FARMERS THREATENED BY PLAGUE OF RABBIS

The finest caption I ever read appeared in the old, forever-lamented *Herald-Tribune* of New York:

GIRL SEDUCED ATOP 65-FT. FLAGPOLE

The story was as much of a stopper as the caption. It recounted that a car salesman in El Paso, Texas, was charged with the 'statutory rape' of a fifteen-year-old girl he allegedly seduced atop a flagpole that was sixty-five feet high. The hanky-panky took place in this novel locale because the Don Juan was a flagpole-sitter by profession, and he had spent no less than sixty-four days on the flagpole before committing libidinal acrobatics *in situ.*

The girl, whose name the authorities did not reveal, told the police she had actually been seduced five times, 'after climbing a rope ladder to the top of the pole a number of times.' The fact that this lass had climbed a sixty-five-foot rope ladder 'a number of times' made me wonder whether the maiden could make the charge of seduction (except the first, of course) stick. Sixty-five-foot ascents are strong prima facie evidence of a not entirely traumatic experience. That certainly does not suggest forcible entry.

from my *Passions and Prejudices*

9 VOLUNTEERS PUT
IN NEW CHURCH FURNACE

FLORIST ASKS GIRLS TO
DROP STRAPLESS GOWNS

BABIES FLOOD HOSPITALS

ESCAPED LEOPARD
BELIEVED SPOTTED

See also **Bloopers, Radio and TV, Boo-boos, Graffiti, How's That Again?, News Items That Haunt Me, Typos**

Heaven

Heaven: God's country

Zelda Szold, aged eighty-two, appeared before the Golden Gates of Paradise and rang the golden bell.

An Admitting Angel opened the gates. 'Welcome, good soul, welcome. Follow me to the Registrar.'

Mrs Szold trod light clouds that wafted her to the radiant, kindly presence of the Registrar of Heaven. 'Your name, dear one?'

'My name is Zelda Levy Szold.'

'S-z-o-l-d?'

'The same.'

'And what was your last address on earth, Friend Szold?'

'On earth, my last address was eighty-four Beersheba Lane, Haifa.'

The Registrar swiftly ran down the list of *S*'s in the ledger emblazoned 'Expected Arrivals'. He ran his finger down one page, then down another... 'Szold ... Szold ... from Haifa... Aha ... Yes.' The Registrar frowned. 'Well, well, can you imagine that?' He looked up. 'Mrs Szold, age eighty-two, from Haifa – you are not due in Heaven for another six and a half weeks!... Listen, who is your doctor?!'

THE MAN WHO COULD NOT SIN

Mr Toplovitz stood before the Chief Admitting Angel anxiously. And the Chief Admitting Angel exclaimed, 'But this is fantastic! I have read your records three times. This is unprecedented. In your entire lifetime did you not commit *one* little sin?'

'I tried to live in virtue,' faltered Mr Toplovitz, 'as a God-fearing man ...'

'But not one – little – sin in an entire lifetime?' sputtered the Admitting Angel. 'We can't let you into Heaven! You are practically an angel already. No, no. You must be *human*, fallible, subjected to temptation ... at least once. So, I am going to send you back to earth – for twenty-four hours. During that time, you must commit a sin – at least one little sin, Mr Toplovitz. It is now seven A.M.!'

The bewildered innocent found himself back on earth, determined to try to take one step from the path of righteousness. An hour passed, then two, then three; poor Mr Toplovitz simply could find no opportunity to commit a sin.

Then a buxom woman winked at him.... Mr Toplovitz

responded with alacrity. The lady was neither young nor beautiful – but she *was* willing. And when she blushingly hinted that he might spend the night with her, Mr Toplovitz was in sixth heaven.

At last, in bed, having truly sinned, in the dark, wee hours – Mr Toplovitz looked at his watch: only one more hour before the Angel would whisk him back to heaven . . . only half an hour . . .

And as Mr Toplovitz quickly put on his clothes, preparing for his return to the celestial region, his blood froze as the old maid in the bed sighed, 'Oh, Toplovitz, Toplovitz – what a good deed you have performed this night!'

See also **Faith, God, The Occult, Religion**

Heroes of Mine

DEAR ROBERT BENCHLEY

Robert Benchley, known to one and all as 'Bob', was the gentlest of men, a lovely humorist, and a prince of drollery. He once confirmed to me a story making the rounds of Hollywood. He had recently asked his doctor what he (the doctor) was going to prescribe for his (Benchley's) stuffed head, runny nose, clammy palms, and romping fever.

The MD briskly said. 'One of the new miracle drugs.'

Benchley, a devout hypochondriac, complained: 'But I don't *like* to try new drugs; they might have funny side effects . . .'

'Nonsense! This will make you fit as a fiddle,' said the doctor, whose name, I think, was Stradivarius. 'I'll drop in to see you tomorrow.'

The next morning, Benchley arose to find his fever vanished, his head clear, his anxieties allayed. His spirit soared so high that he decided to brighten the doctor's day. Benchley considered several ways of doing this, then found a pot of glue, slit open his pillow, and glued feathers to both his thighs. This manoeuvre completed, he drew the sheet up to his neck carefully, high above his waist, cautiously lowered the sheet and waited for his healer.

The moment Dr Stradivarius appeared in the doorway, Benchley exclaimed, 'Doc, you're a whiz! That new drug you gave me certainly worked miracles!'

'You can say that again,' said the doctor.

Instead of saying it again, Benchley blinked innocently. 'There's just one thing, Doc: What do you make of' – he flung back the sheet to reveal two thighs thick with feathers – '... this!'

I have whiled away many an hour imagining what the expression on that doctor's face must have been, and what horrified apparitions – of incredulity, panic, guilt – beset his thunderstruckness.

from my *People I Have Loved,*
Known or Admired

THE PRINCE OF PASTA

Joseph Pellegrino, who owned a little restaurant in Rome, was lunching in a country *trattoria*. He was served a steaming plate of spaghetti. It was possibly the one hundred thousandth plate of spaghetti Signor Pellegrino had been served during his lifetime, but this one caused his jaw to drop, his fork to fall, and his eyes to pop: the spaghetti was not round! It was square.

Pellegrino stared at this farinaceous heresy, lifted some on his fork, tasted the pasta, and rushed into the kitchen. There he saw the Mamma of the *trattoria* rolling a slab of dough across a wooden frame on which was stretched a grid of – guitar strings...

Pellegrino began to serve quadrilateral spaghetti in his restaurant in Rome. It was made on a frame of wire (instead of catgut) strings and has delighted Italians and tourists alike.

This unorthodox – nay, revolutionary! – pasta offers many advantages over conventional spaghetti: it does not slip off the fork so often; it does not slide on the plate so readily; it is also firmer, and holds on to the tomato sauce better than run-of-the-mill pasta. I think square spaghetti also inspires confidence in its character, because of its sturdy, self-reliant appearance.

So far as I can see, this splendid pasta *may* have one trivial fault, a defect implied, though not foreseen, by Christopher Morley, who once said: 'No man is lonely while eating spaghetti; it takes so much *attention*.'

I have long admired the unknown genius, larcenous though he must have been, who ran this one-line ad in a Los Angeles newspaper:

LAST DAY TO SEND IN YOUR DOLLAR.
Box 153

Thousands of idiots sent in their dollars.

from my People I Have Loved,
Known or Admired

THE UNBELIEVABLE LAIBOWITZ

'Good morning,' said Captain Newman brightly.

The soldier touched a finger to his forehead, confirming its existence, and studied us through lugubrious eyes. He made no effort to conceal the fact that he did not approve of what he beheld.

'Sit down, Corporal. What's your name?'

'Laibowitz,' came a sepulchral suspiration.

'First name?'

'Jackson.' (Sigh.)

'How old are you?'

'Twenty-five.'

To my surprise, Captain Newman leaned forward and said frostily, 'I *believe* it is customary for a soldier to address an officer as "sir"!'

Corporal Laibowitz shrugged. 'What's "customary" for a soldier can be tough for a civilian.'

'But you aren't a civilian,' said Newman acidly.

'I *feel* like a civilian,' said Laibowitz.

'Congratulations.' Captain Newman held out his cigarettes. 'Would you like to smoke?'

'Nicotine,' announced Laibowitz, 'is bad for the eyes.'

'Oh. Do you have trouble with your eyes?'

'No, sir.'

'Then why – '

'That's because I never touch nicotine,' said Laibowitz.

Captain Newman looked startled. He leaned back in his chair to study the man before him with new interest. This did not present the slightest problem to Laibowitz, who suffered the scrutiny with the resignation of a man accustomed to the slow-witted. He was, all in all, rather goodlooking – well-shaped features, a firm mouth, large liquid eyes. It was only his manner – an amalgam of acid stomach and apocalypse – which celebrated despair.

Captain Newman said, 'I assume you've worked in a hospital before.'

'Yes – sir.'

Captain Newman waited. So did Laibowitz.

'Go on, Corporal.'

'Go on where?' blinked the dour one.

'Tell me about your hospital experience.'

'What's to tell? The camp I just came from wasn't fit for a dog! Maybe a Nazi dog, not a US citizen. They had me working in the wards day and night. I didn't like it.'

'You mustn't hide your feelings,' said Captain Newman dryly.

'I agree,' said Laibowitz.

Newman winced. 'What kinds of wards did you work in?'

'All kinds.'

'Give me a hint,' crooned Newman.

'It would spoil your lunch.'

'I'll skip lunch.'

'I advise you shouldn't; ask any doctor – '

'I *am* a doctor,' leered Newman.

'OK. General, general surgery, infectial diseases, where I caught everything – '

'Did you ever work in – an NP ward?' asked Captain Newman, rather too casually.

Laibowitz's eyes widened. 'A *mental* ward?'

'I mean psychiatric cases – '

'*Nuts?*'

'They are not "nuts,"' said Captain Newman firmly. 'They're men who – '

'My God, Doc,' cried Laibowitz, 'you gonna put me in a *loony* bin?'

'It is *not* – '

'I'll drop dead!' Laibowitz struggled to his feet, 'I give you my word, Doc, inside one hour you can start digging my grave!'

'Sit down.'

'Better ask me to *lay* down! I'm already a patient.'

'Now listen!' said Captain Newman sharply. 'I don't know where the hell you guys got all these cockeyed ideas! Most of the men in my ward are simply depressed – '

'So am I,' proclaimed Laibowitz.

' – miserable – '

'*They're* miserable? Look at me!'

'Sit *down*!'

Corporal Laibowitz sank into the chair with noises suggestive of strangulation and verging on emphysema.

Crisply, firmly, Captain Newman launched into a lecture explaining the functions of his ward, the nature of our tasks, the duties of a wardman. He was simple, direct, and, I thought, remarkably reassuring. It made not the slightest dent on Laibowitz, who kept uttering woeful lamentations.

Captain Newman explained that we had a staff of excellent doctors ('For me alone you'll need one full time,' said Laibowitz), that the patients were not permitted razors, matches, blunt artefacts, or sharp objects ('But *teeth* they've got?'), that an encouraging proportion of our cases responded favorably to therapy ('Don't spoil your record, Captain!') and were dismissed from Ward 7 to return to either army or civilian life ('I will gladly join them!'), that orderlies were pampered with frequent passes ('You mean of their own free will they come *back*?'), and that when he was off duty, Corporal Laibowitz, along with the other wardman, would sleep in complete comfort and safety in the finest barracks on the base, a good five hundred yards away ('Who will drag me back and forth?' asked Laibowitz).

'That's it,' said Captain Newman efficiently. 'Do you have any questions?'

Laibowitz rose. 'Doc, I appreciate your trying to raise my morale. But let us face facts. You are putting me in a booby hatch. You are asking me to buddy up to cuckoos, crazies, dumdums, and scrambled-eggs-in-the-head ... I got problems of my own, you know. I'm practically a nervous wreck. I'm high-strung, sensitive. I promise you if you send me into your nuthouse, by Sunday – the *latest* – you'll have to fit me for a straitjacket!'

Captain Newman, who had listened to this oration somewhat open-mouthed, braced his shoulders and narrowed his eyes. 'That will be all. You may go now. You will report to Sergeant Kopp.'

'Who's he?' said Laibowitz.

'My wardmaster.'

'Where does he keep his whip?'

'Laibowitz,' snapped Captain Newman, 'what the *devil* is the matter with you? You look intelligent – '

'Don't be fooled by my looks!'

'You're making a mountain out of a molehill!'

'So I'm no good in geography.'

'You'll get the best food on the post in my ward!'

'I already lost all my appetite.'

'You have my deepest sympathy,' said Captain Newman sarcastically.

'From plumbers I expect sympathy; from psychiatrists I expect understanding,' cried Laibowitz, glancing toward the Judge in heaven.

Again, Captain Newman cleared his throat. 'You may go now. . . . Ring the bell outside the door. Sergeant Kopp will show you the ropes.'

'He should only *give* me a rope; I'll hang myself.'

'Dismissed!'

Laibowitz reaffirmed the location on his forehead and sagged out of the room. He might have been en route to the firing squad. . . .

Laibowitz was a master of the art of standing military authority on its head. Take his way of dealing with orders from officers. Written orders of which he approved, he executed with lightning dispatch; written orders of which he disapproved, he 'mislaid', misread, or misrouted.

His response to verbal instructions was even more exasperating: when he disagreed with a superior's instruction, he simply pretended he had not heard it; when it was repeated to him, he concluded it had not been communicated correctly the first time, which made the second exposition no more reliable than the first; when it was driven home to him in an indisputable manner that whatever his personal views, such-and-such a command *had* to be obeyed, he got 'sick' and took to his quarters. Achilles had his tent; Laibowitz had his symptoms. Rarely has medical science been confronted with such symptoms – such coughs, aches, pains, wheezes and vertigos – as Jackson Laibowitz could summon to his cause. He never directly *disobeyed* Captain Newman's will, for instance; he managed to modify it through reinterpretation. He never refused; he simply outflanked. He simulated deafness with an innocence that defied exposure, and stupidity with a poise that demanded admiration. . . .

No one ever won an argument from Laibowitz. He rarely expressed an opinion without framing it as an axiom. He could not, indeed, conceive of having mere opinions; they were propositions in a larger, majestic philosophical system.

Take a matter as mundane as shaving. Laibowitz hated to shave. But he would never say – simply, directly – that he hated to shave. He wrapped his prejudice in the raiment of cosmology: 'If God meant men should have clean cheeks, *would He have invented hair*?'

One morning, when Laibowitz looked like the 'before' version in an advertisement for razor blades, Captain Newman asked him testily, 'Why didn't you shave this morning?'

'The major in Room C didn't shave this morning, either,' said Laibowitz.

'You know perfectly well that the major is forbidden to use a razor.'

'So give me the same break; *forbid* I should use one.'

'Major Slater is suicidal,' said Newman.

'That's exactly what I'm becoming, with your fetish about hair.'

'I asked you a question!' snapped Newman. 'Why didn't you shave this morning?'

'Is this morning different from other mornings?'

'No. That's why you should shave.'

'Excuse me. There is a hole in your logic. That's why I shouldn't.'

'Laibowitz – '

'A man can be born with very delicate skin!' cried Laibowitz. 'Touch it with metal, it bleeds. Scratch it with steel, it gushes. Douse it with witch hazel, my whole body breaks out in a rash.'

'I'll report these original symptoms to the AMA,' said Newman.

'Put in that I also itch from the brush.'

'Shave!' said Captain Newman.

'Why do you treat me like I was *normal*?' complained Laibowitz. 'If I was a patient, you'd call it a phobia and bring me breakfast in bed.'

'But you're *not* a patient – '

'That, you can arrange in a second.'

Captain Newman assumed his most forbidding expression. 'That will be enough, Jackson. Shave!'

Laibowitz rolled his eyes around in anguish. 'I think I'll lay down. I feel dizzy.'

'That-is-an-order.'

'It's against human nature,' muttered Laibowitz.

This apothegm, 'It's against human nature,' was the last, unyielding bastion of Laibowitz's creed. Whatever he opposed, he transformed into an enemy of natural law. He believed that he knew more about 'human nature' than any man on earth. He also seemed to think that *his* human nature was different from others' and required unquestioning acceptance. 'Today I am depressed,' he might announce, 'so do not aggravate me with details.' Or: 'Some men God gave big muscles; others He gave big brains. Don't ask me to move furniture.'

I often heard him invoke the Deity – but in a peculiar way: He called upon God the way a coach sends in a pinch hitter . . .

One day I saw Captain Newman stalk out of the ward, his face a cloud. Laibowitz was in his wake. 'I suppose,' scowled Newman, 'that Sergeant Kopp is on leave.'

'How did you guess?'

'I didn't have to guess, Corporal; I smelled. The bedding in the ward.'

'What's that got to do with Arkie?'

'When Kopp is on duty, that ward is as clean as a whistle!'

'Today it's 110 in the shade,' cried Laibowitz, 'so naturally, the bedding smells!'

'If you *aired* it, Laibowitz, it wouldn't smell.'

Laibowitz regarded his captain with solicitude. 'I have been studying your behaviour. When you're mad, you call me Laibowitz; when you're annoyed, you call me Jackson; when you're happy, you call me Jake.'

'You're damn right I'm mad! That bedding is a disgrace!'

'*Today* you think it smells?' cried Laibowitz. 'You should have smelled it yesterday! It's a miracle my patients didn't faint like flies! I could have bottled that smell and sold it to Secret Weapons!'

'All sheets, mattresses, and pillowcases are to be aired each morning,' said Captain Newman firmly. 'Do you understand?'

'Deaf, I'm not.'

'That is an order!'

To a direct command, which Laibowitz regarded as the unfair advantage the Chiefs of Staff had given officers as against GIs who might best them in man-to-man combat, Laibowitz unfailingly responded with a surprise manoeuvre on the flanks. 'I'm only human.'

'So are the men who have to sleep in those beds!' snapped Newman.

'I only have two hands.'

'But you have four orderlies to help you!'

'They're human the same as me.'

'That's enough!'

Corporal Laibowitz studied his captain with the utmost sympathy. 'Doc, you look tired.'

'Thank you. The condition of the bedding has tired me.'

'If it tires you, imagine what it does to *me*.'

'Stop playing ping-pong with my sentences! Get that bedding out of the ward and into the open air.'

'That goddam sun could make the mattresses explode!' wailed Laibowitz

'Then put them in the shade.'

'By the time you get any shade around here it's time for my patients to go to sleep!'

'Don't talk like an idiot.'

'That,' Laibowitz grumbled darkly, 'is what will lose us this war.'

'Airing the mattresses?' exclaimed Captain Newman.

'Treating Americans like slaves.'

'Welcome, Patrick Henry,' scowled Newman.

'Sarcasm is for dentists; from psychiatrists I expect honesty.'

I thought it was Captain Newman's excessive indulgence that encouraged Laibowitz's unmilitary conduct, but I learned how wrong I was the day Laibowitz passed my office, on his way to Central Supplies, and asked if there was anything he could get me.

'Yes, thank you.' I gave him a list. I needed PPS forms, red pencils, and thumbtacks.

In an hour, Corporal Laibowitz returned – with PPS forms, red pencils, and Scotch tape.

'Didn't they have thumbtacks?' I asked.

'You wanted *thumb*tacks?' he asked incredulously.

'Why, yes, that's why I wrote them down.'

Laibowitz found fascination in the ceiling. 'I can't read your writing.'

'But I *printed* that list.'

'Lieutenant, your printing is even worse than your writing!'

Suddenly I saw a rare opportunity to achieve a miracle – make Laibowitz admit that he had made a mistake. 'Did you by any chance keep that list, Jake?'

'Am I the type to destroy official documents?' He reached into his pocket and produced the list with an expression that warned me that where trust is stunted friendship will soon die.

'Read it,' I suggested.

'With pleasure. . . . Item number one,' he read, 'PPS forms.'

'Check.'

'Item two: Red pencils.'

'I thought you said you can't read my printing,' I smiled.

'*This* you call reading? I'm breaking a code!'

'Try item three.'

'Is that the one that says "Thumbtacks"?'

'Ah!' I sang out in triumph. 'So you *did* understand.'

'Scotch tape is better! Put a thumbtack in deep, you need a crow-bar to pry it out! Stick your thumb, you get blood poisoning. Be honest, Lieutenant; did you ever hear a man should get hurt from Scotch tape?'

'That's not the point. I *wanted* thumbtacks!'

Laibowitz bestowed a considerate expression upon me. 'You got too much on your mind, Lieutenant. I don't blame you for not knowing what's best for your own welfare.'

I often wonder what orders Laibowitz is upsetting, ignoring, transforming, or subverting now . . .

from my Captain Newman, M.D.

See also **Chutzpa, Ingenuity, Repartee, Sarcasm, Scoundrels**

Hollywood

Hollywood

Siberia with palms.

Malice in Wonderland.

The place where girls look for husbands and husbands look for girls.

The biggest electric train any boy ever had.

ORSON WELLES

Scene: The Pearly Gates

ST PETER: Where are you from?
APPLICANT: Hollywood.
ST PETER: Come in . . . but I'll bet you won't like it.

∽

Casey Krausse and Jordan Hilgard, two Hollywood writers, were going to the same psychoanalyst, Dr Helmut Pforzheimer. 'Nothing ever *throws* him,' remarked Krausse. 'Have you ever seen or heard him act surprised?'

'Never,' said Hilgard.

They bemoaned their healer's inhuman unflappability, his total 'cool', his 'laid-back' response to even the most painful (to the patient) material.

'I have an idea,' said Hilgard. 'Let's make up a dream! A really fantastic, hair-raising dream. I'll report it at my hour – nine to ten – and – '

'And I'll report precisely the same dream at my hour: five to six!'

With many a laugh and gloat of anticipation, the two writers concocted a dream: 'A naked boy with a sword, in a green gondola, is drifting under a large, golden Gothic archway – ' (consider that symbolism!) ' – and suddenly a huge bearded warrior, with a hissing serpent in one hand and a fearsome club in the other, jumps into the gondola – at which point a woman all in white gauze cries, "Rape! Snake! Don't club the boy!" . . . The dream breaks off – '

'What a beaut of a dream!' Krausse chortled.

'Wait until Pforzheimer hears *that* twice in one day!' gloated Hilgard.

And so, the next morning, at around 9:05, from his perch in Couch Canyon (as Roxbury Drive is called), Jordan Hilgard reported the bizarre dream to Dr Pforzheimer. . . . And at 5:05, Casey Krausse reported the identical phantasmagoria – then stopped and waited for his shrink's response.

'That dream . . .' Dr Pforzheimer cleared his throat. 'Strange . . . very strange. That's the *third* time I've heard it today.'

∽

'*My* mother,' said little Heather, 'just got married again, so I have a new father.'

'What's his name?' asked little Margy.

'Hanley Droob,' said Heather.

'Oh, he's *nice*,' said Margy. 'You'll like him.'

'Do you know him?'

'Certainly I know him. Last year, he was *my* father.'

☙

The movie writers' lament: 'They change our stories, ruin our characters, distort our ideas – and what do we get for it? A *fortune*.'

☙

It is reliably reported, by those who were on the scene at the time, that Louis B. Mayer, head of lofty Metro-Goldwyn-Mayer in its dazzling heyday, was trying to get the incomparable Marlene Dietrich to do a movie for MGM, for whom she had not made a film in fifteen years.

'Miss Dietrich,' said the persuasive Mr Mayer, 'you can practically name your own ticket. I personally guarantee you will get anything you want.'

After several more persistent invitations, Miss Dietrich said, 'Mr Mayer, let's first do a test . . . *if* you give me Joe Ruttenberg as the cameraman. You know, Joe lighted me more beautifully, more perfectly, when I made my last picture at Metro, than any photographer I ever had before or since. He knows every angle of my face, my bone structure, my profile – above all, my *moods* . . .'

'Say no more, Marlene!' said Mayer. 'You've got Ruttenberg.'

And so the critical screen test was made. . . .

Now Mayer, Ruttenberg, and the great Dietrich were in a projection room. When the test was finished and the lights flashed on, Miss Dietrich cried, 'I – look – just – awful! My skin, my neckline – ' She turned to Ruttenberg. 'Joe, what's *happened* to you? Remember how gorgeously you lighted me before?'

Ruttenberg said, 'Miss Dietrich, please remember – I was fifteen years younger at that time . . .'

☙

Clifford Voultarian, the famous movie director, on a trip to New York, met Wanda Parton, a beautiful, though not particularly bright, model. He fell madly in love with Wanda. After a whirlwind courtship, he married Wanda and brought her home to his mansion near Malibu Beach. And there, very soon after they arrived, Voultarian arranged for twenty of his closest friends to meet his bride at a formal dinner.

As they were dressing to go down to greet the guests, Wanda said, 'Cliff, I hafta tell you – I'm as nervous as a knocked-up cat!'

'Now, now, doll,' said Clifford. 'That's one thing you don't have to – '

'But, Cliff, sweetie. These famous writers and directors and producer pals of yours! They're – they're such great *talkers*. I just ain't got the faintest idea of what to say to such brainy people!'

Voultarian put his arms around her and kissed her on the forehead. 'Sweetie, you don't have to say a *word* to these people. With your looks, they'll just take your ears off. All you have to do is be charming. Just listen – as if you're absolutely *fascinated*, no matter what they gab about. And every so often say, "How *interesting*!" or "That's *marvellous*!" or "How clever of you!" They'll adore you. Trust me!'

Voultarian was entirely right. His bride charmed one and all with her ready smile, her animated expression, her occasional laughs and compliments.

Only after the dessert did Wanda Voultarian make the slightest *faux pas*. Clifford rose from the table saying, 'Well, gang, shall we have coffee and liqueurs in the library?'

To which his beautiful darling trilled, 'Cliff, honey, do you think it's still open this late at night?'

ᔕ

The actor Sherman Caldwell (né Sidney Calish) turned his profile toward his friend David and said, 'So? What do you think?'

'Hey,' exclaimed David. 'You've had a nose job! That's a fantastic change. You look like a Barrymore or a Basil Rathbone!'

'Do you mean that? Or are you just trying to make me feel good?'

'It's the God's honest, Sid. You look like a thing of beauty – and a *goy* forever.'

ᔕ

Beverly Hills is *very* exclusive. For example, the fire department won't make house calls.

MORT SAHL

See also **Actors, Goldwyniana**

Hotels

In the lobby of the Sterling Hotel, Mr Ottenheim beheld a large, fat man, sprawled in a chair, smoking a large, fat cigar.

Mr Ottenheim sniffed the smoke, made a face, and said, 'That is some cheap cigar.'

'It costs fifty cents,' the smoker said.

'Fifty – and how many do you smoke a day?'

'Nine – ten.'

'Let's say ten. That's five dollars a day, right?'

'Right.'

'Three hundred sixty-five days a year. That's – for cigars – over eighteen hundred dollars a year!... And how many years have you been smoking?'

'Forty, forty-five.'

'My God!' said Mr Ottenheim. 'That's like – let's see – eighty-five *thousand* dollars! Did you ever stop to think that if you hadn't burned all that money in smoke, *you* could – oh, own a little hotel like this!'

The fat man studied his cigar. 'Mister,' he said, 'do *you* happen to smoke?'

'God forbid! Not even a cigarette! In my whole life, I never took one puff – '

'So do you own this hotel?'

Mr Ottenheim blinked, 'Certainly.'

P.S. The same story may be told with this ending:

'My God!' cried Mr Ottenheim. 'Did you ever stop to think that if you hadn't literally burned up eighty-five thousand dollars in smoke, you might – why, you might own a little hotel, like this one!'

The fat man nodded. 'I do.'

$\backsim$

'How did you like Atlantic City?' asked Morton.

'Fine. Good hotel. Good weather. Good food. Good gambling.' Spratt hesitated. 'The only thing wrong was – the help.'

'Really? Were they rude?'

'N-no. Just cunning.'

'What do you mean "cunning"?'

'Well, when you phone down for a deck of cards, the bellboy delivers them one at a time.'

○

A young buyer from Des Moines, in Chicago for a convention, filled out her first hotel registration card this way:

Name: Selma Hansley
Address: 806 Oak St., Des Moines, Iowa
Firm: Not very.

○

'So Nate, tell me, how is your little hotel in the Poconos doing this year?'

'Sensational!' replied Nate. 'We have guests sleeping under our beds!'

'No kiddin'?'

'No kiddin' . . . The roofs leak.'

○

Notice in Rooming House in Anchorage, Alaska:

1. Guests arriving without baggage, must leave wife's at desk with Harold.
2. Please do not smoke pot in hallways.
3. Do not clean shoes with a towel, unless it was stolen from another hotel.
4. In case of fire, do not use central stairway. It is highly inflammable. The moment you smell smoke, or hear our central fire alarm, jump out of nearest window.
5. If you see a mouse in your room, notify desk promptly. We will send up two heartless cats.
6. To prevent consistent loss of fresh fruit from centre of dining-room table, there will no longer be fresh fruit in centre of dining-room table.
7. Gambling is permitted only in areas designated 'GAMBLING SALON'. The nearest one is LUCY'S WHEEL, four blocks down the street.
8. We do not supply bottles, nipples, or wet nurses for babies.
9. All bribes to our help will be turned in to the Welfare Fund for Our Three Children. All our help are our children.
10. If you like our rooming house, service, food, or atmosphere, please tell others. If you do not, tell us. We will add 20 per cent to your bill.

How's That Again?

Lovingly collected, from newspapers, magazines, talk shows:

Reverend Hammond was congratulated on being able to get his parish plastered.

The jury's verdict showed they were of one mind: temporarily insane.

The driver of the car swerved to avoid missing the woman's husband.

The ball struck Berra on the right temple and knocked him cold. He was taken to Ford Hospital, where X-rays of his head showed nothing.

The congressman sat on the carpet and discussed the rise in prices and the high cost of living with several women.

Push back the cuticles on one hand with the orange-stick while you soak the other.

The doctor felt the man's purse and said there was no hope.

... There were only three other people in the big room, half of them waiters.

I live so far out of town, the mailman mails me my letters.

HENNY YOUNGMAN

The jury retired at 10 A.M. and deliberated twenty-four hours before returning a verdict of guilty of manslaughter. This conviction carried a penalty of one to ten years in Alabama.

He had a stroke, and didn't recover until he died.

A son was born to Mr and Mrs William Kleintop, Lehigh Avenue, during the past week. Congratulations, Pete!

No governor in many years has been able to love on the salary paid him, even though he is supplied with a furnished home rent free.

He was born in Hartford. Prior to that he worked for the American Silver Company.

People in search of solitude are flocking here from the four corners of the world.

CANADIAN HOTEL PROSPECTUS

He's a real eager-beaver. Why, he gets up six o'clock in the morning no matter what time it is.

THANKS TO HYMAN KAPLAN

Dance-hall marquee

GOOD CLEAN DANCING
EVERY NIGHT
EXCEPT SUNDAY

Mrs Beardsley, who is knitting a complex shawl for the church raffle, said, 'I am knitting as swiftly as I can, to be sure to get to the end of the garment before the wool runs out.'

Dogs are getting bigger, according to a leading dog manufacturer.

He is so honest that he worked in a bathhouse for three years and never took one.

PRIEST SAYS PUTTING CRONIN TO DEATH
Eliminates all Hope of
Rehabilitation

Ladies who have undertaken to act as school-crossing wardens are reminded that if they attempt to carry out their duties without the clothing on, motorists may not take notice of them.

Sign on hotel elevator door in Bucharest:

Lift is being fixed. Until then, we regret you are unbearable.

On lifeguard's stand in Florida:

GIRLS: DO NOT BOTHER LIFEGUARD
UNLESS ACTUALLY DROWNING

Fortunately for the deceased, he had deposited all of his money in the bank the day before, so he lost virtually nothing but his life.

The grandstand was so crowded they had to turn hundreds of people down for seats.

She held out her hand. The young man took it, and departed.

On photocopier in office

The typist's reproduction equipment is not to be interfered with without my specific permission.

MANAGER

'This young lady walked very close to me,' the witness testified, 'and it was obvious that underneath her clothing she wore nothing.'

See also **Boo-boos, Graffiti, Headlines That Haunt Me, Signs**

Immigrants

Hyman Soper entered Shona Mincus's kosher restaurant on lower Broadway. The waiter who poured his water was – clearly an Oriental. Perhaps a Korean? Perhaps from Thailand? And the man proceeded to rattle off the menu – in fluent Yiddish!

When Hyman Soper was paying his bill, he told the cashier, 'I enjoyed my dinner – and even more, I can't get over the fact that your waiter speaks such excellent Yiddish!'

'Ssh!' hissed the cashier. 'He thinks we're teaching him English.'

☌

Social column: 'I's very pleased,' said Sushi, a medical student, in perfect English.

☌

Muttel Friedman, newly arrived from Romania, got a job as a janitor in a theatre on Second Avenue. One afternoon he started for a backstage room on the door of which was this sign:

CHORUS GIRLS ONLY
ENTRY TO ALL OTHERS FORBIDDEN!

Just as Muttel put his hand on the knob of the door, the stage manager shouted, 'Stay out of there!' and hurried over. 'What's the matter with you, you greenhorn?' He pointed to the sign. 'Can't you read English?!'

Muttel drew himself up in righteous indignation. 'Who's smoking?'

☌

1919. Myron Bolitsky glowed with pride – as he stood before Judge Cranborn, to become a citizen.

'How many states are there in the Union?' asked Judge Cranborn.

'Forty-eight,' said Bolitsky.

'Good. And into how many branches is our government divided?'

'President, judges, and Congress.'

'Fine. . . . Now, Mr Bolitsky, will you solemnly swear to support the Constitution?'

A moan escaped Bolitsky. 'I would like to, *believe* me, judge. But I have a mother, wife, and two children in Romania.'

☌

Paddy O'Reilly met his cousin Mike, who had arrived in the United States only ten months ago. '*Ay* there, Michael, me boy. Y're lookin' peaked. Are ye not well?'

'Nay. It's in hospital I was, three days.'

'For what, man?'

'A tech of flu they said. 'Tis gone now 'tis. But d'ye know what that hospital charged me, Paddy? Fair on a hoondred and twelve dollars!'

'Mike, lad, that's not much – '

'Not *much?*' echoed Michael. 'Why back in County Cork, ye can be sick three *months* for money like that!'

Dennis Offaly was an immigrant, arrived but one week earlier from County Sligo. Now, for the first time, he was in an automat, with his cousin Gilly. Dennis fed nickel after nickel into the pie slots, – and soon a row of pies – apple, blueberry, cherry, peach – was arrayed before him. And still he kept dropping nickels in the slots.

Gilly exclaimed, 'Is it *mad* y've gone then, Denny? Y've got fourteen – fifteen – sixteen! – pies b'fore ye, man!'

Said Dennis, 'Faith, why is it botherin' ye that Oy've a lucky streak an' keep winnin'?!'

See also **Accents, The English Language**

Ingenuity

Police who arrested two men on car-theft charges in New York said they belonged to a gang who offered their customers an unusual guarantee. They sold stolen Cadillacs on the understanding that they were in sound mechanical condition. But if a defect developed, the gang guaranteed to resteal the car, so the illegal owner could collect from the insurance company – usually about four times what he had paid for the car.

Sign on shoeshine box on lower Broadway

FREE! FREE!
One shoe shined absolutely free.

At the nurses' desk on the sixth floor of Mount Sinai Hospital, the telephone rang. Nurse Juanita Campaña lifted the receiver, ''ollo. Seex floor.'

'Is this the nurse?'

'*Sí*. I can help you?'

'I hope so. I'm calling about one of your patients – Sol Bloomberg. That's B-L-O-O-M-B-E-R-G. He was operated on – four days ago.'

Nurse Campaña was consulting the charts. 'Sí.'

'Nurse, tell me, what's his condition? How is he coming along?'

'Hees condision is ajust fine. In foct, Doctor Shapeero say he can go home Duesday. . . . Who I should say telephone to heem?'

'No one. *I'm* Sol Bloomberg, and Doctor Shapiro don't tell me a goddam thing!'

In San Antonio, a large sign in the window of Miguel Gonzales's store read:

$$ BIG SALE!! $$
EVER TING
for
HOME, PORCK, KIHTCEN!

An English teacher from the nearby school, Carlotta Mendino, entered the store, and in Spanish inquired, 'Who is the owner?'

'*Yo*,' said Miguel Gonzales. 'Miguel Gonzales.'

'I am the teacher of English, Señor Gonzales. I think you should know that the sign in your window – contains some – several *bad* mistakes in spelling.'

'*Sí*,' nodded Gonzales.

'You know?'

'*Sí, sí*.'

'Would you like me to point out those mistakes, and correct them?'

'No,' the proprietor said. 'I do not wish *corrección*. People come in all the time – to tell me I have this mistake or that mistake in the sign. And at least *half*, señora, once inside, load up on bargains!'

Scene: Telephone Exchange: Cleveland

OPERATOR: This is Long Distance. May I help you?

MR KIRSCHBAUM: You soitinly can, operator. Give me in the state New York, the town is Quaquaga, the phone is number two-seven-six, four, four, three, eight –

OPERATOR: Would you mind repeating the name of that city, please?

MR KIRSCHBAUM: Qua-qu-a-ga. In New York.

OPERATOR: Sir, would you mind *spelling* that?

MR KIRSCHBAUM: Listen, lady; if I could spell it, I would send a postal card.

⌒

Scene: Plaza de la Independencia, Havana

Sergeant Robert Fiana of the Cuban Special Police, on duty at the vast Plaza de la Independencia, spied a man carrying a heavy briefcase. Sergeant Fiana stopped the man, flashed his identification card, and asked, 'Your name, señor?'

'Charamazo.'

'Christian *nombre?*'

'Vicente.'

'What you carry in thees beeg case?'

'In thees case,' smiled Charamazo, 'are pesos.'

'Pesos?!'

'*Sí.*'

'Open thees bag!'

Vicente Charamazo opened the brief case. There, indeed, were pesos – thousands of them.

Sergeant Fiana's eyes bulged. 'How you did get all thees pesos?'

'Gombling.'

'Gombling?' echoed Fiana. 'Thot ees most easy explanation – you think I am fool?'

'I prove to you, comrade,' said Charamazo. He thought for a moment. 'I – I bet you feefty pesos you no can take you pants off before I ron to that monument and back.'

'To the monument and *back?*'

'*Sí.*'

'That, up and back, take you at least four minutes!'

'So?'

'You want bet me feefty pesos I no can take off my pants in four whole minute?!'

'*Sí!*'

'Done!' Sergeant Fiana chuckled. 'Ready? Go!'

Vicente Charamazo started to trot toward the monument; Sergeant Fiana swiftly untied his boots, dropped them, undid his zipper, pulled down his trousers, stepped out of them, and cried, '*Finito!*'

Charamazo stopped trotting and came back to the pantsless sergeant.

'Well?' grinned Fiana.

'You ween,' said Charamazo, and handed the sergeant fifty pesos.

As Sergeant Fiana pulled on his trousers, he chuckled, 'Charamazo, you are worst gambler I did ever seen! How you could ween all that money in bag?!'

'Would you like know?' asked Charamazo.

'Sure.'

'Okay. Sergeant, how many people you see over there, in crowd?'

'Oh, ees thirty – forty.'

'Forty-seex,' said Charamazo, then beamed. 'And every one of them did bet me five pesos I no could talk you into taking off you pants in meedle of Plaza de la Independencia!'

Andrew Selkirk and Currie Stour, two Scotsmen visiting New York, decided their trip could not be considered complete unless they ventured down and took a ride on the legendary subway.

They were hurtling along toward Chambers Street when two armed hoodlums entered their car.

'Don't anyone try to move or I'll blow them to hell!' cried the first hoodlum.

'Just hand over all your valuables!' said the second hoodlum. 'Wallet, watch, rings, necklaces...'

Selkirk and Stour swiftly removed their wallets.

Just before the collecting hoodlum reached them. Selkirk murmured, 'Currie...'

'Ay?'

Selkirk handed Stour a ten-dollar bill.

'What is this for, Andrew?'

'Dinnae y' remember, mon? That be the ten dollars I'm owin' ye.'

☙

Mendel Tarshov fell off a bridge in Moscow. He could not swim. He thrashed around and shouted for help at the top of his lungs.

Two policemen heard his cries and ran to the rail, but when they saw Tarshov's skullcap, they simply laughed.

'Help! Help!' cried Tarshov. 'I'm drowning!'

'So drown, *Zhid* [Yid]!'

Just as Tarshov started under for the proverbial third time, he had an inspiration: 'To hell with Marx! To hell with Lenin! Down with the Politburo!'

At once, the policemen jumped into the water, pulled Tarshov out, and arrested him for spreading anti-Communist propaganda.

☙

One day, to the border post separating Russia from Poland, Yuli Probovnie came riding along on a bicycle – with a heavy sack slung across his shoulders. He stopped at the sentry box and showed the guard his passport, permission to travel, visa . . .

The chief border guard found the papers in order. Then he asked, '*Tovarich*, what's in the sack?'

'Flour,' said Probovnie.

'Humph. Open it up. I want to see for myself if *all* you're taking to those damn Poles is flour!'

So Probovnie opened the sack. The contents certainly looked like flour. But the chief guard stabbed his bayonet into the flour, six – seven – eight times, in eight different places. Nowhere did he strike metal, or a box, a can, a bottle. . . . 'Okay, *tovarich*.' He lifted the border gate, and Yuri Probovnie retied his bag, slung it across his shoulder, and pedalled across the border.

A week later, to the same sentry box, came Yuri. Again he presented his passport, his papers, his visa. And again the chief sentry asked, '*Tovarich*, what are you taking into Poland this time?'

'Grain.'

'Grain, eh? Open up the sack. I want to see for myself . . .'

Again Yuri opened his sack. The contents certainly were grain. The border guard stabbed his bayonet into the grain – six, seven, eight times once more. His bayonet struck no metal, no can, no bottle. . . . 'All right.'

Once a week, for a whole year, the same scene was re-enacted. Each time Yuri Probovnie was stopped by the chief of the border customs control. 'And what are you carrying this time, *tovarich*?'

One week Yuri said, 'Beans.' Another time he said, 'Sugar.' other weeks he carried a sackful of salt, meal, rice . . .

Each time the customs chief examined Yuri's sack and found the contents to be as described.

At the end of the year, the border chief defected. He made his way to Vienna, where, drinking tea in a café one afternoon, he beheld Yuri Probovnie. *'Tovarich!'* he exclaimed. 'You here? Come. Have some tea.'

As they drank, the defector asked Yuri, 'Listen, my friend. I have escaped from the Soviet Union. I'll never go back. So you can talk frankly to me. Will you?'

'Sure.'

'Look, I *know* you were smuggling stuff across the border! I felt it in every bone in my body – but I could never prove it! Now you can tell me the truth. . . . *Were* you smuggling?'

'Certainly.' Yuri smiled.

'What?'

'Bicycles.'

Amos Harvey, in a taxi, noticed he had forgotten to take his wallet along. The meter read $3.25. He thought for a moment, then said to the driver: 'Stop at the next place I can buy some cigarettes.' The cab stopped in front of a drugstore. 'I'll only be a minute,' said Harvey. 'Oh, by the way, I dropped a fifty-dollar bill in the back. Couldn't find it in the dark. Remind me to look for it when I get back.'

Harvey opened the door to the drugstore. The taxi roared away.

Two Jews, Gumbiner and Ohrbach, were walking down a street in Berlin when they saw an SS cop approaching. Only Gumbiner had an identity card. Ohrbach said, 'Quick, Hans, *run!* He'll chase you. You'll show him your identity card – and I'll get away!'

So Gumbiner broke into a run.

'Stop! Stop!' cried the policeman.

Gumbiner kept on running.

The SS cop finally caught up. 'Jew!' he roared. 'Show me your papers!'

Gumbiner, gasping, produced his papers.

The Nazi examined them and saw they were in order. 'But why,' he asked in surprise, 'were you running away from me?!'

'Eh – I wasn't running away from you,' said Gumbiner. 'My doctor – told me to run half a mile after each meal.'

The Nazi frowned. 'But you saw me chasing you! You heard me yelling! Why didn't you stop?'

'I – uh – thought maybe you go to the same doctor.'

Amos and Myron, brothers, not particularly friendly, inherited a large plot of land from their father. They argued and argued about how to divide it. Unable to agree, Myron said, 'Let's go to Rabbi Sampson and ask him the fairest way to divvy up the land.'

Rabbi Sampson was the right man to ask. He said, 'Toss a coin. The one who wins the toss, divides the land.'

'But *rebbe*,' complained Amos, 'I don't believe in gambling!'

'Nor do I,' smiled Rabbi Sampson. 'The one who wins the toss divides the land; but the other one gets first choice.'

High in the ranks of the ingenious must be the Jewish beggar who, at the height of Hitler's power, stood on a busy Berlin corner with a tin cup and this sign:

I DO NOT ACCEPT
MONEY FROM JEWS

The approving *Herrenvolk* dropped coins in the cup in a veritable shower.

The owner of a new drugstore put a large glass fish tank in his window, filled it with water, then placed this sign in front of it:

THIS BOWL IS FULL OF
INVISIBLE PERUVIAN DEVIL-FISH

The sidewalk in front of the window was packed all day.

Jackson lent Maxon five hundred dollars. Maxon promised to return it within a month. A year later, Jackson still had not received a dime. Jackson consulted a lawyer.

'Do you have Maxon's IOU?' asked the lawyer.

'No. I didn't ask for one.'

'Do you have his personal note?'

'I have nothing in writing. I thought I was dealing with a friend.'

The lawyer thought for a while, then said, 'Write Maxon and tell him you have to have the seven hundred dollars he borrowed – '

'You mean five hundred.'

'No, I mean seven hundred. He'll write back indignantly that he only owes you five hundred. You'll have it in writing.'

Sign in pilots' lounge at airport

ATTENTION
By Order of Navigation Control
**Absolutely no flying is permitted over
the nudist camp which is 18.3 SSW on a
true course of 149 degrees.**

After his first day as a bus driver, Patrick Flynn handed in receipts of $165. The next day his receipts were $194. The third day's income was $172. But on the fourth day, Flynn, beaming with pride, placed $483 on the desk before the cashier, whose eyes popped.

'Flynn,' said the cashier, 'this is fontostic, for sure. Never, never has your route brought in such sums! What happened?'

'Well, after me first three days on the route that dispatcher give me, I figured business would never improve. So I drove over to Main Street . . . I tell you, that street is a very gold mine!'

A learned rabbi used to ride from town to town in old Lithuania to preach. He loved to answer questions. Now, the rabbi's driver always listened to the sermons, and especially to the questions and answers.

After many years, one day the driver said, '*Rebbe*. I have

listened to you for over twenty years. I can recite your sermons in my sleep. . . . Before I die, I'd like to be as respected as you are. Tomorrow we're coming to a village we've never seen before. Why can't we change places?! Just this once. I'll wear your broad hat and caftan, and deliver the sermon; and people will ask *me* questions and I'll answer every one – exactly the way you would!'

The idea intrigued the rabbi. So he and the driver changed clothes. . . . The driver delivered an excellent sermon. Then the congregation began to ask questions, which he answered with ease from memory. But the last question asked was so new, so profound, that the poor driver was flabbergasted. Finally, with altogether admirable presence of mind, he drew himself up and thundered, '*Me* you ask a question as simple as that! Why, even my driver, sitting back there, a poor, hard-working man who never set foot in a *yeshiva*, can answer it. Driver!' he sang out to the rabbi: 'Stand up! Did you hear the question?'

'Yes, *rebbe*,' said the rabbi.

'Answer it.'

See also **Aplomb, Graffiti, Reason, Scoundrels, Signs, Stratagems**

Ingratitude

The Padraic Hannegans of Sydney, Australia, were taking a holiday at the sea near Wollongong. Mrs Hannegan was playing in the water with her little son, Carson. Suddenly, an unexpected, powerful wave rolled in, knocked the little boy down, and, roaring back, scooped the child up and carried him out to sea.

'Carson! My boy!' screamed Mrs Hannegan. 'Help! Help!'

People leaped to their feet. Several waded into the water. But all stood frozen, for they could not see the lad who was being sucked out to sea.

'Help! My boy! Drowning!' shrieked Mrs Hannegan.

From his high tower, a lifeguard leaped down to the sand, hurled his torpedo-buoy ahead in the direction he had seen the boy being carried, and with powerful strokes swam out, reached the lad, slung him across the orange torpedo, and propelled both on to a huge wave that carried all three back to shore.

Mrs Hannegan smothered her son, who was coughing, but definitely alive, in her arms.

The lifeguard beamed. 'Fit as a fiddle he is, mum.'

Mrs Hannegan noticed something, drew herself up, and, with considerable indignation, declared: 'He – was – wearing – a – hat! . . .

See also **Chutzpa**

Insomnia

Poor Mr Gittelman could not sleep. No pills from his doctor, no advice from his friends, helped his tormenting insomnia. Mr Gittelman began to look so haggard that his partner, Mr Feigenbaum, said, 'You'll end up in a loony ward!'

'So what can I *do?*' moaned Gittelman. 'I drink hot milk. I take warm baths. I play soft music. I take every sleeping pill the doctor prescribes . . .'

'What about the oldest trick of all: counting sheep?'

Gittelman smote his forehead. 'Harvey, so help me, I forgot that one. You're a life-saver. Tonight, I'll count sheep and if I have to count up to ten thousand, I'll fall asleep at last!'

The next morning, the moment Gittelman entered the loft, Feigenbaum asked, 'Did it work?'

'No,' groaned Gittelman. 'I counted sheep. Oh, how I counted sheep. I counted up to two thousand without getting tired. So I sheared the sheep – all two thousand – and still I was wide awake. So I had an idea, and I made up two thousand overcoats. Do you *know* how tiring it is to make two thousand overcoats! I was exhausted and practically snoring – when it happened!'

'What happened?'

'All night I was up, worrying; where could I get two thousand linings?'

The two friends were at their favourite bar, feeling nice and friendly.

'An' did y' know I was on the wagon, I was, for all of Lent, me boy? Not a drop, not a *drop* so much as touched me lips!'

'Fancy that, Emmet. A reg'lar saint y're gittin' to be.'

'What about you, Terence?'

'It grieves me to confess to ye, I drink a pint of Irish – a whole pint, mind y', ivery single night. In fact I do it on the express orders of Doctor McGonigle.'

'A pint of whiskey, is it? Ah, tell me, Terence, me foine friend – has the doctor's prescription helped y'r not sleepin' so bad?'

'T' tell ye the truth, Emmet, the whiskey hasn't even *tetched* me insomnia – but I sure don't mind staying oop the way I used t'.'

See also **Doctors**

Insults

The last time we met was in my nightmare.

You have a wonderful head on your shoulders; too bad it's not on your neck.

You have the manners of a perfect gentleman: whose are they?

HENNY YOUNGMAN

I don't know what I would do without you – but I'd rather.

Our club is having a membership drive – to drive him out of the club.

You're just what the doctor ordered – a big pill.

He hasn't been himself lately: let's hope he stays that way.

I'd like to rent her out to a nearsighted knifethrower.

LOUIS SAFIAN, *2,000 Insults*

See also **Curses, Groucho, Put-downs, Retorts, Sarcasm, Squelches**

Israel

In 1949, Gerald Harmon, from Manchester, was visiting Israel, and was invited by his Israeli cousin, Simeon, to the historic ceremonies dedicating the Tomb of the Unknown Soldier.

Speeches were made by the president of Israel, the minister of defence, by the commanding general of the army; and at last the tarpaulin that covered the monument was pulled aside – to reveal a simple tomb. On the front was engraved:

BARUCH BARZELAI
Born: Vilna, 1903
Died: Sinai, 1948

All rose as the military band played Israel's national anthem. Soldiers saluted. Civilians placed their right hands over their hearts.

Then Ben Gurion stepped to the lectern to address the throng. And Gerald Harmon whispered to his cousin: 'Simeon . . . I say . . . isn't this supposed to be the Tomb of the Unknown Soldier?'

Simeon nodded.

'But – forgive me, old man. "Unknown?" Absurd. Why, there, plainly inscribed, is the man's name, his birthplace, his – '

'Ssh,' hushed Simeon. 'You don't understand. As a *soldier*. Baruch Barzelai was unknown; but as a pants-maker – !'

ᔓ

In Israel, an American visitor saw an elderly Jew praying, tears simply pouring down his face.

The American, who could not bear the old man's wailing, asked, '*Zayde* [grandfather] . . . please . . . why are you weeping so bitterly?'

'Because – I want to be with my people!' sobbed the old man.

'But you *are*, in Israel, the Promised Land.'

'I mean with my people in Miami!'

ᔓ

Mr and Mrs Gelfarb, from Denver, were visiting Israel. Driving around Tel Aviv, their car was stopped by a traffic patrol car. The officer addressed him: 'Don't you know you're going down a one-way street?!'

'No, officer.'

'Well, you're not blind, are you? Don't you see that great big arrow?'

'Sure I can see that arrow,' said Mr Gelfarb. 'But in Israel, who expects to find *Indians*?'

ᔐ

In El Al cabin   **FASTEN YOUR SEAT BELTS**
                              NO SMOKING
                                EAT FRUIT

ᔐ

Jewish dropout: A student who didn't get a Ph.D.

Sign in a café in Jerusalem

SELF-SERVICE
'For you are servants unto Me,' said the Lord.

ᔐ

Mendel Dresselberg, who was extremely active in Jewish affairs, and had raised a considerable sum for the Bonds for Israel drive, was in Israel for an election – and the day after, he was in the office of the newly elected prime minister. 'I want you to know that if you – well, if you see fit to appoint me to an important position in your government, I can come here, become a citizen, settle . . . I mean, after all – I hope you haven't forgotten how much I've done . . .'

'Forgotten? Never!' said the prime minister-elect. 'In fact, I was just telling a member of my new cabinet that our great friend, Mendel Dresselberg, is the perfect appointee for minister of health and transportation!'

Dresselberg's face broke into a great smile. 'Minister – that's wonderful. But' – he frowned – 'isn't that an unusual combination?'

'Unusual? No, no, my friend,' smiled the prime minister. 'What this job involves is this: the minister – you – gets an apartment in Haifa, preferably with a balcony, overlooking the harbour. And you sit on that balcony, where everyone can see you. And whenever a ship prepares to leave Haifa, you, the minister, stand up, holding a huge bullhorn, and as the ship begins to pull away from the dock, you wave at it like crazy and, in a strong, official voice, through the bullhorn, you holler, "Sail in the best of health! Go, go! Sail in the best of health!"'

∽

Two Israeli spies, caught in Syria, were put up against the wall. The firing squad marched in. The Syrian captain asked the first spy, 'Do you have any last wish?'

'A cigarette.'

The captain gave him a cigarette, lighted it, and asked the second spy, 'Do you have a last request?'

Without a word, the second spy spit in the captain's face.

'Harry!' cried the first spy. '*Please!* Don't make trouble.'

∽

Charley Gans, a congenital wise guy, visiting Israel, stopped at a vegetable stand. He picked up several large cantaloupes, hefted them for weight, then *utzed* the farmer, 'Hey, can't you *sabras* grow bigger peaches than these?'

The farmer fixed Gans with an icy stare. 'Peaches? Those you call peaches? Do me a favour, mister; put down the two grapes and go away.'

∽

Sign in a barracks of the Israeli army:

Privates will refrain from giving advice to officers.

∽

In Tel Aviv, one dark night, Special Agent 6-Z-4 looked up and down the street, then darted into the apartment building. He slipped the Colt into his outer pocket, knocked on the door of 2D twice, paused, knocked once, paused, knocked twice again.

From inside, a voice inquired, 'Who's dere?'

'Goldblatt?' whispered 6-Z-4.

The door opened; a bald-headed little man in pyjamas said, '*Sholem aleichem.*'

'The ostriches,' murmured 6-Z-4, 'have arrived in Greece.'

'*Ha-anh?*' goggled Goldblatt.

'The ostriches,' repeated 6-Z-4 slowly, 'have arrived in Greece . . .'

A light entered the eyes of the bald-headed little man. 'Ah-*aha*!

Mister, I am Goldblatt, the piano teacher. You want Goldblatt the spy. Upstairs, 4B.'

Israel's prime minister at a cabinet meeting lamented: 'Our inflation is unbearable, our deficits are increasing by leaps and bounds – I don't know what to do that's best for our country!'

The minister of finance said, 'Why not – declare war?'

'War?' frowned the prime minister. 'Against whom?'

'Against – the United States of America.'

This astounding suggestion created gasps and groans. 'You must be crazy! War? Between Israel and America? Why, such a war would not last ten minutes!'

The finance minister nodded. 'Quite so. We declare war – and immediately acknowledge defeat. "You are the victors!" we tell the Americans. So immediately the US will send us relief: food, supplies, oil. They will give us huge grants, rebuild our roads and harbours, send us – '

'*Just* a minute,' growled the prime minister. 'All that is fine, and would certainly happen. But tell me, if you're so damn clever, what if we *win?!*'

See also **Anti-Semitism, God, Jews, Rabbis, Stratagems**

Jews

Either Hilaire Belloc or A. N. Ewer coined this quatrain:

> How odd
> Of God
> To choose
> The Jews.

This jingle was answered by some unknown wag:

> Not news,
> Not odd,
> The Jews
> Chose God.

To which a Jew responded:

> Not odd
> Of God:
> Goyim
> Annoy 'im.

Young Mrs Pollack, pushing a pram with two baby boys in it, encountered Mrs Miller, who said, 'Good morning, Mrs Pollack. My, what beautiful boys! So – how old are they?'

'The doctor,' said Mrs Pollack, 'is two. The lawyer, tomorrow is his first birthday.'

Mrs Zolotow was proudly pushing the perambulator down Ocean Avenue, where her neighbour, Mrs O'Leary, stopped her. 'Well now, Mrs Zolotow, an' which o' y'r children has made y' a grand-mother again?'

'My daughter, Rosalie.'

Mrs O'Leary looked into the carriage. 'Oh, my, *my*, Mrs Zolo-tow. Sure an' this is a pretty bundle o' joy.'

'You think *she's* pretty?' Mrs Zolotow sniffed. 'Wait until you see the pictures!'

Jackson, Waybrook, Buchanan, and Isaacs was one of the finest law firms in the city. One day a friend of Eli Isaacs asked, 'Why does your name appear last, Eli? Everyone knows that Jackson is ga-ga, Waybrook spends most of his time in the country, and Buchanan never won a case in court. Your name should be first!'

'You forget something,' Isaacs smiled.

'What's that?'

'*My* clients read from right to left.'

Mrs Galitzki, visiting London, went shopping at world-famed Fortnum & Mason. She bought jars of marmalade, jams, pickles, tins of fine cookies.

'And where,' asked the striped-trousered salesman, 'shall we deliver these, madam?'

'Don't bother. I'll take them.'
'But madam, we'll be *happy* to deliver this order – '
'I know, but I don't mind, I'm from the Bronx.'
'I understand, madam,' said the clerk. 'Still – why *shlep*?'

Roses are reddish,
Violets, bluish;
If it wasn't for Christmas
We'd all be Jewish.

Harold Schussler and Norman Meyerson, both widowers, were passing the time by playing cards in Meyerson's old apartment on Amsterdam Avenue. After several hours, Schussler glanced at his wrist. 'Oh, damn. My watch has stopped again. Norman, what time is it?'

Meyerson shuffled the cards. 'I don't know.'

'So Norman, look at *your* watch.'

'I don't have a watch.'

'So take a look at the clock in the kitchen,' said Schussler.

'I don't have in the kitchen a clock,' said Meyerson.

'So in the bedroom, Norman. The clock – '

'In my bedroom also is no clock.'

Schussler's brow furrowed. 'Listen, Norman. Are you telling me that you don't have on your wrist or in a pocket, a watch – and that in this whole six-room apartment you don't have one single clock?!'

'That's right.'

'For God's *sake*, Norman! What do you do when you have to know what time it is?'

Meyerson shrugged. 'I use my bugle.'

'Your *what*?!'

'My bugle.' Meyerson leaned over and from the floor lifted an old, battered bugle, went to a window, raised the pane, put the bugle to his lips, and blared a forceful: 'Ra-ta-ta-ta-*tah*!'

And from a dozen flats in the courtyard came this litany: 'What's the matter with you, you crazy man, playing the bugle at a quarter to eleven at night?!'

Note: No collection of humorous episodes would be complete without the following well-known exchange – which, no matter how often told, loses nothing by repetition.

The hostess was making the rounds, at her tea for the ladies, with a platter of freshly baked, home-made cookies. 'So, Mrs Pearlstein,' she smiled, 'have some cookies.'

'No, thank you,' said Mrs Pearlstein. 'They're absolutely delicious – but I already had four.'

'You already had *five*,' said the hostess. 'But who's counting?'

Said Mrs Heffelman, 'Listen, Goldie. I hear you had this year a very, very bad time.'

'Why "had"?' said Mrs Kopman. 'You think everything is by me now hotsy-totsy?'

'No?'

'No.'

'So tell me what's happened?'

'What's happened is, in May, my darling little dog was run over. In June, my daughter Freda ran away with a married man. In July, my son lost his job. In August, my husband had a fatal heart attack. And next Tuesday,' Mrs Kopman sighed, 'the painters are coming.'

When Messrs Motzner and Krupnick opened their new store, they decided, for tactical reasons, to call it 'Donahue and Donahue.'

On their first day, a customer asked one of the salesmen, 'I want to talk to Mr Donahue.'

'Which Mr Donahue do you want?' replied the salesman. 'Motzner or Krupnick?'

The resident pediatrician was making his morning rounds in the ward, trailed by six interns. 'Sickle-cell anaemia may be found in black children, especially if their parents come from the Caribbean. Tay-Sachs syndrome occurs in adult Jews, of course; but

Jewish children are more easily identified by one fact. Can anyone tell me what that is?'

'Certainly,' said one intern. 'Heartburn.'

ᔓ

Father Malachy was walking down a street in Boston when he saw a large banner over a store:

GREENBERG AND O'SULLIVAN

Father Malachy hastened in with a broad, broad smile. He was greeted by a bearded man wearing a *yarmulka*.

'Well, sir,' beamed Father Malachy, 'I just want ye t' know how foine it is afther all these years, for a simple Irishman to see your people and mine working together – and as partners! What a sorprise. What a sorprise!'

'Father, I thank you. But I'll give you a bigger surprise,' said the old man. '*I'm* O'Sullivan.'

ᔓ

THE WALLS OF JERICHO

ACT I   Scene: Classroom, Sunday School at Beth Hillel Synagogue

MR AARONS: Well, children, who can tell me the answer to this question: who was it who blew down the walls of Jericho. . . . Jonas?

JONAS SPRINGER: Don't look at me, sir. *I* didn't!

ACT II   Elias Springer's Home.   The phone rings.

MR SPRINGER: Hello.

MR AARONS: Hello, Mr Springer?

MR SPRINGER: Yeah.

MR AARONS: This is Mr Aarons, from Beth Hillel. I'm sorry to bother you, but I must talk to you about your boy, Jonas. When I asked him, during Bible class this morning, who it was who blew down the walls of Jericho, he answered, 'Don't look at me! *I* didn't.'

MR SPRINGER: Look, Mr Aarons. If my Joney says he didn't do it, he didn't do it!

(hangs up abruptly)

ACT III   *Rabbi's office*

RABBI LOWENSTEIN: Mr Aarons, I hear that when you asked Jonas Springer, in your class, 'Who blew down the walls of Jericho?' the boy answered 'Don't look at me, *I* didn't!' Is that so?

MR AARONS: Yes. But the boy's father *assures* me that if Jonas says he didn't do it, he didn't do it!

RABBI LOWENSTEIN: Well, I have known Elias Springer for fifteen years. And I can vouch for his honesty!

ACT IV   *Office of Nathan Fardroos*

RABBI LOWENSTEIN: Since you are the chairman of our synagogue's board of trustees, there is one little matter I ought to bring to your attention. You know Mr Springer, of course. Well, his son Jonas is in our Bible class. And when the teacher, Mr Aarons, asked who blew down the walls of Jericho, little Jonas replied: 'Not me.' Mr Aarons told this to Mr Springer, who insisted that his son could be trusted! I asked Mr Aarons what he thought, and he said he believed the father! When Mr Aarons asked me what *I* thought, I told him that I have known Elias Springer for many years, and if *he* says Jonas is telling the truth –

MR FARDROOS: All right, enough! I'm a busy man, rabbi. There's no need to make a big deal about this. Just have the wall fixed, and send the bill to me.

In the card room of a resort hotel in the Poconos, four strangers arranged a bridge game. As they sat down, the first man said, 'Let's introduce ourselves. I'm Albert Carman.'

'My name,' said the second player, 'is William Cohane.'

'I,' said the third man, 'am Joe Cronin.'

The fourth man: 'I'm Jack.'

'Jack what?'

'Also Cohen.'

Ephrian Gerbner could scarcely believe his eyes. There, on Yom Kippur, the most holy feast day, the Day of Atonement, at a table right in the window of the Sea King Restaurant, sat his old friend, Meyer Perlmutter – eating oysters!

Into the Sea King dashed Gerbner. 'Meyer! My God! Eating?! Today?! And *oysters* yet?'

'So?' shrugged Perlmutter. 'Isn't there an *r* in Yom Kippur?'

⌒

A bearded old man once patted my head, when I was ten, and chuckled fondly. 'You look like a nice boy. You should live to a hundred and twenty-one!'

When I told this to my father, he explained, 'Jews say that – because Moses, according to legend, lived to be a hundred and twenty.'

'Oh ... but why did the old man tell me "a hundred and twenty-*one*"?'

My father smiled. 'Maybe he didn't want you to die suddenly.'

⌒

The four ladies were on the porch of Mrs Ruttenberg's Villa d'Esther resort, in the Poconos, rocking back and forth, taking in the scenic beauties. After a bit, the first woman sighed, '*Oy* . . .'

The other three sighed in sympathy.

Soon, a second woman sighed, '*Oy vey* . . .' The others nodded. A third woman said, '*Oy, Gottenyu!*' and the others again nodded.

At last, the fourth rocker said, 'So. Enough talk about the children. Let's go for a walk.'

⌒

On its maiden voyage, the SS *Shalom*, the first great ocean liner of Israel, steamed into the harbour of New York to a truly tumultuous greeting. But one observer was not tumultuous. He frowned. 'That boat ... you know something: she doesn't *look* Jewish!'

⌒

Note: 'Bialy' is the abbreviated name of Bialystock, in which Russian or Polish town bakers first (supposedly) made those slightly underbaked rolls, shaped like a tiny, tiny rubber wading pool, with baked onion sprinkled in the declivity, that have become second in popularity only to bagels.

L. R.

The Richard F. Lowenfelds bought a fine house in Sands Point, Long Island, staffed it with a French cook, an Irish maid, and an English butler, and invited three couples from New York out for the first Sunday brunch of the season: the Goldsmiths, the Rubloffs, and the Chertoks.

On Sunday morning, Mrs Lowenfeld noticed that the table was set for twelve. She rang for the butler. 'Earnshaw,' she said, 'did you set the table for *six* couples?'

'Yes, madam.'

'But I told you were were having three couples – plus Mr Lowenfeld and myself. That's eight in all.'

'Yes, madam.'

'Then why did you set the table for twelve?'

'Because, madam,' said the butler, 'Mrs Chertok telephoned an hour ago to say that they are bringing the Bagels and the Bialys.'

The waves were high and rough and pounded at the shores of Pompano Beach, and the lifeguard pulled the limp form of Maxwell Sonnenfeld out of the angry waters. A crowd formed around them.

'Stand back!' boomed the lifeguard.

'Get a doctor!'

'Give the man air!'

'Get his wife!'

'Stand *back*!' the lifeguard shouted. 'I'm going to give him artificial respiration.'

'Never!' cried Mrs Sonnenfeld, pressing her way to the fore. 'My Max gets real respiration or nothing!'

On the train from Boston to New Bedford, Mr Josephson sat down opposite an attractive young man. After a moment, the young man said, 'Sir, may I ask you what time it is?'

Mr Josephson pulled his gold watch out of his vest pocket, snapped the cover open, and said, 'Twenty-two minutes past eleven.'

'Thank you.'

Mr Josephson put his watch back, studied the young man, and said, 'Are you by any chance going to New Bedford?'

'Yes, I am.'

Mr Josephson stared at him, said, 'Go to hell – and don't say a word to me again!' and opened his newspaper with a flourish.

The young man had turned red. He said. 'Sir, I resent that! . . . Do you hate Jews?'

'Oh, no. I'm a Jew myself.'

'Then why – just because I asked you a polite question – did you –'

Mr Josephson placed both hands on his chest. 'Don't jump to conclusions, young man. . . . Listen. Suppose I gave you a polite answer, after you said you were going to New Bedford – like "That's good" or "Nice day" or "Staying long?" We would start a conversation. You would ask me, "Do you live in New Bedford? . . . Do you take this train often? . . . What business are you in?" and I would ask you what you do for a living – and so on, for a half-hour, maybe. And then, because you are a nice-looking young man, I would ask you to come to dinner at my home – where you would meet my wife and my daughter, Sylvia, our only child, a *lovely* girl, beautiful, talented, a wonderful cook, loves music, reads a lot. . . . You would undoubtedly ask her to go out on a date. So you and my Sylvia would go out, and – believe me! – young man, you would fall head over heels in love! . . . So soon you would come to me and say, "Mr Josephson, I would like your consent to marry your daughter" . . . Young man, I would absolutely break your heart! Could *I* let my only daughter marry a fellow who doesn't even *own a watch*?!' Mr Josephson shook his head. 'No. . . . So I figured it best for me, for Sylvia, for you, too – to stop the whole business before I can even start. That's why I said, "Go to hell!" before – and that's why I say, "Go to hell!" now. . . . Do me a favour. Don't say another word to me until we get to New Bedford!'

Mrs Gorshky sent this telegram from Leningrad to her husband in Kovno:

SAYS TO OPERATE OPERATE

RUCHEL

To this message, Mr Gorshky replied:

SAYS TO OPERATE OPERATE

NAHUM

The police at once arrested Mr Gorshky, beat him up, threw him into a cell, then asked, 'All right now, you agent of the capitalist bourgeoisie! What secret code are you using?'

'What code? What secret?' asked bewildered Gorshky.

'Do you think we're fools? Just read these messages!'

'Certainly,' said Gorshky. 'But first I must tell you that my Ruchel is sick, and the doctors in Kuvno couldn't help her. So she went to Leningrad to consult a famous surgeon. And after she saw him, she wired me like this – ' He picked up her telegram and read: '"Says to operate . . . *Operate?*" . . . . I thought over the surgeon's recommendation, and I answered her – ' Gorshky picked up a copy of his reply. '"Says to operate? Operate!"'

∽

No Jewish girl reaches the age of thirty without having been asked to marry at least four times – once by her father, three times by her mother.

∽

At the festive table, during the Sheineman's Passover party, the conversation sparkled. At one point, Mr Sheineman asked Mrs Glantz, on his right, 'Someone told me you're an expert on Omar Khayyam.'

'Who's a *maven*?' she asked. 'I only know what I like and what I don't like.'

'So? What's your feeling about the Rubaiyat?'

Mrs Glantz shrugged. 'Not bad, not great. But speaking personally, *I* prefer Chianti.'

When the Glantzes left the party, Mr Glantz said, 'Mildred, why do you always have to show off? Why do you have to pretend you know it all? The Rubaiyat isn't a *wine*!'

'Omigod,' moaned Mrs Glantz.

'It's a cheese.'

∽

One of the telephone operators at the famous law firm Fleming, Boyd, Harwood, and Kassenbaum answers the electronic beep from the electronic switchboard, 'Fleming, Boyd, Harwood, and Kassenbaum.'

'Hello, may I please speak to Jacob Kassenbaum?'

'I'm sorry sir, but Mr Kassenbaum is not in today. This is Yom Kippur.'

'Well, Miss Kippur, please tell Mr Kassenbaum his bifocals are ready.'

∽

WHY DO JEWS SAY 'WHY?'

Lord Strathmore asked Lapidus, his tailor, 'Why is it that you Jews always answer a question with another question?'

Lapidus pursed his lips. 'Why not?'

The next day, Strathmore asked the driver of his taxi, one Isaac Lipsky, 'Driver, why is it that Jews always answer a question with another question?'

'Who told you that?' sneered Lipsky.

That Sunday, Strathmore asked a Jewish neighbour, 'I say, Herbert, why do Jews seem to answer every question with a question?'

Herbert smiled, 'But who doesn't?'

A week later, Strathmore asked Dr Shulman, his dentist, 'Why do Jews always answer a question with another question?'

Shulman's eyes rounded. 'They *do*?'

Aboard the Concorde to New York, Lord Strathmore asked the bearded man in the seat next to him. 'Why do you Jews always answer a question with another question?'

'How should I know?' replied the stranger.

And at dinner, several days later, Strathmore asked the famous banker, Roger Lehmann Loebel, 'May I ask you something, Roger? *Why* do Jews always answer a question with another question?'

'*Do* they?' exclaimed Loebel.

So Lord Strathmore, utterly frustrated, asked a priest, 'Father, perhaps you can help me.'

'I'll try.'

'Well, it is said that whenever a member of the Jewish faith is asked a question he answers with another question. You serve on several interreligious committees. Is that true?'

Sighed the priest, 'Now what idjit iver told ye a silly thing like that?'

∽

Mr Lurie, a resident of Los Angeles for fifty years, approached a young man who was waiting for a bus on Wilshire Boulevard. 'Young man, excuse me. Can I ask a personal question? Are you Jewish?'

'No, I'm not.'

'Are you sure?'

'Of course I'm sure!' The young man laughed.

'You're not just teasing me?'

'No. Why should I tease you?'

Mr Lurie sighed. 'Well, excuse my question. I didn't mean to embarrass you.'

'Wait, mister,' the young man glanced around and, lowering his voice, said, 'can you keep a secret?'

'Absolutely!'

'Well, not a soul in the world knows it – except you. The truth is: I am a Jew.'

'My, my,' clucked Mr Lurie. 'You certainly don't *look* Jewish.'

Herbie Klonsky came into his boss's office with trepidation. 'Mr Rodolovitch, I don't like to bother you, but – well, maybe you wouldn't mind too much if – if I take off tomorrow?...'

'Tomorrow?' Mr Rodolovitch said. 'What type of holiday is tomorrow?'

'It's not exactly a holiday,' said Klonsky. 'It's – our anniversary. Wedding anniversary. For me and my Shaindl. Twenty-five *years*, Mr Rodolovitch.'

'Oh... Well, I suppose it will be all right you shouldn't come to work.... Take the day off.'

'*Thank* you, Mr Rodolovitch.'

Just as Herbie was going through the door, Rodolovitch cried, 'But one thing, Klonsky. Do I have to go through this nonsense every twenty-five years?!'

The teacher said, 'Children, since this is the first day of a new term, I want each of you to stand up, give us your name – clearly – and your age, and mention your favourite hobby.'

The first child rose and said, 'My name is Andrew Blake. I'm almost ten years old .... I like to swim.'

The second student rose: 'My name is Jimmy Cort. I'm nine and a half years old. My hobby is collecting stamps.'

The third student rose: 'My name is Morris Wexler. I'm ten, and I pledge five dollars.'

∽

'Hey, Pete,' said Waldman, 'have you heard the latest joke about the two Jews who – '

'Hold it. Wait,' said Pete Hyman. 'Why does it always have to be two Jews? Are the Jews the only people in the world you can tell funny stories about? Wouldn't a story be just as funny if it was about two Mexicans? Or two Japanese?'

'Okay, okay,' said Waldman. 'I'll try it your way. Once there were two Japanese, partners in a *teffilin* [phylacteries] factory. One day, going to a meeting of the UJA, the first Japanese said to his partner, "Menachem, next Yom Kippur, I hope to be in Boston, because my grandson, Erwin, will be *Bar Mitzva*!' So the second Japanese answered, "Israel, I'm going to a circumcision...'"

Said Pete, 'Forget it.'

∽

Beckman and Moscot, old friends, had sat in silence on their favourite park bench for hours, lost in thought. Finally, Beckman gave a long, sad sigh.

Moscot said, 'You're telling *me*?'

∽

'Hello, Mandel. What's new?'

'Good. With me, everything is good!'

'Really? Everyone knows you almost went broke. So how can you say everything's *good*?'

'Because it is. I get up every morning good and tired. I come home every night good and depressed. I'm good and disgusted with my children, and I'm good and sick of my wife. In fact, my whole life is so rotten, I'm good and tired of living!'

∽

Into the posh aisles of Kensington Gourmet Foods came a bearded figure in a black hat with a broad, flat rim, a white shirt, no necktie, and wearing the long black caftan of a *Chasid*, a most pious disciple of the sainted holy man, Itzkhak Ben Mendelovitch.

The *Chasid* surveyed the fine, rare comestibles for which Kensington Gourmet Foods was known, then stopped in front of the station where, behind a glass partition, slabs of meat were arrayed: roast beef, turkey, bologna, liverwurst. . . .

'Can I help you?' asked one of the men behind the counter.

'Eh . . . mmh . . . yeah . . .' The *Chasid* appeared to be debating his choice. 'Eh – yeah! I'll take, please a helf-pound that nice corn biff . . .'

The clerk cleared his throat. 'Sir, that is not corned beef. It's baked Virginia – *ham*.'

The *Chasid* eyed the clerk frostily. 'Tell me, young man . . . did I *esk* you?!'

Old Hyman Sisselberg, crossing Fifth Avenue in front of St Patrick's Cathedral, was knocked down by a hit-and-run driver.

He lay there, half conscious, as people crowded around him. A priest pushed his way through the crowd, knelt beside Hyman Sisselberg, and out of force of habit quickly said, 'My son, do you believe in God the Father, God the Son, and God the Holy Ghost?'

'*Gottenyu*,' croaked Sisselberg. 'I'm dying, and he asks riddles.'

Two old friends were sitting on a park bench observing their prolonged, familiar, silent communion. At last one said, 'How are things?'

'Eh!' shrugged the other. 'How about you?'

'Mnyeh.'

In an hour they rose. 'Well, goodbye. It's always nice to have a heart-to-heart talk.'

A lady from Brooklyn was watching a parade on Fifth Avenue.

'Look!' someone cried. 'There goes the mayor of Dublin – and he's a Jew!'

'*Ai-ai-ai*,' clucked the matron. 'Where could such a thing happen? Only in America!'

Two men sat opposite each other in the Amtrak train. One was reading a newspaper. After a while, the other man said, 'Uh – going to Philadelphia?'

The first man lowered his newspaper. 'No,' he said. 'I'm going to Baltimore. My business is insurance. My name is Henry Slott. I live in Great Neck. I'm not rich, I have a son at Swarthmore and a daughter who's married. My wife's maiden name was Portanow and she comes from New Haven. I'm a Republican. I can't play golf. I do play bridge. I spend my summers in Westhampton and in winter I spend two weeks every December in Pompano Beach. I go to a Reform temple, contribute to the UJA and the Community Chest. I don't have a brother of the same name because I don't have a brother, and my sister you couldn't possibly have known because she died thirty years ago in Detroit. So: if I've forgotten anything you're interested in, please ask me right now, because I want to finish this paper and take a nap until I get to Baltimore.'

ᔆ

Azriel Chyet, a Jewish patriarch, was on the witness stand in Brooklyn.

'How old are you?' asked the district attorney.

'I am, thank the Lord for His goodness, eighty-two years old.'

'What was that?'

'I said, "I am, thank the Lord for His goodness, eighty-two years old."'

'Just answer the question!' snapped the DA. 'Nothing else. Now, how – old – are – you?'

'Eighty-two,' said the old man, 'thank the Lord for His – '

The judge banged his gavel and cut in, 'The witness will answer the question – *only* the question, without additional comment, or be held in contempt of court! Do you understand that?'

Up rose the counsel for the defence: 'Your Honour, may I ask the question? . . .

'Try,' said the judge.

The lawyer said, 'Mr Chyet, thank the Lord for His goodness, how old are you?'

Beamed the old man, 'Eighty-two.'

ᔆ

During a gigantic celebration in Red Square, after Trotsky had been sent into exile, Stalin, on Lenin's great tomb, suddenly and excitedly raised his hand to still the acclamations: 'Comrades, comrades! A most historic event! A cablegram – of congratulations – from Trotsky!'

The hordes cheered and chortled and cheered again, and Stalin read the historic cable aloud:

> JOSEPH STALIN
> KREMLIN
> MOSCOW
>
> YOU WERE RIGHT AND I WAS WRONG.
> YOU ARE THE TRUE HEIR OF LENIN.
> I SHOULD APOLOGIZE.
>
>   TROTSKY

You can imagine what a roar, what an explosion of astonishment and triumph erupted in Red Square now!

But in the front row, below the podium, a little tailor called, 'Pst! Pst! Comrade Stalin.'

Stalin leaned down.

The tailor said, 'Such a message, Comrade Stalin. For the ages! But you read it without the right *feeling*!'

Whereupon Stalin raised his hand and stilled the throng once more. 'Comrades! Here is a simple worker, a loyal Communist, who says I haven't read the message from Trotsky with enough feeling! Come, Comrade Worker! Up here! *You* read this historic communication!'

So the little tailor went up to the reviewing stand and took the cablegram from Stalin and read:

> JOSEPH STALIN
> KREMLIN
> MOSCOW

Then he cleared his throat, and sang out:

> YOU WERE RIGHT AND I WAS *WRONG?*
> *YOU* ARE THE TRUE HEIR OF LENIN?
> *I* SHOULD APOLOGIZE???!!!
>
>   TROTSKY

Mr Korshack had only one grandson, a sixteen-year-old named Bruce. But what could Mr Korshack and his grandson possibly have in common? Whatever the old man wanted to talk about, bored Bruce. The things Bruce was immersed in, bewildered his grandfather. The greatest passion in Bruce's life, it seemed, was – basketball. Every moment of his spare time was spent in watching professional basketball on television.

One night, Bruce went to a school dance – and Mr Korshack glued himself before the TV to watch the game between the Milwaukee Bucks and the Los Angeles Lakers.

When Bruce came home, after midnight, Mr Korshack leaped to his feet. 'Bruce! Bruce! I watched that game for you! The whole game!!'

Bruce was properly excited. 'Oh, great, gramps! What was the final score?'

'The final score,' said Mr Korshack, 'was ninety-nine to one hundred and two!'

'And who won?'

The old man hesitated. 'Eh – one hundred and two.'

When Solly Nayfack returned from a tour of Israel, Greece, and Italy, he told his partners in Lochinvar's Men's Wear, 'The climax of our whole trip through Europe was the Vatican. You know, we had a little audience with the pope!'

'The *pope*, Solly? You kidding?'

'Absolutely not. The pope – in person!'

'So Solly, what type man would you call him?'

'Very fine,' said Solly. 'Spiritual. Dignified. Size forty-six long.'

'If you want to live forever,' Mendel Minkoff told a very rich cousin, 'come to live in our little town.'

'Is it that beautiful?'

'Beautiful? It's the ugliest town you ever saw in your whole life!'

'Is the climate that good?' asked the cousin.

'The climate is without a doubt absolutely terrible!'

'Then why in God's name do you tell me to live there?!'

'Look at the statistics!' exclaimed Mendel. 'In three hundred and fifty years, never – not once – has a rich man died there!'

Three women were discussing their sons, with customary pride.

'My boy,' said the first, 'is a famous surgeon, and president of his medical association!'

'My son,' said the second, 'is a professor in the law school.'
'My son,' said the third, 'is a rabbi.'
'A *rabbi*! What kind of career is that for a Jewish boy?'

See also **Accents, Anti-Semitism, Curses, God, Ingenuity, Israel, Rabbis, Stratagems**

Just Jokes

A travelling salesman came to the door of the farmhouse and said, 'My car's broken down, it's too far to walk to town – do you have a room I can sleep in tonight?'

'The only spare bedroom I got,' said the farmer, 'is my son's. You'll have to sleep with him.'

The salesman turned white. 'My God, I'm in the wrong joke!'

Why is it that the walls in a hotel room are very thin when you try to sleep and very thick when you want to listen?

ARTHUR GODFREY

Colonel Fairlie Strothingham, as respectable and impressive a Son of the South as you could ever hope to find, telephoned his mansion from his office. 'Hello. How are you?'

'Ah'm jest fine.'

'Everything all right at home?'

'I – uh – giss so, suh.'

'What do you mean you *guess* so? Anything wrong with my wife?'

'No, suh. She ain't sick – '

'Then put her on the phone.'

Silence.

'I said, "Put – her – on – the – phone!"'

'Well, suh, that's jest it. Yo' wife is in the bedroom – but she ain't alone.'

'*What?!*'

'She's in that there bed with a man from Atlanta – '

'Now, listen. Listen carefully,' seethed Colonel Strothingham. 'Go into my study. There's a gun in the desk. Get it. Go upstairs. Open the bedroom door – and if you see my wife in bed with that man, shoot! Shoot them both!'

'Oh, sir. Ah cain't do that!'

'You do that right now, do you hear? If you don't, I'm coming right home and *I'll* kill the two of them – and you, too!...'

'Oh, Lord,' moaned the servant.

'Now go and do what I told you.... I'll wait on this phone...'

In five or six minutes, the quavery voice of the servant returned on the line. 'Okay, suh. Ah's through.'

'Did you shoot them both?'

'Yas, suh. An' Ah was so nervous, Ah ran to the back garden, and Ah threw the gun in the swimmin' pool, and now –'

'Swimming pool?' echoed the colonel. '*We* don't have a swimming pool.... Listen! Is this Fairfax-eight, seven, seven, oh, three?'

⸺

Judge Christie leaned forward and said, 'Are you trying to tell this court that the defendant actually strangled his wife in a disco, in front of three hundred people?!'

'Yes, sir.'

'But didn't anyone try to stop him?'

'No, sir. Everyone thought they were dancing.'

⸺

The plumber rang the doorbell. The housewife answered.

'I come to fix your broken hot-water pipe.'

'We no got broke pipe,' said the woman.

The plumber consulted a note-paper in his hand. 'Are you Mrs Gonzales?'

'No. She move. Four month back.'

'How do you like that?' said the plumber in disgust. 'All you people are the same. You call for a plumber, hollering it's an emergency and can I rush right over – and before I can even answer the call, you pack up and move!'

⸺

Mr Nathan was going through some old files when, to his aston-

ishment, he found a claim check for a pair of shoes he had brought
to Aristides Narikos's Shoe Repair – fourteen years ago!

That afternoon he went over to the shoe repair store. 'Mr
Narikos, I know this is going to surprise you – and maybe this is all
too late – but you were supposed to put new heels on a pair of my
shoes – '

'Sura!' smiled Narikos.

' – fourteen years – ago!'

Narikos turned pale. 'Four-a-tin yiss? . . . Eh, you got to have
check!'

'I do.' Mr Nathan handed Narikos the old faded check.

Narikos gulped, scratched his chin, muttered to himself in
Greek, disappeared behind a beaded curtain. After a bit, he
returned. 'Boss, you shoes – dey brown?'

'I think so.'

'And got da buckle, not da laces?'

'That's right!' beamed Mr Nathan.

'Need new heel?'

'Exactly.'

'They be ready Wenadsday.'

Joel Glickman met Weissman at Feuerman's Delicious, a cafeteria
near Union Square. No sooner did they sit down at a table than
Glickman exclaimed, 'I had a year, Phil, it shouldn't happen to a
dog. In June, business was so bad I thought I'd go bankrupt. In
July, I had to get a loan from the bank. In August, I wished it was
still July. In September – '

'Stop!' cried Weissman. 'Why are you ruining my lunch? I don't
get one word out before you clobber me with all your problems.
You want problems? *I'll* give you problems! Last year, my wife ran
away with my partner. Then a fire burned my whole apartment to
a crisp. On New Year's, my daughter told me she had to have an
abortion. And you pepper my head with your problems?! You
heard my troubles. Could anything have been worse?!'

Glickman sighed. 'November.'

'I don't know what to get my wife anymore. First she wanted a
mink, so I got her a mink. Then she wanted a silver fox, so I

bought her a silver fox. Now she wants a lynx – but that's ridiculous. The house is already full of animals.'

HENNY YOUNGMAN

⌒

'Do you know what it means to come home every night,' says Henny Youngman, 'to the woman who will give you a little affection, a lot of tenderness, and an ocean of love? It means you went to the wrong house, that's what it means.'

⌒

Edward Fothersby bought £400 worth of scuba-diving equipment and went down, down into the water off his estate in Barbados. Intrigued by the magnificent fish, he swam on. . . . Soon, to his astonishment, he beheld a stranger in swimming trunks!

Fothersby grabbed his underwater pad and on it wrote, with his underwater pencil:

> I spent £400 on gear. You have
> *none*. How can you stay down so deep?

He handed the pad and pencil to the swimmer, who hastily scribbled on the pad and shoved it back to Fothersby.

> I'm drowning, you jerk.

⌒

JIM: What did the usherette say when her brassiere strap broke?
JOE: What?
JIM: 'I have two down in front.'

⌒

Old Isaac Arp handed Mr Zeligman, the pharmacist, his latest prescription. In half an hour, Zeligman gave him three little bottles of pills.

'All these?' asked Arp. 'Why so many types pills?'

'The red ones calm your nerves,' said Mr Zeligman. 'The white ones will help your headache, and the blue ones are to relieve your sinuses.'

Mr Arp clucked in admiration. 'How do you like that? Such little pills, and each one knows exactly where to go!'

The Friends of Douglas Park in Chicago met to consider ways of improving the pretty lagoon. Mrs Mary Lou Stopes suggested, 'In my opinion, brothers and sisters, the best thing to do is to put in a flock of gon*d*olas. I seen pictures of gon*d*olas in a place in Italy where all them Eyetalian folk was havin' the *time* of their life!'

'I do agree with Sister Stopes about them most pleasin'-to-the-eye gon*d*olas,' said the chairman. 'But they is bound to be *mighty* expensive. We cain't afford such improvements!'

After many sighs, up shot the hand of Rufus T. Pratt. 'Brothers and sisters, I make a motion we get jist *two* of them gon*d*olas – one male, one female. I hear they breed faster'n rabbits!'

It was old Mr Eizenstat's first ocean voyage. And the third day out, the ship ran into a terrible storm. The heavings and lurchings and rollings of the vessel forced ashen Mr Eizenstat to the rail, where he hung and retched in agony.

A voice from a kindly steward piped up, 'Don't be too alarmed, sir. No one has ever died of seasickness.'

'Oh, God,' moaned Eizenstat. 'Don't say that. Only that hope is what's keeping me alive.'

WIFE: Wasn't today the day everyone in the plant had to take an intelligence test?
HUSBAND: That's right, dear.
WIFE: Did you take the test, too?
HUSBAND: Absolutely.
WIFE: How did you do?
HUSBAND: Let me put it this way: thank God I own the company!

A friend once asked Bob Hope: 'What went through your mind, Bob, the first time you got a look at Dorothy Lamour in that sarong?'

'I never gave it a second thought,' said Hope.

'Truly?'

'Sure. I was too busy with the first one.'

Mrs Anderson asked her new maid: 'Vesta, did you remember to clean out the refrigerator?'

'Oh, *yes*.' The maid smiled. 'And everything was really delicious!'

Keir MacAfee, a congenital non-picker-up of bills, was eating with his old classmate, Jock Thwaite. They had a fine meal of kippers and stout at a pub. The waiter left the bill exactly between the two men.

Thwaite was determined not to pay the bill this time. The conversation flagged, the time passed, and finally Keir MacAfee said, 'Jock, it has just occurred to me, it has, that ye've paid our restaurant bills for many and many a moonth now.'

'True, aye, true,' smiled Thwaite.

'That has been thoughtless of me, lad,' said MacAfee. He reached into his jacket. 'Now f'r *this* bill, Jock – let's toss a coin.'

When Mr Hennessey returned from a visit to his cousin, Emmett, in the psychiatric ward, Mrs Hennessey bombarded him with questions. 'And was he glad you come? Did he then talk sense?'

'Pore Emmett, pore lad,' sighed Mr Hennessey. 'Carries on, he does, somethin' fearful! He rants, he raves – Nora, he jist talks *crazy*! I tried to bring him down to earth – I talk about the weather, will he be needin' anything, do they let him have a nip now and thin, the thirty dollars he owes us . . .'

'Ah, an' did pore Emmett remember?'

'*That* crazy,' said Hennessey, 'the lad ain't.'

Elbert Rowley, a wealthy car dealer from Cincinnati who was visiting Palm Beach for the first time, was swept out to sea by a huge wave. 'Help! Help!' He thrashed about in the water. 'I'm drowning! He-e-e-e-lp!'

A lifeguard plunged into the surf. With powerful strokes he reached Rowley, swam behind him, gripped the drowning man across the chest, and pulled him to shore. Rowley was unconscious. The lifeguard gave him mouth-to-mouth revival, blowing air into Rowley's lungs, and for ten minutes applied pulmonary resuscitation. When at last the lifeguard rose, dripping perspiration from his exertions, Rowley was breathing normally. The life-guard helped him to his feet. 'Okay now, mister?'

'Yes, thank God,' said Rowley. 'Wait here, young man.' He went over to several men sprawled in beach chairs. 'Say, can you guys give me some information?'

'What about?'

'How much do you tip for a thing like that?'

◠

A teacher of English in Gotham, the legendary city famous for the not-so-bright, told his class of aspiring writers, 'Any good short story always contains one or more of these essentials: religion, emotion, sex, mystery, surprise, royalty.... For your next exercise, write a story using as many of these essentials as possible.'

The best composition was only one line long:

'My God!' wept the beauty-contest queen. 'I am pregnant! Who can the father be?'

◠

Old man Mulligan fell out of his third-storey window. An excited crowd gathered around him. A police car roared up, sirens shrieking, and a cop hopped out and bent over the old man. 'Don't move! We'll have an ambulance here in a jiffy.... What happened?'

'How the devil should Oy know?' snorted Mulligan. 'Oy jist got here!'

◠

On her first trip out of Llandriddon Wells, Branwyn Abertwyth, a strong, buxom lass, stood admiring the grand railway terminal in Liverpool. 'Coom here,' said her mother, 'and stond on th' scale machine.'

'Whaffor?'

'T' weigh y'r own self.' The mother dropped a penny in the slot. 'T' chart is to show hoo mooch y' should be weighin' f'r your height.... This is something' we never hov in Llandriddon!'

Branwyn mounted the scale. The needle spun around. The girl read the number, studied the chart, and moaned, 'Oh, moother. It's a freak, I am. For I should stond four full inches higher!'

◠

Alvin Silverman, C.P.A., and Dana Shaw, D.D.S., classmates at Erasmus High, decided to go on their own safari. Their wives refused to join them. So Alvin and Dana flew to Africa, hired a native guide and porters, and struck off down the Congo.

On the fourth day, emboldened by the absence of any misadventure, Alvin and Dana rashly ignored their guide and struck off through dense jungle – when a snarl and a ferocious roar froze them in their tracks. 'Dana . . .' quavered Alvin.

'I heard it, Alvin.'

'Don't *talk*. Whisper . . . for God's sake . . .'

The roar roared closer, louder.

'Alvin,' quaked Dana. 'It's behind me . . . take a look . . .'

'I'm looking . . .'

'Is it a lion? A leopard?'

'How should I know?' wailed Alvin. 'I'm an accountant, not a furrier.'

See also **Embarrassing Moments, Jews, Shaggy Dogs, True Tales**

Kibitzers

Note: A *kibitzer*, to those who (though it is hard to believe) have never heard the word, is (1) a know-it-all, who offers unasked-for advice – especially at a game in which he is not a player (poker, chess, checkers, bridge), or (2) a buttinski, who sticks his two cents into a discussion that is none of his affair, or (3) a wisecracker, a needler, or (4) a chronic second-guesser; or (5) a self-appointed expert who irritates everyone else, or (6) most favourably: an amicable kidder.

L. R.

Julius Kovalski started to mount the ladder, to hang up this new sign:

FRESH FISH
SOLD HERE
DAILY

Kovalski's neighbour, Finestein, sang out, 'Hey, Julie. You nuts, puttin' up a sign like that?'

'What's wrong with it?'

'Why do you say "*Fresh* Fish"? You want your customers to think you ever sold them *stale* fish?'

'You're right.' Kovalski took his brush and painted out FRESH. He started up the ladder.

'Hold it,' called Finestein. 'Why "*Sold*"? Could anyone think you gave fish away *free*?!'

Kovalski expunged SOLD.

'And why "*Here*"? Obviously, you don't sell fish over *there* . . .'

'You're right.' Kovalski painted out HERE.

'That leaves "Daily",' said Finestein. 'Is that smart? If fish are fresh, they *must* be caught and sold daily. Right?'

'Absolutely!' Kovalski crossed out DAILY The sign now read:

FISH

As Kovalski started up the ladder again, along came another neighbour. 'Why are you putting up that ridiculous sign?'

'What's wrong with it?' bridled Kovalski.

'You don't have to put up a sign, Kovalski. Anyone can smell your fish a mile away!'

So Kovalski put up no sign at all.

᠎⌒

Manny Klopfer was the most persistent, inveterate *kibitzer* in all of Miami Beach. One day he took his place behind a new arrival from New Jersey. For two hours, Manny offered unsolicited advice. To the New Jerseyan's delight, he kept winning all that time.

During the third hour, the new arrival got a hand of unusual complexity. He rearranged it several times, pondering deeply. Finally, he turned to the *kibitzer*: 'What card do I play now?'

Klopfer frowned, then whispered: 'What game are you playing?'

᠎⌒

The regular cardplayers at Kolinsky's Spa in the Catskills were cursed by a *kibitzer*. Most *kibitzers* are mild-mannered, but this *kibitzer*, one Sy Potachek, was a *kibitzer* of such persistence and spurious omniscience that the cardplayers met to decide how to put an end to his activity.

'Let's tell him, once and for all, to mind his own goddam business!' said Mr Schreiber.

'You think you can insult a guy with his gall?' scoffed Mr Garfinkel.

'Let's stop playing in the game room,' suggested Mr Danenberg.

'So where should we play? In the laundry?'

'Wait, I have an idea.' That was Henry Kruger. 'Let's invent a game! A cockamamy way of dealing and bidding – a game so crazy that Potachek won't be able to figure out what's going on! That'll shut him up good.'

The others applauded this altogether superb idea.

The next day, the four men appeared in the game room as usual; and, as usual, Sy Potachek pulled up a chair.

'Suppose today – we play "Shmeitz and Kreitz"?' suggested Mr Kruger.

'Great!'

'Fine!'

'I *love* "Shmeitz and Kreitz"!' exclaimed Mr Garfinkel.

'How about a penny a point?' asked Mr Danenberg.

'And double for a *plotch*!' said Schreiber.

'And twice over, split-the-pot for *Kashenoy*!' said Kruger.

'Agreed! Cut the deck!'

During all this astonishing nonsense, Sy Potachek sat, frowning, but silent.

Henry Kruger took the deck of cards, divided it into four parts, handed one part to each of the other players, picked up his portion, and tossed a card before Mr Danenberg. 'I bid one *Jiffel*.'

'Double – with a *Schmeitz*,' said Danenberg.

'I have a *Knotch*!' exclaimed Garfinkel. 'So I raise you a blue, in spades!'

'Oh, boy!' chortled Mr Schreiber. 'I have a *Shmatzer*! A red *Shmatzer*! So I call you both and raise – '

'*Psst*!' the *kibitzer* hissed. 'Shreiber, don't be a fool!'

'What do you mean?'

'A red *Shmatzer* can't beat a Double *Jiffel* – especially when there's a blue raise, and in *spades*!'

See also **Advice, Chutzpa, Salesmen, Squelches, Texans**

Kids' Stuff

Little Morris Ephron came home from his Hebrew school lesson one day.

'And what did you learn today?' asked his father.

'Wow! What a story!' said Morris. 'The teacher told us about Moses leading all the Hebrews out of Egypt, with Pharaoh's Egyptians chasing them. At the Red Sea Moses dropped an atomic bomb! Bang! Pow! The waters of the Red Sea opened up, the Jews got across, the waters closed, and all the Egyptians were drowned.'

'Tell me truthfully, Morris. Is *that* what your teacher told you?' gasped Mr Ephron.

'Naw,' said little Morrie, 'but, pop, the way he did, you'd never believe it either!'

The man patted the little boy on the head and asked, 'Larry, is your mother still as pretty as she used to be?'

'Oh, yeah,' said Larry. 'It just takes her a lot longer.'

Sunday School teacher: 'Now, children, who can tell me why there is only one God?'

Little Susan Lawson waved her hand energetically.

'Yes, Susan?'

'There is only one God because He is *everywhere*, so there's just no room for any other one.'

Mrs Halper marched her son into Dr Shinkin's office. 'Doctor,' she demanded, 'is a nine-year-old boy really qualified to perform an appendectomy?'

'What?!'

'I asked you: is a nine-year-old boy qualified to take out someone's appendix?'

'Certainly not!' exclaimed Dr Shinkin.

Mrs Halper turned to her son. 'Okay, Melvin. You heard the doctor. . . . Now go put it back!'

JOHNNY (age 8): How did Princess Diana *know* she was going to have a baby?

CONNIE (age 9): She can *read*, can't she? My goodness, Johnny, it was in *all* the papers!

Children's clothes store

> **Get your real Cowboys outfits at**
> **Hopalong Kassidy's (formerly**
> **J. Kaminsky's)**

The little girl soberly studied the goodies in the case at the candy store.

'So what do you want?' asked the owner.

'I want a chocolate Easter Bunny – a boy,' she said.

'A boy?' the owner laughed. 'Why, there isn't that – ' (snapping his fingers) ' – much difference between a boy bunny and a girl bunny.'

The little girl said, 'But there's *that* – ' (snapping fingers) ' – much more chocolate.'

Little Antonio was watching his mother bake cookies. After a long time, he said, 'Mama, why don't you ask me something?'

'Tonio, what you want your mama shoulda ask you?'

The lad replied, 'You could ask, "Hey, Antonio, you want a cookie?"'

Elsa and her brother were visiting their aunt, who placed two apples on the table. One was large, red and shiny, the other small, dull, and withered.

'Now, children,' said Aunt Charlotte, 'I want to see which of you has the better manners.'

'He does,' said Elsa as she took the big red apple.

Father Ortiz asked one of his students, 'Josita? You say your prayers before each meal?'

'N-no, *padre*,' said Josita.

'*Hanh?* You no pray before you eat?!'

'I no have to. My mama is good cook.'

∽

Little Arthur was a fine, healthy six-year-old. There was only one thing his father and mother worried about: little Arthur had never spoken one single word.

One day, his mother sprinkled sugar over half a grapefruit and placed it before Arthur. Arthur ate one spoonful, made a face, and exclaimed, 'I *hate* it! This is bitter! Don't ever serve me anything like this again!'

'Arthur!' cried his mother. 'You can talk!'

'Arthur!' cried his father. 'You know so many words!' He hugged the little boy.

'How *wonderful!*' said Arthur's mother.

His father laughed. 'Arthur, son, why didn't you ever talk before this? Not one word all these years?!'

The lad said, 'Until this grapefruit, everything you gave me tasted dandy.'

∽

Said a five-year-old. 'The nursery school is where they tell the children who hit someone, not to; and they tell children who don't hit, to hit back.'

∽

Tommy Gans, age six, was taken by his mother to the ballet school where his older sister was enrolled. Tommy watched in fascination as the girls practised their dances on their toes. After a while, he whispered, 'Mommy . . .'

'Yes, dear?'

'Can't they just get taller girls?'

∽

When little Filbert learned that his cousin, Peter, whom he had never met, was coming to stay with them for a month, he could scarcely control his excitement. But when cousin Peter finally arrived, Filbert's jaw dropped in astonishment and tears of dismay rolled down his cheeks.

'Why, *Fil*bert,' his mother chided him. 'What's the matter?'

'I thought,' the lad sniffed, 'that Peter would be a rabbit!'

ᔆ

Little Earl, age seven, came running into the house from the yard, screaming at the top of his lungs.

'*Darling!*' Earl's mother clasped the crying lad to her bosom. 'What happened?'

'D-daddy,' sobbed the lad, 'was fixing – the – the fence – and hit – the hammer – *right on his thumb!!!*' And the boy burst into a new flood of caterwauling.

'Now, now, Earl, dear,' his mother cooed. 'You must learn not to cry over things like that. Why didn't you just laugh – '

'I did,' wept Earl.

See also **Children, Famous People (as seen by Children), Mothers**

Languages: Pitfalls

The guidebooks urge any American venturing abroad to learn the basic phrases of a foreign language. Tourist tip-sheets assure you that natives adore hearing a visitor roll his tongue around theirs. Well, I hate to say this, but the advice is cockeyed, and if you fall for it, you'll end up to your armpits in the quicksands of phonetics.

The terrible truth is that the slightest slip in pronouncing a little vowel, in any language, can throw you straight into bedlam. Take English. The difference between 'Call me' and 'Kill me', for instance, is only 1/64th of an inch of air space, so a greenhorn in a hurry can wind up being throttled by an American trying to oblige a visitor from abroad.

Or take a simple sentence such as: 'I want my meat well done.' Naïvely uttered by, say, a Papuan, that sentence comes out, 'I want my mate walled in.' Very few restaurants will brick up your wife on such short notice.

The same booby traps await the American who is fool enough to plunge into the jungle of any alien argot. The first time I went to Paris, I entered a neighbourhood bistro and hailed the *propriétaire* with a buoyant 'Áh, m'sieur, but I am very hungry tonight!'

That, at least, is what I thought I was saying. What I actually uttered was, 'Ah, but I shall have many a female tonight.'

You can hardly blame the astounded man for hustling me to a shadowy corner, where my lust would cause no trouble. On the other hand, you can hardly blame me for having fallen victim to the treacherous nasalities of French, where the ever-so-slight difference in sound between *faim* and *femme* had converted a hungry adolescent into a sex maniac.

In Tokyo, I carefully read aloud (from a phrase book called *You, Too, Can Speak Japanese*) the phonetic syllables for 'I – would – like – a massage.'

To this the Oriental attendant replied, with ceremonial hisses of joy and abnegation: 'I would be honoured to carry you there on my back, exalted thimble, but the cat is already late for the wedding.'

I think I had misled him. Either that, or he was relying on his vest-pocket copy of *You, Too, Can Spoke Engrish*.

from my Passions and Prejudices

Occidental places can be just as disorienting. I once entered a splashy men's store in Madrid and, in my buoyant high-school Spanish, informed the clerk that I wanted to purchase a pair of gloves and an umbrella. The man turned white and dashed off, bleating for his superior.

To this person in a morning coat and striped trousers, I calmly repeated: 'I want – a – pair – of – men's – gloves – and an umbrella.'

The superior Iberian flinched. 'But, señor,' he quavered, 'why do you wish to wallop yon horse with a parachute?'

What happened, as I reconstruct the linguistic mishmosh, was this: the Spanish for umbrella is *paraguas*, which I mangled into *paracas*, which they took to mean *paracaidas*, which means parachute. Gentleman is *caballero*, which I blithely rendered as *caballo*, which means horse. It was a cinch to nose-dive from *guante* (glove) to *guantada* (wallop), even though I have never laid a glove on a horse, much less walloped one with a parachute. I have never even chastised a chihuahua. Not with so much as a feather, which is *pluma*, much less a *plancha*, which is flatiron.

So, I don't care *how* easy the guidebooks tell you it is to toss off a few fruity phrases in the natives' Flemish or Plattdeutsch. The depressing truth is that *any* language simply bulges with laryngeal pitfalls and idiomatic ambushes.

If you're lost in Mozambique, stop any native with a bright 'Blessings from your patron saint, and how do I get to the flea market?' Five will get you twenty if the chap doesn't take you by the hand and lead you there himself.

Why drive the locals *loco* by asking them to wallop yon horse with a parachute?

from my *Passions and Prejudices*

Leonard and Manny, both lovers of Yiddish, were comparing its charms to those of other languages, and Lenny observed, 'Do you know something remarkable? There's no word in Yiddish for "disappointed"!'

'I can't believe it. You must be wrong. Wait, I'll call my mother.'

And to his mother, who barely spoke English, Manny said in fluent Yiddish, 'Mameleh, listen. Suppose I told you I was coming to dinner on Friday. And suppose you worked all day Friday to make me the finest meal ever – from chopped liver and *gefilte* fish and down through the chicken and *kugel* and two kinds of strudel for dessert. And on Friday, two minutes before I'm supposed to arrive, I telephone and say that something so important has come up that I just can't come to dinner! What would you say?'

'What I would *say*?' wailed his mother. 'I'd say, "*Oy, bin ich* [am I] disappointed."'

See also **Accents, Advertisements, Boo-boos, English, Goldwyniana, Malaprops, How's That Again?, Signs, Typos, Yinglish**

Lawyers

A very successful lawyer was being badgered by his wife. 'You say you will, you *say* you will! But whenever the time comes, you find some excuse – '

'Okay, dear, I'll do it – right now.' The legal wizard stalked into his son's room. 'Junior, the time has come for us to have a man-to-man talk!'

'Sure, dad. About what?'

'About – the alleged facts of life.'

∽

Ignorance of the law excuses no man from practising it.

∽

Scene: Town in New England

VISITOR: Sir, do you have a criminal lawyer in this town?

LOCAL RESIDENT: We-ell, we're pretty sure we do, but . . .

VISITOR: But what?

LOCAL RESIDENT: But we've not been able to prove it.

∽

The lawyer was briefing his star witness, Sam Peurifoy. 'You realize that before you sit down on that chair next to the judge you're going to have to swear to tell the truth, the whole truth, and nothing but the truth?'

'Yes, *sir*.'

'And Sam, suppose you don't tell the truth, the whole truth, and nothing but the truth? Do you know what'll happen?'

'Yes, *sir!* Our side'll win.'

∽

In the elegant offices of Mannheim, Mannheim, Mannheim, and Mannheim, the phone rang. It was promptly answered: 'Mannheim, Mannheim, Mannheim, *Mann*-heim.'

'Hello,' said the caller. 'I'd like to speak to Mr Mannheim.'

'I'm sorry, but Mr Mannheim is in Washington.'

'Oh . . . then can I speak to Mr Mannheim?'

'Sorry, sir, but Mr Mannheim is in court today.'

'Well, then, I'll speak to Mr Mannheim.'

'Mr Mannheim won't be in his office until four.'

The caller sighed. 'Okay, then can you connect me to Mr *Mann*-heim?'

'*Spea*-king!'

∽

HARLEY AND SMITHERS
BARRISTERS
CHAMBERS 43-C
LINCOLN'S INN FIELDS
LONDON

JURY ANNOUNCED VERDICT IN CROWN V. LASSITER.
JUSTICE HAS PREVAILED.

ATKINSON

J. R. ATKINSON
BARRISTER
KINGS BENCH WALK
PLYMOUTH

APPEAL AT ONCE.

HARLEY

The prosecutor, a terror for any defence witness on the stand, leaned forward and, steely eyed, asked Mr Aaron Rattner, 'Are you positively sure, beyond a smidgeon of a doubt, that the woman you saw entering the building was the plaintiff?'

Rattner hemmed and hawed. 'Vell, I t'ink – '

'Stop!' The prosecutor raised a minatory palm. 'In this court, we do not care what anyone *thinks*. I only want you to tell the court what you *know*.'

Rattner blinked. 'Excuse me. How I can tell vhat I know unless I t'ink? Don't forget: I'm not a lawyer.'

See also **Courts, Evidence**

Lectures/Lecturers

Moses Trelawney, a candidate for the city council in Yazoo City, Mississippi, was being introduced to an audience in flowery and extravagant phrases. To his neighbour on the platform, Moses whispered, 'How long you think all these folks fixin' to hear my oration?'

'You jist hold forth as long as the spirit done move you, Moses,' said the neighbour. '*We* all go home aroun' two forty.'

∽

At a banquet which went on and on and on, the presiding officer of the club finally said, 'Ladies and gentlemen, we have run considerably over-time – so I am particularly pleased to introduce our distinguished speaker for the evening, William Collier, who will now give you his address.'

The audience applauded, Collier rose, said, 'Mr Toastmaster, ladies and gentlemen: my address is Two thirty-nine East Thirty-eighth Street, New York City,' and sat down.

The ballroom shook from the applause.

∽

When the speaker of the evening was introduced, with extravagant praises, at a banquet in his honour, he responded nervously: 'You know, I came here in the hope of hearing a fascinating speech. I was hoping to hear my lips drip brilliant phrases and memorable epigrams. Now I have to tell you: I'm afraid I'm going to be disappointed as hell.'

∽

The luncheon speaker boomed into the microphone, 'Gentlemen, your chairman promised me – and I quote his exact words, "a *vast* audience." But judging from the number of empty chairs, I can only come to the conclusion that I have a half-vast audience . . .'

∽

My friends – (I know you much too well to call you 'ladies and gentlemen) . . .'

∽

On and on droned the British sociologist at the final banquet of their annual convention in London. It was past eleven o'clock when the chairman rose to announce: 'We shall now hear our distinguished guest of honour, our main and final speaker, who will speak to us on the subject: "Current Research on Sex". Since the hour is so late, I have begged him to condense his long speech somewhat – and he has most graciously agreed to do so. Milords, ladies, and gentlemen, I give you Professor Horace Brownlow.'

Up rose Professor Brownlow. When the tired applause trailed off, he said, 'My topic is sex. Milords, ladies, and gentlemen: sex gives me *considerable* pleasure. Thank you.'

See also **Boo-boos, Education, Jews**

Letters

Maine Angler
Peconsquet, Me.

```
Lemuel Edwards
P.O.B. 270
Jonesport, Me.

Dear Mr Edwards:
    Renewal form is enclosed.  Your sub-
scription has expired.
                    Yours,
                        J. Walton
                        Business Manager


J. Walton
Maine Angler
Peconsquet, Me.

    So has Lem.
                        A neighbour
```

Mrs Forsberg received two letters:

```
Dear Mrs Forsberg:
    I had a good time at your party last
night.  Thank you for asking me.
                    Yours,
                        Jordan Balder
```

```
Dear Mrs Forsberg:
   What a wonderful hostess you are!
               Yours,
                 Ralph Parmenter
```

Mrs Forsberg read both letters, consigned Balder's to the waste-basket, picked up the phone, and called Parmenter. 'Ralph? . . . Are you free for dinner Saturday?'

(What do you mean, you don't get the point?! Read the two notes again.)

⌒

It is said of Julius Rosenwald that he rarely had trouble with people who owed Sears-Roebuck money. Whenever a bill went unpaid too long, and 'Past Due' notices were to no avail, Mr Rosenwald would write the debtor:

```
Dear Mr Jones:
   Your bill is long overdue.  If you do
not pay it within 48 hours, we shall
notify all your other creditors that you
paid us in full.
               Yours,
                 J. Rosenwald
```

See also **Business, Ingenuity, Salesmen, Stratagems**

Life

Life is a dream, but please don't wake me.

Ever since dying came into fashion, life has not been safe.

Life is the greatest of all bargains: you get it for nothing.

When life isn't the way you like it, like it the way it is.

The only thing you get free in this life is garbage.

YIDDISH FOLK SAYINGS

◌

April Fool: A joke repeated 365 times a year.

SHOLEM ALEICHEM

◌

A pollster was telephoning a sample of Americans for their responses to: *'When do you believe that human life really starts?'*

Terence O'Malley said: 'Right at the moment of conception.'

Charles Manders replied: 'At birth, when the embryo leaves the womb.'

Abraham Kotinsky said: 'When the children have left home and the dog (may he rest in peace) has died.'

◌

Life. It's full of such sadness and sorrow, sometimes I think it's better not to be born at all! . . . But how many people do you meet in a lifetime who were that lucky?

YIDDISH SAYING

Scene: The Porch of Villa Mitnick in the Poconos

Mendel Kalbfiess, aged eighty-nine, and Avrum Gottschalk, ninety-one, are in rocking chairs. They rock in silence, save for an occasional sigh or *zifts*, or phatic grunts, 'Hmph!'s and 'Ai's, and clucks. Finally, Mr Kalbfiess clears his throat and announces: 'Gottschalk, I made op mine mind. All mine life I been torturing mineself – mit vun qvastion. "Vat's de minnink of life?"'

'And now you fond de enswer?' asked Mr Gottschalk with irony.

'Corract. Life? Life is a tremandous fontain in de middle of a lake. And de lake is insite a blue montain mit saventy angels sitting in a coicle, seenging to God.' Mr Kalbfiess nodded his satisfaction and smiled.

Mr Gottschalk took thought, stroking his chin, tugging at his forelock, closing his eyes the better to visualize Mr Kalbfiess's poetic vision. After some time, Mr Gottschalk opened his eyes – and, with a polite sigh, said 'Kalbfiess, I hoid avery void you sad; and I been t'inking dem over, every void. But I have to tell you, I am not convinced. *Vhy* is life like a tremandous fontain in de meedle of a lake, and dat lake itsself is insite a blue montain, and saventy angels are in vun big circle singing to the Almighty, blessed be His name?'

Now it was Mr Kalbfiess's turn to harumph and hack and close his eyes in thought. And after some time, he, too, sighed, opened his eyes, and murmured, 'So, Gottschalk. You are right! Life *ain't* a tremandous fontain in de middle of a lake, mit de lake itsalf insite a blue montain, mit saventy angels in a coicle singing to God.' He rose. 'Now I'm gung to take a nap. Philosophy tires me ot.'

Two old men sat in rocking chairs on the front porch of the nursing home, rocking gently, back and forth, in silence. Finally, the first old man, Lupowitz, sighed, turned to the second old man, said, 'Life.' And with that, saying no more, he went back to his rocking.

Janovich, the second old man, coughed, then screwed up his eyelids, '"*Life*" you said?'

Lupowitz nodded. 'Life...'

'So – what about Life?'

Lupowitz cleared his throat. 'I have decided that life,' he declaimed, 'is like a bowl thick, cold sour cream!'

Janovich went '*Tchk-tchk-tchk!*' After taking thought, he quavered, 'So why is Life like a bowl thick, cold sour cream?'

Lupowitz shrugged. 'How should I know? Am I a philosopher?'

See also **Faith, God, Heaven, Religion**

Logic

'Have you anything to say before I pass sentence on you?' asked the judge.

'Yes, Your Honour.' The prisoner took a deep breath. 'How can I be convicted of forgery when – when I *can't even write my own name!*'

The judge stroked his chin. 'Because you were not *charged* with signing your own name.'

∽

A commuter came running along the platform at Knobby Vale, in Sussex, crying, 'Stop! I say – train, *stop!*' But the train pulled away. 'Confound it, missed the bloody thing by no more than two seconds!'

Another Englishman, waiting for an incoming train, lowered his newspaper in annoyance. 'The way you're carrying on, old boy, one might have thought you missed it by two hours!'

∽

'Lloyd Morgan! Lloyd Morgan!' cried Mrs Morgan, as she ran into the pub in Llandudnorvon. 'Is it then true, Lloyd Morgan, that ye did win a thousand quid in th' lottery?!'

'That it is, Mrs Morgan,' laughed the lucky man. 'One o' me tickets had th' right number. . . . Have a pint, woman!'

'A pint it is,' chortled Mrs Morgan. 'But wait, mon. What is it I heerd you t' say? That *one* 'v your tickets – ?'

'Aye. I bought meself five tickets, and one – '

'*Five* tickets?!' the woman cried. 'By me blessed mother's memory, Lloyd Morgan, why did ye need to buy them other four?!'

See also **Evidence, Ingenuity, Reason, Shlemiels**

Love

The triumph of imagination over intelligence.

H. L. MENCKEN

'Tis better to have loved and lost than never to have lost at all.

SAMUEL BUTLER

The delusion that one woman differs from another.

H. L. MENCKEN

The only fire against which there is no insurance.

EDITH PIAF

The alliance of affection and lust.

L. R.

The Comedy of Eros.

EVAN ESAR

> At twenty, a girl will ask: 'Is he good-looking?'
> At thirty, she asks, 'Is he rich?'
> At thirty-five, she cries, 'Where is he?!'

William Faulkner once got into an elaborate discussion with a guest about the difference between 'like' and 'love'. After the guest left, Faulkner asked a servant: 'Sophia, how would you explain the difference between "like" and "love"?'

'Well, Mist' Faulkner,' said the maid, 'it's like this: when Ah likes 'em, Ah lets 'em. But when Ah *loves* 'em, Ah helps.'

Lover's leap: The distance from one bed to another.

Love-talk: The difference between rape and rapture.

Playboy

See also **Bachelors, Hanky-panky, Marriage**

Malaprops

At huge funeral for a widely disliked producer

It only goes to show what happens when you give the public what it wants.

I challenge you to give a frank, affirmative answer: yes or no!

Listen, if people just don't go to see a certain movie, nobody can stop them!

Oh, you three certainly are a pair – if there ever was one.

If his father was alive today he would be turning over in his grave.

If you don't stop nagging me with such details I'll find someone who will!

When I want your opinion, I'll give it to you!

He's the type who'll cut your throat behind your back.

Every time he opens his mouth, he should close it . . .

He always puts his foot in the soup.

He's such a worrier that when he's asleep he dreams he's not sleeping.

That man is such a charmer, he's practically a Don Coyote.

L.R.

He doesn't waste a word; every line he writes is full of pith!

L.R.

Now we've got them right where they want us!

I wonder if Indian parents had a T.P.A.

Does the name Pavlov ring a bell?

They say you can't do it, but that doesn't nearly always work.

CASEY STENGEL

Your remark is either unnecessary, rude, or both.

I wouldn't trust him if his life depended on it!

He was stranded so high and dry he could barely keep his head above water.

I'm not the type who wears my heart up my sleeve.

Women tell everybody not to tell anybody.

There was this terrible woman in the Bible who hated Samson: Phyllis Stein.

Not all that shivers is cold.

See also: **Bloopers, Radio and TV, Boo-boos, Cynics' Dictionary, Goldwyniana, Typos**

Man

Man

The missing link between apes and human beings.

KONRAD LORENZ

The animal that bargains; no dogs exchange bones.

ADAM SMITH

A creature made at the end of the week, when God was tired.... God invented man because he was so disappointed in the monkey.... Man is the only animal who blushes – or needs to.

MARK TWAIN

Of all the ways of defining man, the worst is the one which calls him a rational animal.

ANATOLE FRANCE

Man has been called the rational animal; all my life I have been searching for evidence to support this.

BERTRAND RUSSELL

Educated chimpanzees.

One of God's blunders, or is God one of man's blunders?

NIETZCHE

The only animal who cooks his food.

The only animal who can play Scrabble.

See Also **Life**

Marriage

Long, long before Freud, the Jews had this saying: When a young man gets married, he divorces his mother.

I never knew what happiness was until I got married – and then it was too late.

ANON

Marriage

The only way of finding out exactly what kind of marvellous mate your wife/husband wished she/he had married.

The only adventure open to the cowardly.

VOLTAIRE

A fifty-fifty proposition, if you're a fraction.

Sign on door of matrimonial agency: COME IN, RELAX, SPOUSE AROUND.

HOLTZMAN: I've been married twenty-eight years today, and I'm still in love with the same woman.
GLAZER: That's wonderful.
HOLTZMAN: And if my wife ever finds out, she'll kill me!

John Calverton and his college chum, Dan Malloy, were having lunch. During a heart-to-heart talk about their respective marriages, John blurted, 'What it comes down to, Dan, is – well, my wife just doesn't *understand* me. . . . Does yours?'

Malloy thought for a moment. 'I don't think so, John. I've never heard her mention your name.'

Captain Wayne Cummings wrote his wife long, long letters from his post in Lebanon. 'There's a shortage of books here, but there sure is no shortage of beautiful girls – Lebanese, Druse, Palestinian, and a dozen other nationalities. But you don't have to worry, darling. I would fill up the long lonely hours learning to play a musical instrument, if I had one . . .'

His wife promptly express-mailed a harmonica.

A year later, Captain Cummings came home. At the airport was his wife. 'Sweetheart! Darling!' Cummings ran to his mate, arms wide open.

'Hold it, Wayne,' she said. 'Just stay right there. Before there's any embracing around here – let's hear you play the harmonica.'

The pharmacist said, 'Well, Mr Tsoner, how did that mudpack you bought for your wife turn out?'

'Pretty good,' said Tsoner. 'Pretty good. If not for that one defect . . .'

'What defect?'

'It kept falling off.'

Mr and Mrs Kevin McBride, in their early nineties, were celebrating their seventieth wedding anniversary, and a television crew from Belfast had come to interview them in their small thatch-roof cottage.

'Now thin, Mr McBroyde,' said the interviewer, 'siventy years is a mighty long toyme. In all those many years, did you never – even once – think of gettin' a divorce?'

'Divorce? Me? From me darlin' Kathleen?' blinked Mr McBride. 'Nay, man. Not once.'

'And what about the wife, eh? Mrs McBroyde?'

'Divorce? Never. Not once did the thought enter me mind.' Mrs McBride shrugged. 'But murder? Ay! Often!'

From the marriage announcements column of *The Times*

> On June 3, 1978: Lord Hansford-Blunt, 74,
> to Lady Prunella Vintor-Fleck, 29. The
> bridegroom's gift to the bride was an
> antique family pendant.

'... And *then* I went to see the doctor – Maury, *Maury*!'
'Mmh?'
'Maury, are you listening to me or reading the newspaper?'
'I'm listening, I'm listening.'
'I *said*, this afternoon I went to see Dr Stoller.'
'Mmh.' Maury turned the page. 'So how is he?'

'My wife is such a great housekeeper,' boasted Frackman, 'that she vacuums every room every day and puts a completely clean, empty bag in the Hoover every night!'

'Humph,' said Kolchak. 'I've got a wife who, when I get up in the middle of the night to go to the bathroom, changes the sheets before I get back!'

It was almost midnight on a fearful night – the rain pouring down, the storm blowing in fury. Mr Salovsky was about to close his Golden Door Delicatessen when a wet, wet man staggered through the door, shaking an umbrella that had been turned inside out by the wind.

'I was this minute about to lock up!' said Mr Salovsky.
'So I'm lucky.'
'What would you like?'
'A bagel,' said the bedraggled man.
'All right. One bagel. And – ?'
'That's all.'
'That's *all*?' Mr Salovsky could hardly believe his ears. 'No cream cheese on the bagel?'
'No, thanks.'
'A piece lox?'
'No lox.'
'But a takeout cup of good hot coffee, right?'

'No, thanks. No coffee.'

Mr Salovsky stared at the dripping stranger. 'On a terrible night like this, you came out and walked all the way here for – one – plain – bagel?!'

'That's what she wants,' said the customer.

'She?' echoes Salovsky. 'That explains it. "She" has to be your wife, no?'

'Certainly it's my wife. Do you think my *mother* would send me out for one bagel on a godforsaken night like this?!'

The old friends met in London's St James' Square.

'Why, Hubert, old boy, you look positively *wonderful*!'

'I should,' said Hubert. 'Such a spot of luck I've just had. How *can* one be so lucky?!'

'What happened?'

'What happened dear boy, is that Penelope ran away. Pftt!... My wife simply disappeared – with my best friend.'

'What's his name?'

'Who knows?' grinned Hubert. 'Never even met the bounder.'

BESSIE: I read where a single oyster can lay between one and eight
    million eggs a year!
SOPHIE: Migod, think of what the married ones can do!

As the reception line moved past the bride and groom, one man shook the groom's hand and whispered into his ear, 'Congratulations, fella. My name is Francis Dorn. You could be hearing a lot about me in the years ahead. Don't take it seriously...'

The groom looked puzzled.

'Your bride,' said Dorn, 'will from time to time say I'm the man she should have married...'

Mel Draper, after a night of poker with his pals, was tiptoeing, shoes in his hands, into the bedroom. He stumbled over the bedspread.

Mrs Draper turned in her sleep and drowsily asked, 'Mel, is that you?'

Draper froze. 'It damn well better be!'

⌒

Cried Mrs Horlick to Mr Horlick: 'So okay! I grant you – yes, I admit it – I *love* to spend money! But just name one other extravagance of mine. Go ahead. Just one.'

⌒

'Cynthia,' wheezed Mr Bannister, 'I have been figuring out my estate . . .'

'Oh, Floyd, *please* don't talk of that.' Mrs Bannister sniffed. 'You'll be better in no time – '

'No, no, my dear. I won't be with you long. I don't want you to worry about getting along after I'm gone. So I figured out my estate. It will come to eight hundred thousand dollars.'

'Floyd, *please*. Life won't be worth living without you. You are all I want in the world.' Cynthia dabbed her handkerchief to her nostrils, shed a tear, then said, 'By the way, dear, does that include the cottage in Connecticut?'

⌒

Corky Hearn was in his cups, sniffing and sniveling. 'For eighteen years—*eighteen* years, mind ye . . . me and me wife wuz the happiest man and woman in the whole durn world!'

'What,' asked a barfly, 'happened?'

'Then,' blubbered Hearn, 'we met.'

⌒

The late Joe E. Lewis, a nightclub entertainer with special wit, once ruminated: 'Show me a Jewish man who comes home early every night, is greeted with smiles and coos, has his coat and hat taken, his shoes taken off, pillows arranged for him, made to feel comfortable and welcome in every way, then is served a really delicious meal – and I'll show you a Jew who lives in a Japanese restaurant.'

See also **Bachelors, Hanky-panky, Just Jokes, Love**

Martians

The two men from Mars walked down the empty street, gazing around in wonder. Finally, they stopped before a fire hydrant. 'Take us to your leader!' said the first Martian. . . . 'Hey, didn't you hear what I said?! Take – us – to – your – leader!'

The Martians waited. Silence. The first Martian angrily began to kick the hydrant. 'Unless you take us to your – '

'Oh, lay off,' said the second Martian. 'Can't you see he's only a kid?'

∽

Two men from Mars landed in New York. They drifted about and happened to run into each other on the branch of a tree in Central Park. Each knew the other was from Mars because of the ultrasonic vibrations that emanate from Martians' heads.

'Hello, there,' said the first Martian. 'Been on this planet long?'

'Since Tuesday,' said the second.

'Quite a place, isn't it?'

'You bet.'

'By the way, what's your name?'

'44X306. And yours?'

'92T748.'

The second Martian pondered: 'That's funny; you don't look Jewish.'

∽

Opgdkrf, visiting our planet from Mars, studied the window of Warshawsky's Bakery and entered the store. 'Those little wheels in the window,' he said.

'*Wheels*?' echoed the puzzled Warshawsky.

'Yeah. Like – right there. In the tray . . .'

'Oh, *bagels*,' said Warshawsky. 'Here . . . taste one.'

Opgdkrf bit into the doughy delicacy and exclaimed, 'Wow! You know something? These would go great with cream cheese and lox!'

Military

For many years, SECRET was the designation used in Washington for confidential material whose circulation was to be severely restricted.

When SECRET failed to keep all the secrets, TOP SECRET was created.

When TOP SECRET did not sufficiently guard triple-important information, FOR EYES ONLY appeared.

Now a new, ultra-efficient classification is being considered by the Pentagon: Top, Top, Top Secret materials will henceforth be stamped in glaring red:

D.B.R.

What does D.B.R. stand for? *Destroy Before Reading*

༡

Sign on door to US Army recruiting station: DRAFT CARDS CHEERFULLY BURNED HERE.

༡

The recruit was so exhausted by the day's exercises that, assigned to stand guard duty, he could not keep his eyes open – so he rested his chin on the butt of his rifle, whose bayonet he stuck into the earth, and dozed off . . .

In time he became aware of heavy boots approaching. His heart leaped: the penalty for sleeping on duty was awful. Opening his eyes slightly, he discerned the Officer of the Day, glaring, closing in on him. The soldier kept his head down. The officer stopped.

The soldier raised his head, gazing up to the sky piously, said, 'Amen . . .' then braced into a salute. 'Yes, *sir*?'

༡

Before the entire ship's complement, the navy commander, a staunch believer in psychology and a champion of morale, addressed them: 'Officers, men, before we set foot on our wonderful ship, I want you all to realize how deeply I am committed to one simple principle: the SS *Eldridge* is not '*my*' ship. It is not the *officers*' ship. It is not *your* ship. . . . Gentlemen, the SS *Eldridge* is *our* ship!'

From the far ranks came an ironic voice, 'Great. Let's sell it.'

See also **Behind the Iron Curtain, Just Jokes, Russia**

Miracles

Paddy Kerrigan was going through Irish customs after his trip to France. Among his suitcases stood a brown gallon container. 'And what might this be?' asked the customs officer.

'Sure, and that is holy water I am bringin' back t' me loved ones, from Lourdes.'

The customs officer unscrewed the top, sniffed, blinked, raised the bottle, and tasted the contents. '*Water*, did you say now?' he sputtered. 'This is *brandy*. Strong French brandy!'

'Praise the Lord!' cried Kerrigan. 'Another miracle!'

$\backsim$

In Belfast, Terence Foley stubbed his toe on a two-by-four plank, fell down, then hurried to his doctor, chortling. The doctor substituted a dead patient's X-ray. And Terence Foley, represented by a lawyer named Houlihan, sued the L. E. Construction Company for a million pounds.

In the courtroom, Terence Foley's bandaged toe had become an immobilized leg, plastered solid up to the hip; and Foley's left arm was in a cast bent up across his shoulder; and Foley's neck was in a brace; and the pain in his back was said to be so great he had to be wheeled in and out of the courtroom in a wheelchair.

Lawyer Houlihan's throat choked as he described Foley's family of eight, a wife, a mother, a father, a father-in-law, one grand-mother on her deathbed – all, all dependent on Terence Foley.

It took a softhearted jury less than an hour to find for the plaintiff, and to award Foley no less than five hundred thousand pounds. The cheers from the ranks of Terence Foley's family, friends, and creditors rang through the courtroom.

As Foley was wheeled out of the fateful room, the lawyer for the construction company, Liffey Donahue, stepped over to him. 'Well thin, congratilations t' ye, Terence Foley. A mighty fine windfall y've this day gotten.... But I have bad news for ye,

Terence Foley.' He whispered into Foley's ear so no one else could hear him. 'Ye know and *I* know this is all a made-up crock! Ye got no more'n a wee *sprain* – if that. So the construction company, determined t' stop any forther such rascalry, has hired the foinest detectives in the land! And they will be followin' ye, Terence, day and night, wheriver ye go, *how*iver ye go! Ye will niver enjoy y'r ill-gotten money! Th' first minute ye get out 'f that ridiculous wheelchair, ye will be slapped with a summons, and hauled back to a smarter judge, God willin'; and ye will be exposed as a malingerer and a crook! Ye will be required to return ivery penny 'v that shameliss verdict! Ye will be charged with th' crime of – '

Foley raised a consoling hand. 'Save y're valuable brith, Mr. Donahue. Y'r words do not dismay me. Day and night will y're detictives be followin' me, now? Watchin' me ivery move, is it? Well, I shall *tell* you my ivery move in advance!' Foley signalled Donahue to come closer. 'From Belfast I fly to London, where I shall be carried to a plane to the South of France. There I am taken off and taken in an ambulance to a little town. And if your foine detictives are still watchin', so much the better. Because they will behold a miracle! I shall rise from me chair of pain, an' I shall walk!' Foley smiled beatifically. 'Ah, Donahue, Donahue. Me viry heart pounds with joy as I contemplate the mysterious powers of our blessed Lady of Lourdes . . .'

See also **The Occult**

Modesty

A famous old rabbi was being introduced to a congregation by a trustee who waxed more eloquent by the second: 'We are about to hear from a man of such wisdom that even the most learned sit at his feet, of such kindness that even children flock to him for advice, with such a keen understanding of human problems that men and women bare to him their innermost secrets, a man of such . . .'

At this point, the old rabbi tugged at the eulogist's sleeve, whispering, 'Don't forget my humility.'

Moses

The great throng of Hebrews patiently waited at the foot of the mountain, which was covered with dark smoke. For hours and hours now, Moses, who had led them out of the wilderness, had been gone.... Only the night before, the Great Lord Jahweh had appeared in a Cloud before Moses, who had come down from the mountain with the sacred tablets on which were inscribed the commandments to the Hebrews.... And Moses had gone back now to ...

Suddenly the tip of a white staff was seen moving down the mountain – and the fluttering of a white robe ... A great murmuring possessed the throng. At last they beheld – Moses!

A cheer of acclamation rang out. And Moses stood before the vast assemblage and in a commanding voice said: 'Children of Israel! I bring you tidings from your Lord, God of Israel. For six hours I have been with Him, kneeling in the dust, recounting the petition you assigned me to convey to Him! And I can now give you His answer!'

A weighty silence fell upon the Hebrews.

'The answer of our Lord God, King of the Universe, to your petition about the Commandments contains – good news, and bad news.'

Agitation swept the ranks. 'Tell us, O Moses!'

'What said our Lord?'

Moses spread his arms to still the throng. 'The good news, my children, is that I managed to persuade the Lord to cut the list from fourteen to ten!'

Cheer after cheer rose from the congregation. 'Hurrah! Hurrah!'

'Our Moses is mighty above all men.'

'O Moses, you will be thanked down all the eons ...'

'Finish!' cried someone.

'What is the bad news?'

Moses stared at the throng for a moment, then cleared his throat and declared: 'The bad news ... He would not budge. Adultery is still in.'

∽

This tale is a Hollywoodnik's version of the historic flight of the Hebrews out of ancient Egypt:

When Moses, racing his harassed and desperate people across the desert, came to the Red Sea, he gave swift thanks to the Lord, then called out, 'Manny! Manny!'

From the throng came Manny, a publicity man, 'Yes, Moses?'

'The boats!' said Moses.

'What?'

'The *boats*. The boats you were supposed to arrange – to get us across the Red Sea?!'

'Oh, my God!' said Manny. 'Moses, what with all the news items and human-interest stories – I forgot!'

'You forgot the *boats?!*' cried Moses. 'You moron! The Egyptians will be here any minute! What do you expect me to do – ask God to part the waters, let all of us across, and drown the pursuing Egyptians? Is *that* what you think – '

'Boss,' said Manny with fervour, 'you do that and it's worth at *least* two pages in the Old Testament!'

At the Red Sea, Moses, beholding the astonishing sight of the waters parting, groaned. 'Oh, Lord, I was just going in for a dip!'

RED BUTTONS

Mothers

God could not be everywhere, so he created mothers.

Mothers understand what children do not say.

Why do mothers have big aprons? To cover the faults of their children.

'A mother has a set of glass eyes.' (She cannot see her offspring's faults.)

YIDDISH SAYINGS

Harvey Nesselbaum, the patient, stretched out on the couch in his psychoanalyst's office.

Dr Gupel settled back in his chair behind the couch, notebook in hand.

'A dream,' said Nesselbaum. 'My God, doctor, such a dream!
. . . I was in the kitchen – a nice house, an old-fashioned stove,
chairs painted with – let me think, yes, stencilled, with birds and
flowers. . . . And my mother was making me breakfast. And
while I was eating the cereal, two soft-boiled eggs, toast, a glass of
Coca-Cola – into the room flew – an American eagle! And sat on
my mother's shoulder! Cawing – *cawing* "The Star-Spangled
Banner"! . . . Doc, what can that mean . . . an American eagle . . .
our national an – '

'A Coke?' cried Dr Gupel. 'A *Coke*?! That your mother gives you
for *break*fast?!'

⌒

Rafe ('Knuckles') Blatkin, a 'hit-man' for a Canarsie mob, was
gunned down in front of his building by the Slattery boys.

Bleeding from a dozen bullet holes, Knuckles staggered up the
brown-stone stairs and pushed open the door to his home.
'Mama . . .' he groaned. 'Mama . . .'

His mother sang out, 'Rafeleh!'

Knuckles, clutched his abdomen. 'Mama – they – '

'Rafeleh, don't talk,' beamed Mrs Blatkin. 'First, eat a little
something, *then* we can talk.'

⌒

Scene: A Catskill Hotel

MRS SHEIN: How about we have a cocktail before dinner?

MRS FINE: No, thank you. I never drink.

MRS SHEIN: Why not?

MRS FINE: Well, in front of my children, I don't believe in taking a
    drink. And when I'm away from my children, who *needs* it?

⌒

Mrs Notstein sent her little boy off to his first day in school with
many a kiss and a hug. 'So, *bubeleh*, be a good boy and obey the
teacher. And don't make noise. Be polite, *bubeleh*, and play nice
with the other children. And when it's time to come home, button
up warm, and be careful crossing the street, *bubeleh* . . .' etc., etc.

Off went little Notstein.

When he returned that afternoon, his mother hugged him and

kissed him and exclaimed. 'So – how did you like school? You make friends, *bubeleh?* You *learned* something?'

'Yeah,' said the little lad. 'I learned my name is Irving.'

Mrs Herman and Mrs Gerges were talking about their children. 'My son?' said Mrs Herman. 'Who could ask for a better boy? Every Friday, he eats dinner at my house. Every summer, he makes me spend a month with him in the country. Every winter he sends me for a month to a hotel in Florida.'

To which Mrs Gerges replied. '*I* have a son, an angel. For a whole year, he's been going to the most expensive psychiatrist in New York. Every day, month in and out, he goes there. And he talks each day for an hour. And do you know what he talks about, paying *fifty dollars an hour?!* . . . Me.'

Little Gershon came home from school in considerable excitement. 'Mama, mama! In half an hour there is going to be an eclipse of the sun! Can I go out and watch it?'

'Why not, dollink?' replied Gershon's mother. 'Only one thing; don't stand too close.'

See also **Children, Education, Jews**

Movie Marquees

ADAM AND EVE
with a Cast of Thousands

GEORGE WASHINGTON SLEPT HERE
with Ann Sheridan

THE BRIDE WORE BOOTS
and
Selected Shorts

Double features on movie theatre marquees

GO FOR BROKE
and
THE LAS VEGAS STORM

THE SEVENTH VEIL
and
GREAT EXPECTATIONS

AN AMERICAN IN PARIS
and
THE BIG HANGOVER

HOLIDAY AFFAIR
and
LET'S MAKE IT LEGAL

TRAPEZE
and
EMERGENCY HOSPITAL

I AM A CAMERA
and
OVEREXPOSED

See also **Boo-boos, Goldwyniana, How's That Again?**

Movies

Traditional Hollywood movie: Boy meets girl. Boy loses girl. Boy gets girl.

Science-ficton films: Boy meets girl. Boy loses girl. Boy builds girl.

Current films: Boy meets boy. Boy loses boy. Boy gets another boy.

Newest movie successes: Boy rapes girl. Girl joins gang. Gang rapes girl's father.

L. R.

See also **Goldwyniana, Movie Marquees**

Musicians

Musicians assert that the following episode is absolutely true. Years ago, when the boy Jascha Heifetz made his astounding debut in Carnegie Hall, every first-rate violinist in New York was in the audience. Among the galaxy of virtuosos was the great Mischa Elman, who had brought along his illustrious friend Leopold Godowsky, a famous pianist and a renowned wit.

Young Heifetz stunned the house with his technical brilliance and indescribable wizardry. After one astonishing arpeggio, the audience exploded into thunderous acclamation.

Elman mopped his brow and neck and whispered to Godowsky, 'Lord, it's hot in here!'

'Not,' said Godowsky, 'for pianists.'

The orchestra conductor could not help noticing, during the rehearsal of the Jupiter symphony, how his first cellist was moaning and making horrible faces. This went on so uninterruptedly that the conductor finally ra-ta-ta-taed his baton on the music stand. The orchestra went silent. The conductor turned to the cellist. 'Are you feeling ill?'

'Oh no, maestro.'

'Don't you like the way I'm conducting this symphony?'

'Oh no, sir. Your conducting is very inspiring!'

'Then why,' the conductor demanded, 'are you making those constant groans and tortured faces?'

The cellist sighed, 'I *hate* music.'

Musician: A man who, hearing a female singing in the shower, puts his ear to the keyhole.

Nationalities

This portion comes from a game played by graduate students when I was at the London School of Economics

L. R.

One Englishman, a bore;
Two Englishmen, a club;
Three Englishmen, an empire.

One Frenchman, a lover;
Two Frenchmen, an affair;
Three Frenchmen, a ménage.

One German, a burgher;
Two Germans, a beer-parlour;
Three Germans, an army.

One Italian, a tenor;
Two Italians, a duet;
Three Italians, an opera.

One American, a businessman;
Two Americans, a market;
Three Americans, a cartel.

One Irishman, a drinker;
Two Irishmen, a fight;
Three Irishmen, partition.

One Japanese, a gardener;
Two Japanese, a cult;
Three Japanese, electronics.

One Dutchman, a citizen;
Two Dutchmen, a bicycle club;
Three Dutchmen, irrigation.

One Russian, a melancholic;
Two Russians, a chess game;
Three Russians, a revolution.

One Swiss, one Swiss;
Two Swiss, two Swiss;
Three Swiss, three Swiss.

Nebechs

Note: A *nebech* – often written in English as 'nebbish' – is a meek, weak, unimpressive namby-pamby – the sort of character featured in Woody Allen's films.

L. R.

Nebech

The one in a group you always forget to introduce.

The unlucky soul upon whom a waiter always spills soup.

'Officer, officer!' the driver called from his car on 38th Street.
   A policeman sauntered over. 'Yeah?'
   'Officer, is it okay for me to park here?'
   'Absolutely not.'

'But officer,' the *nebech* protested. 'How about all those other cars parked up and down the whole street?!'

'They,' said the cop, 'didn't ask.'

'Doctor Mertz,' the *nebech* complained, 'why doesn't anyone ever pay attention to me? My wife, my children, my friends – I might as well not even *be* here, the way they just don't listen to anything I say. Why, doctor? Why?'

Dr Mertz thought for a moment, stepped to his door, and into the waiting room called, 'Next.'

Advertisement

BLOTTING PAPER
FOR SALE

The perfect gift for the man who has nothing.

Mrs Bechter began to beat her milquetoast of a husband, who fled her blows by crawling under the sofa.

'Come out of there, Sol, you coward!'

'No!' Sol shouted. 'I'll show you who's boss in this house!'

See also **Dummies, Jews, Shlemiels**

News Items That Haunt Me (All True)

In Kirby Misperton, zoo officials paid out more than £280 to visitors last year for articles stolen from them by monkeys. The monkeys specialized in snatching eyeglasses from the wearers' noses when visitors bent forward to make out a sign on the cage. The sign reads:

WARNING:
THESE MONKEYS SNATCH GLASSES

Daily Mail

A young British surgeon, on his first visit to America, was invited to look up a cystoscope (an instrument for viewing inside the bladder). To his astonishment, he saw the sign:

VISIT JOE'S BAR

For a moment the young surgeon thought he was beholding the final extremity of a national mania for advertisement. Then he moved the instrument, and saw that he was gazing at a segment of a plastic cocktail stick.

How it got there remains a mystery.

Daily Telegraph

ᔆ

BRAZEN HUNGER MARCH BY HARES

Moscow (Reuters) – Thousand of fearless and hungry hares were reported on the march today in Far Eastern Siberia.

Tass, the Soviet press agency, said the hares trooped through ... settlements in the Kamchatka Peninsula, 'showing utter disregard for the frenzied barkings of dogs.'

When they reached the coast of the sea of Okhotsk, the hares ravenously attacked sea kale ... [then] 'marched back to the tundra in the same organized manner.'

Daily Telegraph

ᔆ

HUSBANDS WHO HAVE
SEX OPERATION WILL
GET EASIER HOME MORTGAGES

A plan to allow easier mortgages for husbands who had undergone vasectomies was approved by Sutton Coldfield Town Council, Warwickshire, last night.

The council approved a proposal that 'if a husband can provide medical evidence he can no longer help to procreate children, his wife's income will be taken into account' when advancing council mortgages.

The proposal was described as 'moral blackmail' in a letter from five local Roman Catholic clergymen to Councillor Ron Hudson, chairman of the housing committee.

News of the World

One incident that caused him 'a great deal of personal pain,' Mr Heckscher said, was a bitter argument with Mayor Lindsay over the decision to hire Robert S. Collier, who was convicted two years ago of a conspiracy to blow up the Statue of Liberty.

New York Times, March 24, 1968

A man who removed a stuffed tiger from a zoo's publicity display at Waterloo Station got no farther with it than the taxi rank.

The police arrived as he was trying to get into a taxi-cab with the stuffed animal, with the help of the driver and a porter. The tiger, a rare Sumatran specimen valued at £500, was too big to go into the vehicle.

At Croydon Crown Court, Samuel William Smith, 50, told the court that while he was looking at the display, a youth told him he could have the tiger for £35. He said that as the exhibition was closing that night, the stuffed animals were for sale cheaply.

'I thought it was a bargain at the price.'

Daily Telegraph

WANTED: Typist to copy Top Secret documents. Must be unable to read.

Krokodil (a satiric journal), Moscow

For seven months, the National Park Service has been trying to put out a fire in a 25,000-year accumulation of giant sloth dung, in a remote Grand Canyon cave. So far the agency has not succeeded ... the effort has cost $50,000.

Smithsonian paleobiology curator Dr Clayton Ray said ... the giant sloth ... was not notable except for producing a large and durable stool in the same place for about 25,000 years.

Washington Post, February 1977

From the august *New York Times:*

> Recently, a Queens salesman began wondering if he shouldn't consult a psychiatrist. Every time he drove his car, he thought it was raining. He clearly heard the sound of gurgling water but no rain was falling.

A psychiatrist friend whom I promptly telephoned chuckled as he offered a diagnosis: (1) The salesman *hated* to go out on the road; so (2) the rain he imagined he was hearing was wishfulfilment; (3) this was a perfectly understandable expression of 'the salesman's unconscious', which produced the illusory sounds of rain in order to (4) trick the salesman into going back home to hit the sack.

I thanked my friend and hung up. I did not have the heart to read him the remainder of the story:

> One day, the salesman headed for the nearest service station. It seems that the car's steering column was full of water, which had accumulated from both condensation and leakage.
>
> The mechanic told the salesman it was the first time he had ever run into such a problem.

If you ask me, it's the first time anyone heard of that problem.

from my *Passions and Prejudices*

GOLDFISH SAVED FROM DROWNING

Mr Humphrey discovered the goldfish gasping for air on the surface of his garden pond at Hillside Crescent, Uxbridge. He fished it out and found its mouth was jammed open by a pebble. Gently he went to work and gradually eased the pebble out. Then he put the fish back into the water, where it quickly recovered.

Tonight an RSPCA inspector said: 'Mr Humphrey's

prompt action undoubtedly saved the fish's life. I will be preparing a report to be put before the Awards Committee. Not many people know that a fish could drown if it swallows too much water. I hate to think how many goldfish owners have stood by and let a fish drown because they did not know what was wrong.'

London Star

Note: the names in this editorial have been changed to protect the guilty.

TURN BACK, FOOLISH GIRL, TURN BACK!

Miss Blossom Mae Jetheroe, 23, was sentenced to seven days in gaol for 'accosting' gentlemen on King Street. In passing sentence, Mr Justice Cecil Horstcroft sternly admonished the errant female: 'The wages of sin is surely *death*. O shameless, foolish girl, mend your ways!'

Yes, yes, Blossom Mae, listen to your just sentencer! Wrest your tinkling feet from the primrose path! Spurn those tawdry escapades that imperil your soul! Stray not from the straight and narrow! Think, Miss Blossom Mae, and turn back! There still is time! Let the blush of virtue return to your still young cheeks!

Jamaica Star, Kingston

See also **Advertisements, Bloopers, Radio or TV, Headlines That Haunt me, How's That Again?, Typos**

Nudists

A beautiful young thing walked proudly past a group of men at the nudist colony. Their eyes followed her. One of the men sighed, 'Wow! Can you imagine what she would look like in a bathing suit?!'

EDEN NUDIST COLONY
BARE WITH US

Obscenity

O banish the use of those four-letter words
Whose meaning is never obscure:
The Romans and Britons, those bawdy old birds,
Were vulgar, obscene, and impure.
You stubbornly use any weaseling phrase
That never says just what you mean,
You prefer to be known for your hypocrite ways
Than be vulgar, impure, or obscene.
Let your morals be loose as a libertine's vest
But your language keep always obscure;
It's the word, not the act, that's the absolute test
Of what's vulgar, obscene, or impure.

AUTHOR UNKNOWN, alas

The Occult

The spiritualist gazed into her crystal ball, blinked, gazed again,
then stood up and slapped her beautiful client hard on the cheek.
  'Why are you doing this?' cried the client.
  'For going to bed with my husband – '
  'I never went to bed with your husband!'
  ' – next Saturday.'

**The London branch of the Clairvoyant Society
will not have its regular meeting this month,
due to unforeseen circumstances.**

For months, Mrs Zissel had been nagging her husband, Milty, to go with her to the séance parlour of Madame Froda Pranyakar. 'Milty, she is absolutey *spooky*. A real gypsy – and with such things she can bring out of her crystal ball will make your hair stand on end, do you hear me? She brings the voices of the dead – from the other world – right into her parlour! We all *talk* to them. Last week I talked with my darling brother, Howie. Then my mother, may she rest in peace. Then Uncle Freddie and Tante Sura. . . . Milty, for a lousy twenty dollars you can talk to your old grampa who you say you miss so much you're always telling me you mourn him so much. Isn't that worth twenty lousy dollars – to hear – to *talk* to – your darling *zayde?!*'

Milton Zissel could not resist his Hannah's appeal. At the very next séance at Froda Pranyakar's Gypsy Fortune and Séance Parlour, Milty sat under the multicoloured light, at the green table, holding hands with the pilgrim to his right and the mystic to his left, all humming, 'Ooooom . . . ooooom . . . Tonka Tooom . . .' Madame Froda Pranyakar, heavily made up, glitter on her upper eyelids, wearing huge earrings, three sparkling necklaces, and a heavy braid of bracelets, a paisley scarf tied around her head like a *babushka*, her eyes lost in trance, was making mysterious passes over a crystal ball from which a ghostly light emanated. . . . 'Oom . . . ooom,' moaned Froda Pranyakar. 'My medium . . . Vashtri . . . she keened. 'Vashtri . . . come in, Vashtri . . . Who is that with you. . . . Who? . . . Mr Zissel? . . . Milton Zissel's beloved grandfather? . . . Speak . . . speak, Milton.'

Milty Zissel dared not open his eyes. He swallowed the lump in his throat and called 'Grampa? . . . *Zayde?* My own dear *zayde?*'

'Ah, Milteleh,' a thin, thin voice quavered. 'Is that you, my darling *aynekel?*'

'Yes, yes!' cried Milty. 'This is your grandson . . . *Zayde*, are you happy in the other world?'

'Happy, Milteleh? . . . I am in bliss. Eternal, everlasting bliss . . .'

'And are you with my *Baba?*'

'Yes, yes . . . Sara and me . . . together . . .'

'And do you see other Zissels?'

'All . . . all . . . We eat together every day . . . milk . . . manna . . . fruits of paradise. . . . We laugh . . . we pray . . . we sing . . . we gaze upon the shining face of the Everlasting Lord!'

A dozen more questions did Milty ask of his grandfather, and each question did his *zayde* answer with enthusiasm, albeit in that thin, reedy, ectoplasmic voice – until: 'So now, Milty darling, I have to go back. . . . The angels are calling . . . I am old and weak. . . . Just one more question, Milteleh. . . . Ask. . . . Ask . . .'

'*Zayde*,' sighed Milty, 'when did you learn how to speak English?'

℘

Alec Nadich, carrying his violin case, and with a few minutes to spare in Penn Station, stood on a weighing scale and dropped a penny in the slot.

A deep, resonant voice from inside the machine intoned: 'You weight one hundred sixty-eight pounds . . . you are five feet ten inches tall . . . and you attend the Anshe Emmet Synagogue on Allen Avenue . . .'

Alec was thunderstruck. He quickly dropped another penny in the slot. The needle quickly stopped at 168 again. Now the orotund voice said, 'You play the fiddle in Gussheimer's Resort in the Catskill Mountains . . . and you are waiting to catch the – three twenty-two train to Libertyville . . .'

Alec simply could not believe his ears. He pondered, went into the men's room, put on a pair of sunglasses, altered the shape of his hat, removed his tie, took off his jacket and draped it over his violin case – and again dropped a penny in the scale.

And now that maddening, omniscient voice said, 'You are five feet ten . . . you weigh one hundred sixty-eight pounds. . . . You attend the Anshe Emmet Synagogue on Allen Avenue. . . . You play the fiddle in the Gussheimer orchestra – and you have just missed the three twenty-two train to Libertyville, you idiot.'

℘

In fortune-teller's window:

YOUR PROBLEM SOLVED –
OR MANIA REFUNDED

℘

The Ayatollah Khomeini, plagued by the infirmities of age, cursed by insomnia, and tormented (on those nights he briefly slept) by horrendous nightmares, called in Parsi Fassarjian, 'beloved of the

Prophet,' a mystic renowned throughout Iran for his ability to see into the future.

'My days are numbered as the pages in the holy Koran,' the Ayatollah mused, cross-legged on his golden cushion. 'Tell me then, can you foretell the day of my passing?'

The great seer peered into a brass bowl he had brought along, in which were coiled the entrails of a rare white lion, heavily sprinkled with incense, then closed his eyes and hummed strange phrases, then stirred the entrails – and exclaimed, 'Ah, noble Ayatollah, beloved of Fatima and the Prophet Mohammed, it is foretold that you will soon leave this sordid earthly plane and ascend to Paradise...'

The Ayatollah nodded heavily. 'Soon? ... Soon.... Can you say *when* soon?'

'On a holiday,' said Fassarjian, messing with the entrails and releasing more incense. 'A special Zionist holy day, a day celebrated throughout all of Israel.'

The Ayatollah's eyes opened and flashed. 'What? What? Are you certain?'

'Aye, Reverend One, there can be no mistaking the omens.'

'Which Zionist holiday? Which day celebrated in all of Israel?'

'Oh, Beloved of the Prophet, *any* day you die will be a holiday celebrated throughout all of Israel.'

∽

The sign in the window next to the door, at the head of the flight of brown stairs, read:

MADAM NASTAZIA

SPIRITUALIST

MEDIUM

One night, old Mr Pomeranz made his way up the stairs.... 'Madam Nastazia ... my dear Sadie, my wonderful wife of forty years ... passed on.... If only I – could hear her dear voice ... talk to her...'

Moaned Madam Nastazia, 'Cross my palma ... twenty dollars...'

In a darkened room scented by exotic perfumes, under a beaded lamp, Madam Nastazia invoked the spirit of her finest intermediary, 'Princess Wadlóvi of Molvania,' and soon the quivering voice

of Mrs Pomeranz was heard: 'Shepsel ... can you hear me? ...
Here is Sadie ... your wife...'

'Sadie!' cried Mr Pomeranz. 'I hear you! How *are* you, darling?
Where –'

'I am in heaven, Shepsel; united with my parents, and yours,
and Tante Minnie, and Cousin Mervin ... and we live on the
fruits of paradise...'

The séance lasted eight minutes before Princess Wadlóvi murmured, 'Our vibrations ... weaken ... farewell...'

Dimly Mrs Pomeranz's dulcet tone sounded. 'Goodbye, Shep-
seleh.... Please ... call again...'

Madam Nastazia turned the lights on. 'What fine séance! You
agree?'

'Agree?' echoed Mr Pomeranz. 'It was a miracle! Here! Please!'
He placed two more ten-dollar bills in the spiritualist's palm. 'I'll
be back tomorrow!'

Madam Nastazia beamed. 'You are generous mon, sir.
Tomorrow, I show how moch I oppreciate. All time you talk to
Sadie, I will be drinking a gloss water!!'*

Old Saws Sharpened

Rome wasn't burned in a day.

Give a man enough rope and he'll hang you.

A rolling stone gathers no moths.

Where there's a will, there's a wail.

He's just a wolf in cheap clothing.

He who laughs last, lasts.

That's like carrying Cohens to New Rochelle.

Beware of the Greek who asks for a gift.

Let sleeping ducks lie.

*Don't get it? Well, among professional ventriloquists 'throwing your voice'
while drinking a glass of water is considered the acme of technical perfection.

Never let a gift horse in the house.

People who live in glass houses shouldn't get stoned.

Don't burn your bridges until you come to them.

Don't put all your chickens in one basket.

Let's get down to brass roots.

None but the brave desert the fair.

from my *Rome Wasn't Burned in a Day*

See also **Cynics' Dictionary, Doggerel, Goldwyniana, Limericks, Mala-props, Puns, Put-downs, Sarcasm, Wit**

Optometrists

Sign in optometrist's window:

EYES EXAMINED WHILE YOU WAIT!

Sign in optometrist's window:

**IF YOU DON'T SEE WHAT YOU WANT,
THIS IS THE RIGHT PLACE TO COME TO.**

Sign in optometrist's window:

OH, SAY, CAN YOU SEE?

'Now, then,' said Dr Tsviful, indicating the large eye chart on the wall, 'what's the smallest line of letters you can read on the chart?'
   The patient peered at the wall carefully, then turned to the opto-metrist. 'What chart?'

See also **Dentists, Doctors, Psychiatrists/Psychoanalysts/Psychologists**

Pets

Sign in pet shop over cage of dachshund puppies:

GET A LONG LITTLE DOGGIE

Sign near Dog and Cat Hospital

HOSPITAL ZONE
NO BARKING!

Legend holds that when Noah was loading the Ark, God appointed an angel to name each couple as they filed aboard. This angel, whose name was Meyer, would give a couple a searching look, then choose a name. Take the huge-antlered, yellow-coated deer that lives in the mountains of Mongolia. Meyer named it 'Altai-Wapiti.'

The other angels, who did not like Meyer, were watching him like a whatever-they-called-a hawk before that name was allocated. And when Meyer touched the shoulder of the huge-antlered, yellow-coated deer with his sword, saying, 'I dub thee Altai-Wapiti!' a chorus of cherubs protested. 'Meyer, why are you calling that yellowish-coated, branch-antlered thing an Altai-Wapiti?!'

Meyer answered, 'Because he *looks* like an Altai-Wapiti, that's why!'

I do not believe this.

Meyer named other deer 'Hello' and 'Goodbye', from which comes our custom of saying 'Hello [or Goodbye], dear.'

L. R.

Justin Chernik wanted to give his old grandmother, who still lived in the Bronx, alone and with few friends, a birthday present – and this year, he wanted the present to be something special.

He wandered down many streets, looking into the store windows, until he saw something that made him stop cold in his tracks. In the window of Haley's Pet Shop was a cage, and in the cage was a parrot, and under the cage was this sign:

THIS PARROT SPEAKS YIDDISH!

Justin could hardly wait to enter the shop. 'That sign is not a gag or anything, is it?' he asked the owner. 'Certainly not!' said Mr Haley. 'Do you speak Yiddish?'

'Sure.'

'Okay. I'll get the bird. Talk to him. See for yourself.'

Haley took the parrot out of the window and the bird perched on his finger as the owner came over to Justin. 'Go on.' The following astonishing conversation then took place, all in Yiddish:

CHERNIK: *Sholem aleichem.*

PARROT: *Aleichem sholem.*

CHERNIK: You really speak Yiddish?!

PARROT: Why shouldn't I? Is there a law against it?

CHERNIK: What's your name?

PARROT: Yussel.

CHERNIK: How in the world – ?

PARROT: How, how? It's not such a *tsimmes*. I was born in the jungles of Brazil, captured, then brought up in Rio in an Orthodox Jewish family! The father spoke Yiddish; the mother spoke Yiddish; the family even sent me to a Hebrew school. And when my *Bar Mitzva* approached –

CHERNIK: Enough! That's enough. Yussel, you're the answer to my dreams!

To Mr Haley, Justin said, 'It's absolutely astonishing! This little bird is going to give my dear grandma a whole new world of pleasure to live for! She and Yussel can talk for *hours*. Grandma can unburden herself of all sorts of old grievances and sorrows. Yussel can tell grandma about his unusual life – in the jungle, in Rio with an orthodox Jewish family – ! Mr Haley, how much are you asking for this little bird?'

'Eight hundred dollars,' said Haley. 'And he's not so little.'

'Eight hundred – ! That's a lot of money.'

'Well, Yussel is a lot of parrot. He's young, extremely healthy, he could live for twenty more years – and when can I ever expect to get another Jewish parrot?'

'Five hundred . . .' said Justin.

'No . . . seven.'

'Six.'

'Six-fifty, and that's my final offer!' said Mr Haley (né Horwitz).

'It's a deal.'

So Justin Chernik wrote out a cheque. 'Deliver the bird

tomorrow – Grandma's birthday.' And he carefully wrote out his grandmother's address . . .

The next day, Justin telephoned his grandmother with impatient expectations. '*Bawbe*, this is Justin! Happy birthday, Grandma!'

'Oh, darling, thank you.'

'And you should have many, many happy returns!'

'I'll be glad if I'll have *three* . . .'

'Grandma. Did you get my – present?' laughed Justin.

'Your present! That beautiful bird! Certainly I got it. *What* a present! Only you could think of such a wonderful, unusual gift!'

'*Bawbe*, you really like him?'

'*Liked* him?' said Grandma. 'He was *delicious!*'

Postscript to the reader: I always thought that this story could not be improved – nor provided with a 'topper.' I underrated human resourcefulness. With 'delicious!' the story need not end . . .

'D-*delicious?*' sputtered Justin, 'Grandma, that – bird – spoke – fluent – Yiddish!'

Grandma chuckled. 'Oh, Justin, you are such a joker.'

'I'm not joking, *bawbe*,' cried Justin. 'That parrot – spoke – perfect – Yiddish!'

'Don't be silly,' scoffed Grandma. 'Listen, Justin: if he could talk, why didn't he *say* something?!'

See also **Just Jokes, Shaggy Dogs**

Prayer

On the ten High Holy Days, between Rosh Hashonah and Yom Kippur, seats in a synagogue are often sold in advance to raise funds for the synagogue's yearly expenses. One Yom Kippur, at a small Bronx synagogue, Leonard Krautman came running up to the door.

The sexton barred his way. 'Where's your ticket?'

'I don't have a ticket!' cried Krautman. 'I have to see Chaim Shanker!'

'You have to have a ticket – '

'But it's an emergency! Chaim's house is on fire! I'll just tell him – and come right out!'

'Okay,' said the sexton. 'But don't let me catch you praying!'

See also **Clergy, Faith, God, Religion**

Prejudices

Prejudice: A vagrant opinion without visible means of support.

I believe I have no prejudices whatsoever. All I need to know is that a man is a member of the human race. That's bad enough for me.

MARK TWAIN

∽

The Indians concealed in the thick foliage warily watched the *Santa Maria* lower a boat off its side; then men with sickly, pale bodies and ugly, thick beards plied their oars and the boat approached the shore. The Carib chief sighed, 'Well, fellows, there goes the neighbourhood!'

∽

Q: Why is Sunday morning the best time to drive on a California freeway?

A: Because the Catholics are in church, the Protestants are still asleep, the Chinese are stuffing fortune cookies, the Jews are in Palm Springs, and the Mexicans can't get their cars started.

From Romanian cookbook: Omelet: First, steal two eggs.

Psychiatrists/Psychoanalysts/ Psychologists

Psychoanalyst: A Jewish doctor who hates the sight of blood.

The neurotic builds castles in the air, the psychotic thinks he lives in them, and the psychoanalyst collects rent from them both.

A hysteric knows the secret of perpetual emotion.

A congenitally depressed person builds dungeons in the air.

Neurotic: A person who, when asked 'How are you?' tells you.

Psychiatrist: A doctor who chases ambivalences.

Someone who does not have to worry, as long as other people do.

Psychologist: A man who, when a voluptuous girl enters a room, watches the other men's reactions.

Experimental psychologist: A scientist who pulls habits out of rats.

L. L. LEVINSON

Mr Samuel Goldwyn once remarked, during a dinner-table argument about psychiatry: 'Anyone who goes to a psychiatrist ought to have his head examined.'

When two psychoanalysts meet, the first one says, 'You're fine. How am I?'

'Sit down, Mr Pelham,' said the psychiatrist. 'Now, what brings you here?'

'People!' declared Pelham. 'Stupid people! Doctor, I have to tell you I despair about the whole human race!'

'Mmh. Well, what is it that people actually *do* that makes you so bitter?'

'They call me crazy, that's what they do! No matter what I say or suggest – they say I am a crazy! They won't listen to a word of truth!'

'Mr Pelham,' said the psychiatrist gently, 'perhaps you ought to start at the beginning...'

Mr Pelham said, 'Okay. In the beginning, I created the heavens and the earth. And the earth was without form and void...'

A very depressed woman patient of Dr Homer Byrnes, the well-known psychotherapist, was vacationing in Acapulco, her first

venture out of the United States. She sent Dr Byrnes this postcard:
'Hi, Doc. Having wonderful time. *Why?*'

$\backsim$

THE INSIDE DOPE ON PSYCHOANALYSIS

Psychoanalysis has been used with great success from pole to pole (although it has not been popular with other nationalities). The English, for example, will not even discuss their flower beds with anyone in the medical profession.

The Swiss, for their part, don't pay much attention to Freud because they engage in sex only during the 'r' months. Switzerland has been independent for 300 years.

The French, of course, sneer at the mere mention of psychoanalysis, because by the time he is eight any French schoolboy knows how to add, subtract, and multiply.

As for the Germans, their ideas about sex are very orderly: they never indulge in it in front of their pets, who get nervous during a copulation explosion.

I don't know about the Chinese, who are an inscrutable people; or the Japanese, who shout 'Banzai!' whenever they get excited. That sort of thing would complicate anyone's sex life. Every time a Japanese man shouts 'Banzai!' his partner thinks the Emperor is approaching. This means that a good deal of sex in Japan takes place while the women are bowing.

Now, for the difference between Neurotics and Psychotics. First, they are spelled differently. This is important. Neurotics get extremely upset by incorrect spelling, and psychotics think you are persecuting them.

Second, a *psychotic* is an out-and-out loon. He may think his father is poisoning his yoghurt, that his wife is planning to strangle him with noodles, or that the US government should flood Las Vegas with soda water.

Third, a *neurotic* is a determined sufferer, afflicted by things like depressed cuticles, a fear of pistachio nuts, or underarm humidity.

Fourth, to put it most simply, a psychotic thinks 2 plus 2 equals 7 (4 is the correct answer). A neurotic knows that 2 plus 2 equals 4 – but he just can't *stand* it.

Here are some simple tests you can use to tell the difference between neurotics and psychotics:

1. *Salutation Test*

When you say 'Hello' to a neurotic, he is likely to bridle, 'What do you mean by that?' When you say 'Hello' to a psychotic, he will go to the bathroom.

2. *Dream Interpretation*

A neurotic is happy to elaborate on his dreams for hours. He will even project them for you, along with colour slides of his trip to 'Nature's Winter Wonderland.'

A psychotic, on the other hand, confuses dreams with reality, and he will accuse you of stealing his dreams – and run away. Don't let this worry you, Herm. As Freud taught us, a psychotic is least dangerous when egos away.

3. *Direct Interrogation*

I happen to think that the best way to find out whether someone is neurotic or psychotic is by asking him. Seat the subject in an easy chair and, in a casual tone of voice, smile, 'By the way, John, would you describe yourself as being alive?'

If the answer is 'Yes,' that rules out psychosis. If the answer is 'No,' do not jump to conclusions until you have listened to the subject's heart with a stethoscope. (Of course, you should never address a subject as 'John' if his name is Sam, Percy, or Beulah. You can ruin the Direct Interrogation test by addressing a subject in a way that arouses his suspicions.)

from my 'Dear Herm'

⤺

'Anna,' said Mrs Schlossberg, 'is it true that your nephew Merwin is going to a psychoanalyst?'

'True.'

'Five times a week, an hour each time?'

'True, true.'

'So Anna, for God's sake, what's the matter with him?'

'The doctor says,' sighed Anna, 'that Merwin has a real Oedipus complex.'

Mrs Schlossberg thought this over, then declared, 'Oedipus-schmoedipus – just as long as he loves his mother!'

⤺

DR WEININGER: Well, I think your analysis is now completed. Doesn't that make you happy?

PATIENT: I – suppose so.
DR WEININGER: Why are you hesitant? Do you remember how you
    felt when you first came to me?
PATIENT: Yes. Happier.

∽

The woman patient, stretched out on the couch, dabbed her lace
handkerchief at her nose and sniffed. 'But doctor. If just once – oh,
I would feel *so* much better – if just once – you – kissed me!'

'"Kiss you"?!' the analyst echoed. 'Mrs Forrest, I shouldn't
even be lying *next* to you!'

∽

Distraught Mrs Cooley said to Dr Flint, 'I have to tell ye about a
new craziness that's taken hold of me poor man. He thinks he's – a
refrigerator!'

The psychiatrist frowned. 'Mrs Cooley, that is an obsession I've
never heard of. . . . Uh, how does it manifest itself?'

'Why, the man sleeps with his mouth wide open!'

Dr Flint chuckled. 'That's hardly unusual, Mrs Cooley. Many
men sleep with their mouths wide open.'

'But I can't get any *sleep*, doctor, with that little light on all
night!'

∽

J. J. Javitch owned a fine toy store, called 'J. J.'s Aladdin's Cave.'
But lately, Aladdin's Cave had been having grave problems. The
children loved to try out the hobby-horses, the rockers, the
swings, but never seemed to want to get off. Whenever a parent or
a salesman tried to coax a little one off a toy, the tot would scream
and dig in his heels and throw a violent temper tantrum. The store
often sounded like a madhouse.

One day there appeared before J. J. Javitch a white-haired
gentleman, who said: 'I am Professor Lawrence Hockheimer,
doctor of child psychology, consultant on infant behaviour. I have
heard of your difficulties; I can solve them. My fee is one hundred
dollars.'

'A *hundred* dollars?'

Professor Hockheimer smiled. 'No obligation. If I fail to give full
satisfaction, you don't pay a penny.'

·Mr Javitch led the professor into the toy department. 'Listen. Did you ever hear such craziness?'

On one tricycle, from which his frantic mother was trying to lift him, a little boy was screaming like a banshee. On a hobby-horse, a little girl was screeching at the salesman who was trying to coax her off. On a rocking horse, a child was caterwauling at her father.

Professor Hockheimer observed the howling scene but a moment, went over to the tricycle, patted the screaming lad on the head, leaned over and, smiling, whispered a few words into the boy's ear. At once, the lad slid off the tricycle and leaped into his mother's arms.

Professor Hockheimer went to the little girl on the hobby-horse, stroked her locks fondly, leaned over, whispered something into her ear – and the tyke stopped screaming at once and jumped off the hobby-horse.

With the squalling tyke on the rocking horse, Professor Hockheimer plied his same swift magic. A pat, a smile, those mesmeric words – and decorum replaced obstinacy.

'I can't believe my eyes!' said J. J. Javitch. 'What in the world do you say to them?'

'My fee . . .'

'Fine! Yes! Here's my cheque . . . Now, what's the secret?'

'I pat their hair fondly,' said the great psychologist, folding the cheque into his wallet, 'then I put my mouth close to their little ears, and I whisper, "Listen, my darling. Get off this thing – at once – or I'll give you such a kick in the ass you won't be able to sit down for a month."'

Mrs Stribling stretched out on the couch and said, 'I must tell you, Doctor Ehrenfeld, this whole thing was not *my* idea . . . Doctor Randolph, our family doctor for ever so many years, simply in-*sisted* that I consult you. "Try psychoanalysis for a mere month or so," he said. "I promise you'll be converted. Doctor Ehrenfeld is a very gifted therapist . . ."'

She paused. Behind her, in a comfortable lounge chair, Dr Ehrenfeld, notebook in hand, waited, silent.

'*Why* Doctor Randolph ever got the silly idea that I need psychiatric help, doctor, is something I shall never understand . . . Why, I've never been sick a day in my life, I'm happily married, we have three lovely children, I have dozens of friends – '

'Stop, madam,' Dr Ehrenfeld cut in. 'How long has zis been going *on*?'

⌒

Drs Cassman and Stanley, both psychiatrists, lived on the same floor in a fashionable building in Grosvenor Square, Mayfair. One morning, going to their respective offices, they entered the same elevator.

The elevator operator, a new young man, called out cheerfully, 'Good *morn*ing, gentlemen!'

The two psychiatrists got off on the garage level. As they started for their cars, Dr Cassman said to Dr Stanley, 'I say, old boy: *What* do you think the elevator lad meant by that?'

⌒

'My son,' said Mrs Parker. 'I'm worried *sick* about my son! Doctor, do you know what he does all day, day after day? He makes mud pies!'

Said the psychiatrist, 'I wouldn't worry about that, Mrs Parker. Making mud pies is something all of us once did. His obsession will go away as he gets older.'

'I have to doubt that,' said Mrs Parker. 'And so does his wife.'

See also **Doctors, Hypochondriacs, Jews, Just Jokes**

Punctuation

Don't! Stop!
Don't stop.

Woman! Without her, man would not be civilized.
Woman, without her man, would not be civilized.

Telegrams   NO, PRICE TOO HIGH
                NO PRICE TOO HIGH.

Holland   A low-lying country.
              A low, lying country.

Diet   Don't eat fast.
                          Don't eat, fast.

Death   A: Did he die happily?
                          B: Yes he died, happily.

EVAN ESAR

Apartment Wanted
Secretary about to be married urgently,
needs 2-room apartment

BEATRICE: Is it true you said that that lout Louey looks like a Greek
    god?
SONYA: No, no. What I said was, 'He looks like a Greek. *God!*'

See also **Bloopers, Radio and TV, Boo-boos, The English Language,**
Typos

Puns to Shudder Over

Two destroyers were racing home to port. As one passed the
other, it sent this message:

EXCUSE ME, BUT YOUR SHIP IS SLOWING

Have you heard of the bee who took to wearing a *yarmulka* (skullcap) because he didn't want to be mistaken for a Wasp?

He's not worth her wiles.

GALSWORTHY

VIVIAN: Last night I had a date with a very important guy – an air-
    force general.
MELBA: Major-general?
VIVIAN: Not yet.

'Minnie, tell me honestly: how do you feel about Red China?'
'Please, Dorothy – not with your pink tablecloth!'

Scene: Istanbul

HARKAOI: *Salaam*, Mostroviz. Do you not remember me?
MOSTROVIZ: Your name I do not remember, but your fez is familiar.

See also **Advertisements, Graffiti, Malaprops**

Put-downs

Scene: London; the Apartment of Theodore Benwick-Thorpe, OBE. The telephone rings, Benwick-Thorpe lifts the instrument.

WOMAN: Hul-lo. Is that dear Rupert?
BENWICK-THORPE: No, madam, it is not.
WOMAN: Does not Rupert Carr-Ormond reside there?
BENWICK-THORPE: I'm afraid he does not, madam.
WOMAN: Well, am I connected to nine-oh-four, seven, seven, two, three?
BENWICK-THORPE: No, madam, you are not.
WOMAN: Well to what number *has* Central put me through?
BENWICK-THORPE: This is eight-two-oh, six, four, nine, four.
WOMAN: Are your *shaw*?
BENWICK-THORPE: Madam, have I ever told you an untruth befaw?

☙

'My husband isn't afraid of *any*thing,' said Mrs Kottsen, who weighed over two hundred pounds. 'But me – I have to tell you. I'm afraid of my shadow!'
   'Who can blame you?' said Mrs Nayfish. 'It looks like a crowd is following you.'

☙

Tom Aberfeldy and Lloyd Morgan were having a violent argument right on the main street of Cardiff. ''Tis no wonder th' damn

English say "Taffy is a Welshman, Taffy is a thief!"' cried Aber-feldy.

'*A thief* y're callin' me?!' Morgan shouted. 'Why in all the days of me life, not once – not *once*, mind ye – did anybody hear me honesty questioned!'

'Questioned?' glared Aberfeldy. 'Y'idjit, nobody ever heerd it mentioned!'

$\backsim$

Let's go somewhere where I can be alone.

Would you like to come to my pool? I'll be happy to give you a lesson in drowning.

Didn't we meet in Monte Carlo – the day you blew out your brains?

Send your wits out, to be sharpened.

Generous? Why that man would give you the sleeves out of his vest!

You're the kind of boss who, when dictating, ends every other sentence in a proposition.

See also **Groucho, Insults, Repartee, Sarcasm**

Rabbis

A rabbi whose congregation does not want to drive him out of town isn't a rabbi; and a rabbi they do drive out of town isn't a man.

FOLK SAYING

$\backsim$

Mickey Mitganger went to a rabbi to confess his sins, but he was so shame-stricken that he said, 'Rabbi, I didn't come here for

myself – but – for a friend! He asked me to come. He told me everything to ask you.'

The rabbi thought over this strange request and said, 'What sins
has your friend committed?'

'He often takes the name of the Lord in vain. He fornicates – and
gambles – and he even – '

'Stop,' signed the rabbi. 'Your friend is foolish. Why didn't he
come here himself?'

'He's too ashamed . . .'

'But he could have told me that he came for *you*,' said the rabbi
with a smile, 'thus saving you considerable embarrassment.'

Yagil Rapotkin, a travelling salesman, found himself in the synagogue in a little *shtetl* one Friday night. After the prayers, Rapotkin set off in search of a place to sleep.

'Where are you going?' exclaimed a man. 'A Jew, alone, on the
eve of the Sabbath? Come, man. Come home with me! My name is
Boris Marantz. My wife is a marvellous cook . . .'

The Marantzes could not have been better hosts. They gave
Rapotkin a fine bedroom, urged him to soak in a hot tub, gave him
fluffy towels and scented soap – and fed him a superlative Sabbath
dinner. That night, Rapotkin slept between fine linen sheets . . .

Next morning a sumptuous breakfast awaited him. And as he
made his heartfelt farewells to his host, Rapotkin asked 'How can
I ever thank you both?'

Said his host, 'Just attend to this.' And he handed Rapotkin a
slip of paper, on which was carefully written:

ACCOUNTING

1 Bath: hot water	5 kopecks
1 Cake scented soap	12 kopecks
1 Large fresh towel	10 kopecks
1 Sabbath dinner (complete)	3.00 rubles
2 Fresh sheets	15 kopecks
1 Fresh pillow case	10 kopecks
1 Breakfast	85 kopecks
Total Due	4.37 rubles

(Signed)

BORIS MARANTZ

'B-but – what's this?' gaped Rapotkin.

'Your bill.'

'You expect me to *pay* this?!'

'Certainly,' said Marantz. 'Do you deny that you bathed here, slept overnight, ate like a king – '

'Deny it? I'm absolutely flabbergasted!' cried Rapotkin. 'You *invited* me here! You in*sisted*! I've never heard a more outrageous – '

'Stop!' Marantz held up his hand. 'Let's not argue. Let's go to our rabbi, tell him everything. . . . Will you abide by his decision?'

'Will I?' seethed Rapotkin. 'I can't *wait* to hear what the rabbi says about such outrageous behaviour!'

The two men hurried to the rabbi's house. . . .

Rapotkin told his tale to the rabbi, pouring the words out with great feeling.

The rabbi turned to Marantz. 'And what do you, the host, say? You were the one who invited him, pressed your hospitality on him, urged him – '

'Everything he said is just as it happened,' said Marantz.

'There you are, rabbi!' cried Rapotkin.

The rabbi nodded. 'After hearing you both, and considering all the delicate ethical problems involved, and based on the wisdom – on just such problems – I have studied for years in the Talmud, my decision is clear and simple: Mr Rapotkin, pay the bill.'

Rapotkin could hardly believe his ears. He was shocked; he was speechless. Yet a rabbi had spoken . . .

Rapotkin and Marantz left the rabbi's house. With a heavy heart, Rapotkin started to count out rubles.

'What are you doing?' asked Marantz.

'Paying your bill.'

'*Paying* me? For my hospitality? You must be crazy. Do you think I would accept money from you, my guest – '

Rapotkin sputtered: 'I must be going mad! Didn't you give me a bill?! Didn't you ask me to pay you?! *You* suggested – '

'Oh, *that*,' scoffed Marantz. 'Sure, sure. But I don't want your money. I just wanted you to see what a dope we have here for a rabbi!'

⌒

Three new rabbis, who had been classmates at the Reform seminary, met in a conference and began to discuss their congregations. 'My temple is so modern,' observed the first, 'that after services we adjourn to the social hall for snacks – and ham sandwiches are our most popular item!'

'*My* flock,' said the second, 'are so emancipated that over sixty percent of their children married gentiles!'

The third rabbi cleared his throat. '*My* temple is closed on Jewish holidays.'

This happened many centuries ago, in Persia.

'There's something I want you to do, rabbi,' said the shah. 'Teach my pet monkey how to talk.'

'*What?*'

'He's rather a clever monkey. In any case,' – the shah smiled – 'that's a command: teach my monkey how to talk within one year, or your head will be chopped off!'

'But Your Majesty, to perform a deed like that – I need more than a year; I need at least ten.'

'I'll allow you two years, and not a day more.'

When the rabbi returned to his flock and told them what had happened, they cried in despair. 'Oh, rabbi, rabbi. What will you *do?*'

'Well,' said the rabbi. 'In two years, many things can happen. For instance, the shah can die. Or, *I* could die. . . . Or, the monkey could die. . . . And besides, in two years, who knows: maybe I can teach that monkey how to talk.'

Fischel Kurtzer, a poor tinker walking the streets of Jerusalem, found a fine wallet, in which were eighty shekels, and this notice in a celluloid jacket:

> *If found, please return to*
> *Yitzchak Zelg*
> *29 Weitzman Boul.*
> *20 shekels Reward* – NO QUESTIONS ASKED

So Fischel hastened to the Zelg home, a beautiful house with a fine garden. A servant admitted him to Mr Zelg, a rich, cunning man, who examined the wallet's contents. 'Ah, I see you already took the twenty-shekel reward.'

'Me?' blinked Fischel. 'Never!'

'There were a hundred shekels in my wallet,' smiled Zelg.

'No, no. I swear – '

'Let's not argue about this,' said Zelg. 'Let's let Rabbi Frunkin decide.'

The two men hurried to the nearby synagogue. Fischel Kurtzer told the rabbi what he had found and done. Then Zelg gave *his* canny version of the events, ending, '*Nu, rebbe*. Who do you believe? Me – or that *shlump*?'

'You, Mr Zelg, of course,' said the rabbi.

Fischel's face fell. The rabbi removed the wallet from Zelg's hand – and gave it to the tinker.

'*Rebbe*, what are you doing?' cried Zelg.

'Taking you at your word,' said Rabbi Frumkin. 'You said your wallet contained one hundred shekels. This man says the wallet he found contained only eighty. Obviously, this wallet can't be yours.'

'But – what of my money?'

'We simply must wait,' said the rabbi, 'until some honest soul finds a wallet with a hundred shekels in it.'

⌒

Lewis Browne, author of the immensely successful *This Believing World*, had for a time been a Reform rabbi at a temple in New Jersey. For reasons no one in Hollywood, to which Browne moved, ever found out, Browne had been asked to resign his pulpit.

At a dinner party, a waspish woman remarked, 'So you were really a rabbi. Tell us, were you defrocked?'

'N-no,' said Browne. 'I was unsuited.'

⌒

Shimmel Himmel came to his rabbi, distraught. 'Rabbi, please – you've got to advise me! Every year my wife brings forth another baby. I have nine children already, and barely enough money to even buy them food! . . . Rabbi, what can I *do*?'

The sage thought not a moment. 'Do nothing,' he said.

⌒

The venerable old rabbi called before him young Rabbi Dvorkin, the newest rabbi in town, and sighed, 'My heart is very heavy, Dvorkin. . . . The words I am about to utter come as heavily as if they were made of lead . . .'

'Oh, rabbi, rabbi!' exclaimed Dvorkin. 'Any words you address to me are an *honour*. Please, do not hesitate – speak frankly!'

The old rabbi nodded. 'Very well. I asked you to come see me, because – well, because I heard a fearful rumour – '

'It's not true!' cried Dvorkin. 'I know the rumour, *rebbe*. There's not a grain of truth in it!'

The old man drew himself up in horror. '*True* it should be yet? *Isn't it bad enough there is a rumour?!*'

⌒

'Please, doctor. Save her!' begged Mr Feingold. 'I'll pay you anything.'

'But what if I can't cure her?' asked Dr Zifkin.

'I'll pay you whether you cure her or kill her!' cried Feingold.

A week later, Mrs Feingold died.... The doctor sent Mr Feingold a large bill. And poor Mr Feingold suggested they both go to the rabbi to discuss the fee.

Rabbi Heilbrun, who well knew Dr Zifkin's reputation, said, 'What was your agreement, doctor?'

'He agreed to pay me for treating his wife,' said the doctor, 'whether I cure her or killed her.'

The rabbi nodded. 'And did you cure her?'

'No.'

'Did you kill her?'

'Certainly not!'

'Then,' asked Rabbi Heilbrun, 'under what contract are you claiming a fee?'

⌒

Moishe Zherin, a poor man in a small Polish village, came to his rabbi. 'Oh, rabbi, my life is so miserable! I live above the stable – in one room with my wife and four children and her mother. Rabbi, it is so crowded I just can't bear it any longer!'

'Do you – uh – have a goat?' asked the rabbi.

'Yes, rabbi.'

'Take the goat into your room.'

'*What?*'

'Do as I say, Moishe.'

So the poor man went home and took the goat out of his back yard and put it into his room.

A week later he hurried to the rabbi, sputtering: 'I did what you

told me, rabbi. I took the goat in, and now things are even worse –
much worse than before! Rabbi, what shall I *do?*'

'Moishe, do you have any chickens?' asked the rabbi.

'Yes. Three – '

'Bring them into your house.'

'Rabbi!'

'Do as I say, Moishe. Do as I say...'

So the poor man brought the three chickens into the house. A
week later he returned to the rabbi, wringing his hands. 'It's terrible! Terrible! I can't *stand* if any more!'

The rabbi nodded. 'Very well, Moishe, go home – and put out
the goat.'

The poor man did as he was told, and came back. 'It's a *little*
better, rabbi, but still – three chickens – in a room with seven
people...'

'Throw out the chickens,' said the rabbi.

And the next morning, Moishe Zherin stood before the rabbi,
overjoyed, crying: 'Rabbi, there's no one in all the world as wise as
you! My house – now it is paradise!'

∽

'Well, grandma, how do you feel today?'

'Today, dear, I feel better. And it certainly was nice of that
young rabbi to come in to my room at the hospital to cheer me up.'

'Rabbi? What rabbi?'

'The one with big glasses, reddish hair, tall, thin – '

'Grandma, that wasn't a rabbi. That was Dr Feldman – a specialist we called in!'

'A *doctor* that was? My. That explains everything...'

'What do you mean?'

'To tell you the truth, I thought he acted pretty fresh for a rabbi.'

See also **Accents, Israel, Jews, Just Jokes, Reason**

Reason

A TRIUMPH OF REASONING

A rabbi, famous throughout Lithuania for the power of his analysis and reasoning, was said to be capable of answering any question put to him. One day one of his disciples cried: 'Our *rebbe* can think his way in an instant to the very heart of any problem – and give the perfect answer!'

'It certainly is true that our beloved rabbi has a mind of unparalleled clarity and powers. But what if he is too tired to think hard? Maybe drowsy? Even a bit tipsy? Would his capacity to analyse still prevail?'

This question so fascinated the loving acolytes that they decided to put it to the test. At the next Sabbath feast, they surreptitiously poured enough wine in the rabbi's glass to make him tipsy. Then, while he slept, the disciples carried him, reverently, to the cemetery. There, they laid him on the grass and hid behind the tombstones – waiting to see what the great rabbi would say when he realized where he was. . . .

The rabbi snored away for a time, then yawned, opened his eyes, looked about – and sat up. Stroking his beard, he then proceeded to say. '*Nu?* . . . *If* I am living, what am I doing here? . . . And if I am dead, why do I have to go to the bathroom?'

⌒

Rabbi Tesher, discovering that he had left his comfortable slippers back in the house, sent a student after them with a note for his wife. The note read: 'Send me your slippers with this boy.'

When the student asked why the rabbi had written '*your*' slippers, Rabbi Tesher answered, 'Listen, young man. *Think*. If I wrote "my" slippers, my wife would read "my slippers" – and would send me *her* slippers. What can I do with her slippers? So I wrote "your" slippers; she'll read "your" slippers and send me mine.'

⌒

Two salesmen, carrying their sample cases, met in Pennsylvania Railroad Station. They eyed each other warily. 'Hello, Poppel.'

'How are you, Notkin?'

Silence.

'So – where are you going?' asked Poppel.

'I'm going to Islip,' said Notkin.

Silence.

'Listen, *boychik*,' sighed Poppel, 'when you tell me you're going to Islip, you want me to think you're going to Bellport. But I happen to know that you *are* going to Islip – so why are you lying?!'

꙳

Mr Osterman was awakened from a deep sleep by his wife, who nudged him in the side, saying, '*Get up*, Harry, I'm freezing! Close the window. It's very, very cold outside!'

Sighed Harry, 'And if I close the window, Celia, will it be very, very *warm* outside?'

꙳

Mr Solovy was returning from New York by bus to his little home town in New Jersey. Next to him sat a pleasant young man. Mr Solovy sang out, 'My name is Sam Solovy and I live in Groverville, New Jersey.'

'My name,' said the young man, 'is Spielfogel, Murray Spielfogel, and I'm going to Groverville, too.'

Mr Solovy beamed. 'On business, could I ask?'

'No.'

'Maybe to visit someone in your family?'

'No. I have no relatives in Groverville.'

'Young man, let me ask – are you married or single?'

'I'm not married.'

'Aha.' Mr Solovy leaned back in his seat, closed his eyes, and reasoned thusly: 'He's not going on business; he's got no family in Groverville; he's not married. *Nu*, why is he going to Groverville? He must be going to meet a girl! And if he's going this far, it must be serious. So – which girl? Selma Kromer? N-no. Selma is engaged to that dentist from Red Bank. . . . So is this Spielfogel going to call on the Coopersteins? Nah. Seymour Cooperstein's daughter just got married. . . . Maybe to the Rifkinds? . . . N-nah, Shirley Rifkind is only fourteen – fifteen. . . . Maybe to the Novarskys? But Nancy Novarsky is away at college . . . The Pflaumberg girl? Ah . . . the Pflaumbergs have *three* daughters: Nina, Grace, and Leona. Nina, poor girl, is big and fat, and this young Spielfogel is good-looking enough to pick and choose. Grace? Grace is a divorcée with young children. . . . Leona? . . . Leona. *There* is a live number! And last weekend she went to New York; and the week before that. . . . Aha!' Mr Solovy opened his eyes, beaming, and extended his hand. 'Murray Spielfogel, let me be the first to offer congratulations and best wishes for a long, happy life together!'

'What do you mean?'

'I mean your forthcoming engagement to Miss Leona Pflaumberg.'

The young man blushed furiously. 'But – Mr Solovy! We haven't told one living soul! Not even her mother, her father! . . . How in the *world* did you ever find out?'

'How I found out?' echoed Sam Solovy. 'My boy, it's obvious.'

A chief justice of old was visiting a prison with the warden. Prisoner after prisoner insisted that he was innocent: one said he had been framed, another that the judge who sentenced him had been bribed to do so, another still, that he was the victim of a conspiracy.

The chief justice asked the last prisoner, 'And are you, too, innocent?'

'No, sir, I'm a thief. I was fairly tried and sentenced.'

'You *admit* you're a thief?'

'Yes, sir.'

The chief justice said to the warden. 'Throw this crook out of here!'

'The other prisoners raised a fearful clamour. 'How can you do such a thing?' 'How can you free a confessed criminal, while we –'

'I was afraid,' smiled the chief justice, 'that the evil scoundrel might corrupt all you pure, innocent souls.'

See also **Chutzpa, Logic, Salesmen, True Tales**

Religion

Religion: An old, flourishing prophet system.

Baptism: A sacred rite of such efficacy that he who finds himself in heaven without having undergone it will be unhappy forever.

AMBROSE BIERCE

As Grogan lay on his deathbed, eyes closed, Father O'Donnell

leaned over and said, 'Brian, listen. . . . Repeat after me: 'I renounce the devil and all his evil deeds!'''

Grogan opened one eye, but said nothing.

'Brian!' said Father O'Donnell, 'Can you hear me?' Grogan
nodded.

'Then repeat after me: ''I renounce the devil and all his evil
deeds!'''

Grogan's other eye opened.

'Brian!' snapped Father O'Donnell. 'Don't you *hear* what I'm
tellin' ya?'

'Sure, father,' murmured Grogan. 'But I don't think this is the
time for me to go makin' an enemy of *any*body.'

PREACHER: We are here on earth to help others, Jimmy.
JIMMY: Then what are the others here for, sir?

The Flahertys moved to the suburbs. Their next-door neighbours
were the Spaldings. One day Tim Flaherty, age six, was playing in
the brook with Lucy Spalding, age five. When they had splashed
water all over their clothes, they took them off. . . .

Little Lucy's mother observed all this from the kitchen. And
when Lucy came in, her mother said, 'Lucy dear, did you like
playing with the new boy?'

'Yes, mother.'

'What games did you play?'

'Oh, we didn't play any games. . . . We just cleaned up the
brook and splashed around—and we got so wet we took off our
clothes and played naked.'

Lucy's mother hesitated. 'Well, dear, is there *any*thing you'd
like to tell me?'

Little Lucy reflected. 'Well, mother, one thing: I didn't know
there was *that* much difference between Protestants and Catholics.'

The priest stopped in at the coffee counter and sat down on a
stool. The man next to him said, 'Mornin', father.'

'Good morning.'

'New around here, father?'

'Oh, no.'

'Which is your church?'

'St Joseph's. Just across the street.'

'Now ain't that a coincidence, father?' smiled the man. 'St Joseph's is me own church!'

The priest studied the man and said. 'Strange ... I've been carryin' on my duties at St Joseph's for six years now, and I've not seen you there –

'Well now, father, Oy never said Oy was a fanatic!'

See also **Clergy, Faith, God, Prayer**

Repartee

The aristocratic young lord said to James McNeill Whistler, 'By the way, Whistler, I passed your house last night.'

'Thank you.'

Phone conversation

'Mr Noland told me to tell you he's not in.'

'Fine. Tell him I'm glad I didn't call.'

Hal Knobloch was late returning from lunch. Said his boss, Mr Axelrod: 'You're over an hour late!'

'That's true,' said Knobloch.

'Would you mind giving me a hint why?' asked Mr Axelrod.

'Not at all: I was having my hair cut.'

'Your *hair* cut? Do you think you ought to do that on company time?'

'Why not?' said Knobloch. 'The hair grew on company time.'

Mr Azelrod's eyes narrowed: 'That hair didn't *all* grow on company time!'

'T-true. That's why I didn't have it all cut off.'

'M'sieur Voltaire,' said a friend, 'it is a great surprise to me that you speak so highly of that man. He always says such unflattering things about you.'

'Well,' smiled Voltaire, 'perhaps we are both mistaken.'

See also **Chutzpa, Groucho, Put-downs, Restaurants, Retorts, Squelches, Waiters, Wit, Wordplay.**

Restaurants

Mr Lupowitz, a widower, had for years and years been eating at the same restaurant. On this Friday night, he sat down at his usual table; and his waiter, as usual, put before him the usual chopped liver. Mr Lupowitz ate the chopped liver. The waiter removed it, as usual, and, as usual, replaced it with a bowl of chicken soup.

As he started off, Lupowitz called, 'Eh – eh – eh! Vaiter!'

'What?'

'Please taste this soup.'

'*Hanh*?' the waiter frowned. 'It's the chicken soup you *always* have – '

'Taste it.'

'Listen, Mr Lupowitz: in all the years you are eating here did you ever *once* have a bad bowl chicken soup?'

'Vaiter – *taste – the – soup!*'

'Okay, what can I do?' scowled the waiter. 'I'll taste – where's the spoon?'

'Aha!' cried Lupowitz.

Sign in restaurant window

> EAT HERE AND YOU'LL NEVER
> EAT ANYPLACE ELSE AGAIN.

'Waiter!' sang out Mr Riesman. '*Wai*-ter!'

A waiter ambled over, 'You called?'

'No, you heard a *flute*,' said Mr Riesman bitterly.

'So what did the flute want?'

'What it wanted,' said Mr Riesman, 'is to know the exact nature of my offence!'

The waiter rubbed his chin. 'What offence?'

'That's what I want *you* to tell me, because since I came in here, a half-hour ago, I've been on nothing but bread and water!'

⌒

Sir Lawrence and Lady Runfield were in New York for the first time. To Lady Runfield, Sir Lawrence said, 'Lucinda, my dear, we get plenty of hotel food, and French and Italian cuisine, back home. Might this not be a splendid opportunity to try some authentic – Jewish comestibles?'

'What a *clever* idea, Lawrence,' said Lady Runfield. 'Let's do that.'

That night they taxied down to the Lower East Side, to Olinsky's Excellent Elite, perhaps the best Jewish restaurant in the Western Hemisphere. The owner, Ahron Olinsky, led them to a good table, placed two menus on it, and said, 'Enjoy, enjoy.'

The Runfields examined the items on the bill of fare. They could hardly understand such items as *'Derma ... heldzel ... matjes ... knaydlach...'* When the waiter arrived, Sir Lawrence said, 'Waiter, may I ask – ' he indicated the next table with a nod ' – what are those round, yellowish objects in the soup?'

'In the chicken soup?'

'Yes. They look like quite large dumplings...'

'Oh, them is *matzo* balls.'

'I beg your pardon?'

'*Mat-zo* balls,' the waiter repeated.

'I'll try them ... Lucinda, dear, you?'

'I'll join you. They *do* look lovely.'

The waiter disappeared and soon returned with two steaming dishes of chicken soup glorified by golden *knaydlach* (*matzo* balls).

The Runfields ate this exotic delicacy with *great* satisfaction. Indeed, not a drop of soup, nor a shred of *matzo* balls, were left in their plates.

'How *very* good!' said Sir Lawrence.

'*Super*,' said Lady Runfield. 'Waiter.... Tell me, what other part of the *matzo* do you people eat?'

⌒

Sign in restaurant window

By popular demand
UNDER NEW MANAGEMENT

∽

Scene: Blattberg's Gustatory Haven

CUSTOMER: Waiter, waiter!
WAITER: I'm here.
CUSTOMER: This fish is awful! It smells. It –
WAITER: Wait a *min*ute, mister! You ate here three nights ago and said the fish was delicious!
CUSTOMER: That was four – not three – nights ago!
WAITER: Mister, I give you my word, this is the same fish!

∽

Note on menu in Paris

> *To our American guests*:
> A 10 per cent discount is cheerfully given if you
> do not attempt to order in French.

See also **Chutzpa, Put-downs, Repartee, Retorts, Squelches, Waiters, Wit**

Retorts

An Englishman, visiting New York, passed a store window with nothing in it but a clock. He stepped inside.

From the back, a man with a *yarmulka* (skullcap) came forward.

The Englishman said, 'Hul-lo. May I ask: how long would it take to mend my watch? It's slowing down – '

'How should I know?' shrugged the proprietor. 'I don't fix watches. I'm a *mohel*.'

'A *what*?'

'A *mohel*. I circumcise . . .'

The Englishman sputtered, 'But *I* say – in your window – you have a clock!'

The *mohel* shrugged. 'So what would *you* put in the window?'

A visitor to San Francisco placed a garland of roses on the grave of his grandfather. As he turned to leave, he noticed an old Chinese gentleman placing a bowl of rice on a grave nearby. The American smiled.

The Chinese, noticing this, bowed. 'What pleases you so?' he politely inquired.

'I was just wondering – when do you expect the dead to eat that rice?'

'About the same time,' sighed the Chinese gentleman, 'that your dead smell those flowers.'

An English lord, noted for his arrogance, once asked Dr Chaim Weizmann, 'Weizmann, can you tell me why it is that you Jews are said to be so mercenary?'

To which Weizmann replied, 'For the same reason, milord, that you English are said to be gentlemen.'

During a dramatic moment in the performance of *King Lear*, in Yiddish, at a Houston Street theatre, an actor, at the climax of his great scene, collapsed on stage.

'Doctor!' cried another actor.

'Get a doctor!' shouted a stagehand.

'Is there a doctor in the house?!'

In the fourth row, a man rose. 'I'm a doctor!' He hurried up the stairs to the stage, bent over the prostrate actor, pried open an eyelid, felt the recumbent's pulse.

From the balcony an old lady shouted. 'Give – him – an – enema!'

The doctor leaned over and placed his ear against the fallen one's breast. Not a heartbeat was to be heard.

'Give – him – an – enema!' trumpeted the old lady in the gallery.

The doctor straightened up. 'Lady, this man is *dead*! An enema won't help!'

'It vouldn't *hoit*!' returned the old lady.

Scene: A Community Chest Reception

Mr Manley Emerson, somewhat tipsy, exclaimed, 'I'll have you know, sir – what was your name again?'

'Levitski.'

'I'll have you know, Mr Le-vit-ski, that I come from one of America's first families! In fact, one of my ancestors signed the Declaration of Independence.'

'So?' said Levitski. 'One of mine signed the Ten Commandments.'

See also **Chutzpa, Groucho, Put-downs, Repartee, Restaurants, Squelches, Waiters, Wit**

Revenge

On to Phipps's Fine Foreign Cars lot drove a magnificent Silver Cloud Rolls Royce, out of which stepped a finely dressed woman, all in black. 'I want to sell this car,' she announced.

The owner, Kenneth Phipps, glanced at the speedometer (only 3,050 miles!), got into the driver's seat, turned on the ignition, listened to the motor . . . 'Uh – how much do you want for this car, madam?'

'Fifty dollars.'

Mr Phipps's jaw dropped. 'What is this, ma'am – a joke?'

'No. Just give me fifty dollars and a signed bill of sale.'

'Lady, are you out of your skull?' exclaimed Phipps. 'Don't you know that this Rolls is worth, even secondhand, thirty or forty *thous*and dollars?'

'Yes. Let's not waste time.'

'Madam, is this a stolen car?' asked Phipps.

'Certain not!'

'Is there a lien on it?'

'Absolutely not. . . . Now look, do you or don't you – '

'Certainly I want to buy it! But fifty dollars! There *must* be a trick. *Why* would *anyone* in her right mind – '

The woman in black arched an eyebrow. 'I am entirely in my right mind, sir. I think you will agree. You see, my husband just

died. And in his will, he stated that Flora Delago, who was his secretary – and his goddam mistress – should get the full proceeds
from the sale of his Silver Cloud Rolls Royce! . . . Give me the fifty
dollars.'

∽

Emanuel Gittleman was deep in sleep when his phone rang and
rang. He lifted the receiver. 'Hollo,' he grumbled.

'Mr Gittleman? In apartment three-B?'

'Yeah.'

'This is Mrs Trautman, in Four-G. It's already half past three at
night – and your dog's barking is driving me absolutely *crazy!*' The
phone slammed down . . .

The next night, at 3:45 A.M., Mrs Trautman's telephone rang.
'Hello,' she mumbled.

'Mrs Trautman? In Four-G?'

'Yeah.'

'This is Mr Gittleman, in Three-B. I want to tell you something.'

'At a quarter to *four* in the morning?! Are you crazy?!'

'I don't own a dog.'

∽

Filip Marisol and Enrico Oquendo simply could not bear the
Castro regime any longer. They decided there was only one solution to Cuba's dictatorship: to assassinate Fidel. Both being army
veterans, they got out their rifles, fitted them with precision
sights, and concealed themselves in the doorway of a building
Fidel was scheduled to ride past.

They waited. Hour after hour, they waited.

Finally, Filip whispered, 'Enrico, let's hope nothing hoppened
to the *bastardo!*'

∽

The pretty young thing sitting on the stool at the bar was
approached by an attractive college boy, smiling, 'Are you alone,
miss?'

'What kind of a girl do you think I am?' she cried.

He reddened. 'I just wanted to buy you a drink.'

'No, no, no!' she shouted. 'I won't go up to your room!'

'Hey, calm *down!*' said the young man.

'No! I won't meet you at that motel in twenty minutes!'

Absolutely flabbergasted, the college man made his way through a sea of indignant stares and glares to a table in the far, dark corner.

In a moment, the pretty girl left the bar and, smiling broadly, came to the college boy. 'Sorry to create such a scene. I'm a graduate student in the Psychology Department, doing research for a report: "Masculine Behaviour in Unexpected Situations"!'

The young man stared at her, then leaped to his feet. '*What?*' he shouted. 'One hundred dollars? For twenty minutes? Never!' And with that he stalked out of the bar.

See also **Ingenuity, Hanky-Panky, Scoundrels, Stratagems**

Reviews of Note

The G—— Quartet played Brahms last night at Carnegie Hall. Brahms lost.

PERCY HAMMOND

The plot of this play was intended to be in a light vein, but the vein became varicose.

WOLCOTT GIBBS

The movie version needed something – possibly burial.

DAVID LARDNER

She ran the gamut of human emotions, from A to B.

DOROTHY PARKER

'—— opened last night at the Morosco. Why?'

BROOKS ATKINSON

I have knocked everything in this play except the chorus girls' knees, and there God anticipated me.

PERCY HAMMOND

About the play *The Greeks Had a Word for It*: So did the Hebrews:
lousy.   DOROTHY PARKER

See also **Critics, Sarcasm**

Russia

The applicant for membership stood before the three members of
the Admission Committee of the Fifth District of the Communist
party in Odessa.

'Vladimir Ardjenovic,' said the committee chairman, 'suppose
you received, say – one million rubles from America. What would
you do with it?'

'I would turn it over to the party!'

'Good,' said a member of the committee. 'And suppose you had
two automobiles. What would you do?'

'I would give one to the party for use by members of the executive.'

'And suppose you had two warm winter overcoats? . . .' asked
the third member.

Vladimir Ardjenovic wrinkled his brow, thinking.

'Comrade,' said the chairman, 'after such swift answers to the
other questions, what makes you hesitate on this one?'

'Well, Comrade Chairman, I do have two overcoats . . .'

Azriel Rubinstein stood before the commissar of Passport Controls and with the utmost earnestness pleaded, 'Comrade Commissar Khreznevsky, I am seventy years old, and it is now six *years*
since I began filing applications for permission, from your office,
for me to emigrate from the Soviet Union.'

Commissar Khreznevsky nodded. '*Da.*'

'All of my immigration papers from Israel have been approved
and are in your files – '

Khreznevsky nodded. '*Da, da.*'

'Comrade Commissar, please tell me – why, *why* will you not let me leave the Soviet Union?'

The commissar assumed his sternest expression. 'Becouse in your brain, Rubinstein, you hold vary important secret – *scientific* secrets! Those secrets – if we lat you out of Soviet Union – you will give to Israelis, allies of copitolistic USA – '

'But that's impossible!' cried Rubinstein. 'I no longer *know* a single scientific secret. Have you forgotten? I have been barred from my laboratory for over fifteen years! I have not been allowed to attend any scientific meetings! I have not been given a single classified document about a single weapon or experiment – '

'*Da, da,*' nodded Khreznevsky.

' – And even when I *was* working on missiles, fifteen years ago, we were so far behind the Americans – '

'*Dot,*' thundered the commissar, 'is the secret!'

∽

Hit movie in Odessa:

ESCAPE TO ALCATRAZ!

∽

In the courtyard of the fearful Lubyankow Prison, three condemned men faced the firing squad.

'Andrey Anatovich Narpovikoff,' the commanding officer declaimed, 'for sabotage against glorious Soviet Republic, you have been sentenced to death. Do you have last request?'

'Yes,' said Andrey Anatovich Narpovikoff. 'Please bury my ashes outside Kremlin Wall – near great Lenin's tomb, in honour of glorious Vladimir Ilyich Lenin.'

'All right. Squad: . . . Ready . . . aim . . . fire!'

Down slid Andrey Anatovich Narpovikoff.

'Nikolai Soniavich Premenyev, you have been sentenced to death for trying to smuggle enemies of state across border to Finland. . . Do you have last request?'

'*Da, da,* comrade. Bury me in Tiflis, where Josef Stalin was born.'

'Fine. Squad, reload: . . . Ready . . . aim . . . fire!'

To the stones fell Nikolai Soniavich Premenyev.

To the third condemned man, the executing officer announced: 'Yitzkhok Mandelstein, you have been found guilty of seven attempts to leave glorious motherland, using forged passport and forged exit papers. What is your last request?'

'For me, please,' wheezed Mandelstein, 'just spread my ashes over grave of Comrade Ilya Borganovich, Executive Secretary of the Politburo.'

'Borganovich?' The executioner frowned. 'But Comrade Borga-novich is not dead!'

Mandelstein blinked amiably. 'I don't mind waiting.'

♋

Semyon Grizor trudged along the road, carrying a large load of bread. He beheld a peasant working in the field. '*Tovarich*,' he sang out, 'how far is it to the railroad tracks?'

'Just follow this lane for ten minutes.'

'Thank you.'

'Wait, *tovarich*,' called the peasant. 'You can't get a ticket there. For a ticket, you have to go to the station – '

'I don't want a ticket. I just want the tracks – to lay myself down on. I'm going to kill myself.'

'So why are you carrying that big loaf of bread?'

Grizor shrugged. 'By the time a train arrives in Russia, a man can *starve* to death.'

♋

The Politburo recently received a secret request from one of Russia's Arab satellites: could Soviet experts tell them the age of a mummy just discovered in an archaeological dig, which the sheik was delivering by air?

The Russians promptly cabled the sheik:

MUMMY ARRIVED. INVESTIGATION UNDER
WAY. CERTAIN WE CAN DETERMINE EXACT AGE.

Five days later the chief Soviet expert, Vlasy Ivanovich Barosti-nov, told the Politburo that the mummy was exactly – 5,344 years old.

The head of the Politburo promptly phoned Barostinov. 'Con-grotulation, Tovarich Barostinov. For soch feat, I will give you Commendation. But I most be sure *you* are sure – *ob*solutely sure – the mommy is old five t'ousand t'ree – '

'Comrade Commissar,' exclaimed Barostinov, 'I am positively sure!'

'You used scientific carbon-dating?'

'*Nyet*. Comrade Commissar.'

'Electronic X-ray?'

'No, no,' said Barostinov. 'I found out through most reliable method!'

'What is dot?'

'The mommy made full confassion!'

⌒

'Grampa Vassily,' said the little girl, 'what do you think of Karl Marx?'

'A great man. A very great man!'

'And Comrade Lenin?'

'A great man. A giant.'

'And Josef Stalin?'

'A monster! A lunatic. We learned the truth about him from Comrade Khruschev!'

'And what about Comrade Gorbachov?'

'Hush, Natasha! We won't know until he's dead.'

Old Mischa Gretzkin, aged eighty-seven, lay in his bed in Kharkhov, dying. Came a harsh knocking on the door.

'W-who is it?' quavered Gretzkin.

'The *Malakh ha-movess* [angel of death],' came an orotund voice. 'Fear not –'

'Who's afraid?' shouted Gretzkin. 'I thought it was the KGB.'

Salesmen

In the circles of England's life insurance agents, the name of Humphrey R. Watlaw had become a legend. Many were the tales exchanged about Humphrey R. Watlaw's extraordinary ingenuity and his astonishing sales record.

One day, Chauncey Murk, another salesman in the Phoenix Life Assurance Agency Ltd, was lunching with Watlaw at the

Silver Swan Pub and, over the introductory pint of bitter, asked, 'Humphrey, old bean, you and I have been friends all these many years. You live in Putney and I live and work in Sevenoaks – so neither of us is in the potential customers' territory of the other. I promise to keep your words a secret, my word of honour...'

'What *are* you going all round Robin Hood's barn about, Chauncey?'

'Your astonishing record! I mean, your sales record, old boy. Why, you sell three times the life insurance policies of any of the three hundred agents on Phoenix's staff.... Humphrey, old chap, what *is* your special sales technique? You surely *must* have one...'

'I daresay I do,' chuckled Watlaw. 'And if you promise to take my secret to the grave...'

'Word of honour! Absolutely!'

'Very well, old chap. The truth of the matter is that whenever I have a prospect for life insurance tottering on the edge, so to speak, unsure of his decision, I take the policy, fold it neatly, place it in my briefcase, and, with the utmost friendliness, say, "My *dear* fellow, you need not make a decision as important as this one, so long as you are so beset by reservations. Why not put the worry off for a bit? Think it over – carefully. Sleep on it.... And tomorrow, sometime, I'll ring you up, and you give me your answer – "' Watlaw grinned '"' – if, that is, you wake up."'

☡

On a street in the East Bronx, two hardware stores, directly across the street from each other, sprouted huge, two-storey-high banners. One of these signs announced:

BERNARDO CHAVEZ
BANKRUPTCY SALE
GOING OUT OF BUSINESS!
EVERYTHING MUST GO! 50–75 PERCENT OFF!!

The banner across the street read:

LOST LEASE! MUST MOVE!
TREMENDOUS SALE
BARGAINS – BARGAINS – BARGAINS!
MARGOLIS BROTHERS
FOUNDED 1938

A passerby saw an old man, in shirtsleeves and suspenders, standing in front of Margolis Brothers. A plastic name tag on his shirt pocket read: B. J. MARGOLIS.

'Mr Margolis,' said the pedestrian, 'you must be having quite a problem.'

'What problem?'

'With this going-out-of-business sale, when your competitor, right across the street, is going out of business, too.'

Margolis snorted. 'That Chavez? That Johnny-come-yesterday? Look, mister. Chavez will be out of business inside a week. But Margolis? Me and my brothers? We have built up a *reputation* for going out of business! People know they can *rely* on us. Chavez? Who can take his word for it? But *we* – we'll be here another forty years!'

○

Maurice Einziger, owner of Maurice's Masterpiece Furs, was considered (even by his competitors) to be a master of salesmanship. Once a new customer was trying on a magnificent mink coat, preening before the triple mirror. 'Nice ... yes ... very beautiful, Mr Einziger. But is it – practical?'

'"Practical?"' blinked Eingziger. 'What could be more warm, more light on the shoulders, more long-lasting than a mink coat where every skin is hand-selected by me personally, designed by my designer from Paris, cut and sewed and stitched by the finest craftsmen in the world?!'

The lady hesitated. 'But – suppose I'm wearing this expensive coat and get caught in a terrible downpour – rain, rain, rain?!'

Einziger nodded with complete understanding. 'So tell me: did you ever hear of a mink carrying an umbrella?'

○

'Before I present my company's entirely new and amazing policy, Mr Folger, may I ask: how much life insurance are you presently carrying?'

'I'd say fourteen thousand dollars,' said Folger.

The insurance salesman drew back in shock. 'Good Lord! Mr Folger! How long do you think you can stay dead these days on that kind of money?!'

⌒

Carey Bushnell was a clever sharpshooter and a master of deceit. He had just moved into a new office, on the door of which he had a painter place these words:

BUSHNELL WORLDWIDE INVESTMENT SERVICES
INVESTMENT ANALYSIS AND FINANCIAL ADVICE
C. H. BUSHNELL, PRES.

Carey was sitting in his desk chair, wondering what to do next, when the door opened.

At once he lifted his phone, saying, 'No, I don't think the price of gold will bother us.' He signalled the man in the doorway to enter and sit down ... 'I'd buy a hundred thousand shares.' Covering the telephone speaker with his palm, Carey whispered to his visitor, 'Tokyo calling. Be with you in a moment.' Into the phone he said, 'Michio, I bought you ten thousand Fynborn warrants. Right.... Cotton futures? Not at this time.... I've got a call in to Frankfurt to sell your Deutschmarks.... Thanks for calling. Sayonara.' He put the phone down briskly and addressed his visitor, smiling: 'Well, sir. What can I do for you?'

The visitor said, 'I just came to hook up your phone, Mr Bushnell.'

⌒

Scene: Armenian-American Sports Arcade

Mr Karkorian watched his new salesman, Georgi, expounding to a particularly glum customer. 'An' o' course you need line. *Line:* new, strong line, to fish.'

'Okay,' sighed the customer.

'Also, with you got line, musta have reel, eh? Nice *reel?*'

'Ah – supposa.'

'Also, beeg boots? Up to here – look. Boots? Is no water come in!'

'Yeah, yeah.'

'Maybee – aha! – fish *vest*, also! Becouse today – special price...'

'Suppose.'

'An'a look – hat! *Hat.* Beauful hat!'

'Yeah....'

Georgi wrapped the whole pile of gear and pumped the gloomy customer's hand. 'Goot lock, 'svedanyia.'

The customer departed, sighing.

Mr Karkorian came over to the salesman. 'Georgi, fordy year I be in thees *lafka* – and *never* I see salesman lika you! Customer come – ask fish-hook. One lousy *hook*. An'a you talkin'm in line, rill, boot, vast – '

'Na, na, na,' Georgi interrupted. *'No* come in f'hook. Come in for aspirin.'

'Asprin? Wha' for *asprin*?'

'He think we drugstore. Say to me, 'Aspirin. For wife. Wife she – you know, time month . . .' So I tell 'm, "Ah, so while she outa commish, why you no go fish?"''

⌒

'Hey, Nat, what a day I had yesterday,' said Morty Lazar. 'From the Lamston chain! I got an order for six thousand dollars!'

'Sure, sure,' said Nat dryly.

'You don't believe me?'

'No.'

'Okay, I'll prove it!' exclaimed Lazar. 'I'll show you the cancellation!'

⌒

The old optometrist was breaking in a new assistant: ' – And after you have fitted the new glasses, the customer usually asks, "How much is this?" and you say, "Ten dollars." You wait an instant – and if the customer says nothing you add – "for the frames. The lenses are ten dollars more." Again you hesitate . . . If the customer says nothing, you add, "Each" . . .'

See also **Business, Ingenuity, Just Jokes, Stratagems**

Sarcasm

A flustered bridge player asked his partner. 'How would *you* have played that hand?'

'Under an assumed name.'

An English columnist, noted for the sharpness of his pen and the penetration of his wit, one day wrote:

> – the eminently sensible bill was defeated in the House of Commons. One wonders how much longer the people of Britain can have faith in a body half of whose members are idiots.

Several days later, the columnist printed this memorable retraction:

> A spate of angry mail from readers has denounced the author of this column for saying that half the members of the House of Commons are idiots. I have been urged to apologize for so harsh and incorrect a statement. Herewith, my apology. I am happy to correct my observation: half the members of the House of Commons are not idiots.

An actress shaped like Raquel Welch stepped out of the shower, in her suite at a fine New York hotel, dried off, and, stark naked, stepped into the bedroom.

There she saw a window cleaner, admiring her through the glass.

The actress was so startled that she froze, standing there, speechless, nude. Her trance was broken by the window cleaner: 'What's the matter, sweetheart? Never seen a window cleaner before?'

The bus was jam-packed at rush hour. A very large, very fat woman got in and as the bus started up, gazed about angrily. Michael Killigan, a tiny man, hiding behind his newspaper, slunk lower . . .

In a loud, grating voice the woman declared, 'Isn't there one polite man here who will offer me his place?!'

Killigan sighed, lowered his paper, and rose. 'Well now, madam, I guess I'll make a small contribution . . .'

The diner stared at the waiter who was placing the soup before him. 'Are you the same waiter who took my order?'

'Yeah.'

'Are you *sure?'*

'Sure I'm sure,' huffed the waiter. 'Why do you ask such a question?'

'Because by now, I expected a much older man...'

◅

Our rabbi prayed to the Lord that the rich give more to the poor – and God has answered half that prayer: the poor have agreed to accept.

◅

As old Muldoon, clay pipe and all, entered the elevator of the posh London store, the ex-Coldstream Guard at the controls closed the scissors gate with force and in an insolent tone asked, 'Well now, paddy, what floor would *you* want to get off on?'

'Noomber three,' grinned Muldoon, '*if* Oy'm not takin' Your Lordship out of your way.'

◅

The new arrival at the summer resort sat down in a beach chair. 'I got up at dawn!' he boasted, 'to see the sunrise.'

'You soitinly picked the right time,' said his neighbour.

See also **Chutzpa, Groucho, Put-downs, Repartee, Restaurants, Retorts, Shnorrers, Squelches, Waiters**

Scoundrels

One of my favourite childhood memories involves a men's clothing store in our neighbourhood, which was owned by a pair of partners who, rumour had it, sent eight children through college simply by pretending to be deaf. The ingenious haberdashers' deaf caper is unmatched, I think, for simplicity, duplicity, and punishment to the greedy. Here is how it worked:

One partner would wait on a customer, extolling the excellence of the wool, the styling, the needlework of this or that suit. Often the customer would, naturally, ask, 'How much is this suit?'

'What?' asked the salesman, cupping his ear.

'How – much – does – it – cost?' the customer repeated more loudly.

'Hanh?'

'*How much is the suit?*' the customer would shout.

'Ah, the *price!* I'll ask the boss.' Whereupon the 'clerk' would turn and shout toward the back of the store: '*How much is the beautiful navy-blue, double-breasted suit?*'

The 'boss' would shout back: '*Forty dollars!*'

The 'deaf' clerk would tell the customer: 'The boss says, "Twenty dollars."'

Need I describe how swiftly many otherwise righteous men, young and old, plunked down their twenty dollars and hastened out of the store, chortling?

from my *Passions and Prejudices*

Mr Bradshaw was walking briskly to his house, down the dark street from the railway station, when a thin, woebegone stranger suddenly came out of a parking lot and stepped in front of him. 'Pardon me, sir. Could you help a man who's really down on his luck? So help me God, sir, all I have to my name is this gun.'

'Hey, Sheldon. What's wrong?'

'Wrong?'

'Yeah. You look pretty darn miserable.'

'I'm miserable because I had a sore toe, so I went to a doctor. He examined me and said, "It's not too bad. I'll have you walking by tomorrow morning."'

'And did he?'

'You bet he did. He stole my car.'

W. C. Fields once leered, 'You can't cheat an honest man.' That moralism has become the Eleventh Commandment in American folk thought: but it is not true.

Consider the many victims of a master of skulduggery in Watchung, New Jersey. One Saturday night, just before Labour Day, this scoundrel placed a night-deposit box outside the entrance to a bank in a large shopping centre on Route 22. He set his beautifully made night-deposit box, which was a fake, right next to the bank's night-deposit box. Since banks are closed on Sundays and Labour Day, one of the busiest weekends of the year, storekeepers were tickled pink to deposit their cash, and cheques made out to 'cash,' in the night-deposit boxes.

Early Tuesday morning, the wizard picked up his receptacle. The illicit contents came to over $26,000 in cash and $3,500 in checks, which provided our *Gonif* with much exultation and professional pride.

The police force of Watchung, New Jersey, refused to tell the Associated Press exactly what the fake deposit box looked like. This was quite correct of them in my opinion. Excessive verisimilitude in reporting criminal artefacts is pretty certain to: (a) instruct and (b) encourage imitators. Only a fool would publicly provide a good working description of a fake night-deposit box.

As for the name Watchung, I marvel at the esthetic satisfaction that nomenclature can provide.

from my Passions and Prejudices

Robert and Flora Bascombe received, in the mail, two tickets to the biggest hit on Broadway, a show for which tickets had been sold out for three months. Whoever had sent the tickets had forgotten to include a note with the donor's name. The tickets were for the following night.

The Bascombes went to the show, which they enjoyed hugely. When they returned to their apartment, their bedroom was turned upside down: the woman's furs and jewels were gone, the man's fine cuff links were gone. And on a pillow was this note:

Now you know.

SILKY PINCUS DESCRIBES
THE CASE OF HOKEY SLOCUM

'Hokey' (Hobart) Slocum was one of the most artistic cheque-hikers in the greater Manhattan area. He really *milked* the bank account of Mrs Gwendolyn Blair, who was forty-six and loaded.

Her hubby is a VP at Continental Parachutes, Inc. Hokey nets hisself like twelve grand, with no overhead except pen and ink, before Mrs Blair finds out she is overdrawn – plenty. She gets very mad on her bank when they can't explain things to her satisfaction. So she decides to hire a PI – to find the unknown forger. I take her on as a client and pass the word around our snitch circuit. Soon I get a tip that the penmanship kite has to be the work of Hokey Slocum ... I turn that over to Headquarters.... Inside fourteen hours the forgery boys collar Hokey.... He would of taken a sure 1–5 fall – except for one thing...

Mrs Blair had to confront Hokey in the station house, to tell the cops if she knows him or ever seen him before. Mrs Blair is negative. But Hokey puts on such a cornball act, exclaiming he don't know the difference between right and wrong on account of the brain surgery he had to have for his Korea war wound in the service of our country, that Mrs Blair, who did not know Korea from anaemia, gets all choked up. She informs me that if Hokey will return the boodle and promise never to do such a naughty thing again, she will drop all charges...

So I get a smart lawyer, Lester Plosher, and tell him I have come to love Hokey, as who don't, and can he help that true artist out in his moment of need?... The mouthpiece lays on a deal with an assistant DA he knows and despises, a clown named Hamilcar Strable who happens to be very religious, so he is jumping to save a soul, plus gain a contributor to his forthcoming primary campaign for a councilman from Staten Island. To Mrs Blair, Hokey antes up three grand – and he signs a promissory note that he will cough up the balance in monthly instalments.... So Justice was done and a trial avoided to save the taxpayers' money, plus our overcrowded prisons don't have to cram another sardine into the can.

Well, Hokey makes his monthly payments – the first of each month, on the dot. He borrows the dough from Chomski and Bell, who are actually bondsmen, but they have a sensitive nose for any type buck, and they charge like 19 per cent. ... The kicker is, that brainy Hokey insists on making his monthly payments to Mrs Blair in person.

Hokey is a nifty dresser and a talker so smooth you could use his words for eyeglasses. And when, in the fifth month of fulfilling his legal obligation, he cannot go on the cuff for more scratch, from even the firm of Chomski and Bell, Hokey tells Mrs Blair he is considering hari-kari, even though he never set a foot in Japan. In fact, Hokey cries, 'Madam, I throw myself on your mercy!' – and he throws hisself on her *zaftig* body as well.

One thing Hokey always could spot a mile away in the smog is a middle-age dame who is hungry for love, on account of her hubby is not giving her enough of it. Next thing we hear is Mrs Gwendolyn Blair is filing for divorce. . . . Hokey, who can give lessons in savvy, abets the split by finding the chick in the steno pool at Continental Parachutes from who Mr Blair has been getting nookey.

So Mr Blair don't contest the divorce. Gwendolyn flies to Old Mexico. Inside two hours of getting her decree of freedom, she becomes Mrs Hobart Slocum III. That 'III' did not refer to Hokey's pedigree, as your society columnists assumed, but to the number of nuptials he has committed. . . . So in one shrewd play, admired by all students of the con, Hokey has wiped out his debt, avoided the slammer, and is now residing in the spacious Blair spread in Bucks County . . .

There's a PS. Hokey is now raising Holsteins or some other type animal. I never in a million years would of cast him as a dairyman – except for one thing. Hokey always had a thing for oversize boobies. And Gwendolyn sure had them!

from my Silky!

A classmate of mine at college (let's call him Theobald Prysock) grew so disgusted by the silly hazings he had to endure as a freshman 'pledge' to a certain fraternity that he decided to quit. But moral outrage so burned within the soul of Theobald Prysock that he could not simply return his pledge pin. Theobald spend days on end seeking an act of reprisal that would properly express his feelings for the fraternity 'brothers' he was disowning. What he finally did was masterful.

One night, after his peers were all snoring away, Theobald tiptoed down the stairs to the fraternity house to the fraternity library. He closed the door, removed a book, turned to the flyleaf, and inscribed therein:

GIFT
OF
THEOBALD PRYSOCK

He put the book back on the shelf and proceeded to the next. . . .

It took my pal Theobald a good four hours, I believe, to donate the entire library of Phi Gimmel Epsilon – to itself.

Can you imagine a happier soul than Theo, his lavish philanthropy completed, as he carried his suitcase into the night?

I feel privileged to have known such a rogue.

from my *Passions and Prejudices*

See also **Aplomb, Chutzpa, Ingenuity, Salesmen, Stratagems, True Tales**

Sex

It could be that there are some things in life that are better than sex, and some things are certainly worse. But no man or woman on earth ever found anything just like it.

W. C. FIELDS

Chastity: The most peculiar of all sexual aberrations.

REMY DE GOURMONT

Christianity has done sex an enormous service by making it a sin.

ANATOLE FRANCE

Sex: The most fun you can have without laughing.

The ability to make love frivolously is the chief characteristic which distinguishes human beings from animals.

HEYWOOD BROUN

> The turtle lives 'twixt plated decks
> Which carefully conceal its sex.
> I think it clever of the turtle.
> In such a fix to be so fertile.

A gloss on OGDEN NASH

'Why, Jess Farnow!' cried Mrs Blair. 'I hear you had triplets! Is that so?'

'Oh, yes.'

'Well, gracious me! Congratulations! What a rare, rare blessing. How rarely does one hear of – '

'My doctor said triplets happen only once in two million times!' said Jess.

Mrs Blair blanched. 'Good God, Jess! When did you have time to do the housework?'

࿐

'Oh, my dear, *dear* Violet.' Hensor-Atley murmured, 'I – I – I love you most awfully!'

Violet Penfield-Sym sighed, 'How true . . . how terribly true.'

࿐

When they awakened from their night of love, the lovesick girl murmured. 'Darling, truthfully – am I the first girl you ever took to bed?'

'It's possible. . . . Were you at Disneyland in 1973?'

࿐

'Listen, doc,' sighed old Mr Krantz, 'you been my doctor already forty years. You know I am seventy-eight years old – and naturally things are a little run down.'

'For instance?'

'Well, most important, of course, is sex. My, what a man I used to be between the sheets! Now – well, making love once a month is already something to be glad about. But my friend, Nate Eckel, he is at least eighty-three, eighty-four – and yesterday he told me that he makes love to his wife two-three times a week!'

The doctor studied Mr Krantz. 'So?'

'So?' Krantz echoed. 'Is that all you have to say? *'So?'* I am dying of *envy!* Doc, isn't there something I can *do?'*

'Sure,' said the doctor. 'Tell Eckel the same thing.'

࿐

The marines have perfected survival techniques – that is, ingenious methods of survival if lost on a desert, in a jungle, in a rowboat, on mountains, in forests. . . . In one lecture, the men were being taught about food to be found in any wood: termites, slugs, grubworms. 'And grasshoppers,' said the instructor, 'are a tasty, nutritious food. In fact, King Solomon used to feed grasshoppers to his thousand wives.'

A voice cut in: 'The hell with what he gave the women. What did *he* eat?'

                                    ↪

I wonder what fool it was who first invented kissing.

                                                    JONATHAN SWIFT

                                    ↪

One of the medical staff of British Overseas Air, a psychiatrist, was giving a pilot the customary six-month checkup. 'And about how much alcohol do you consume a week, captain?'

'Oh, perhaps five or six beers. No whisky.'

'And drugs – drugs of any sort?'

'None, doctor. None at all.'

'Cigarettes per day?'

'I do not smoke cigarettes.'

'Cigars?'

'Perhaps one a month.'

'How do you sleep, captain?'

'Extremely well. Go off a moment or so after my head touches the pillow.'

'Do you ever get severe headaches?'

'No, sir.'

'Are you likely to develop emotional tension – during, say, an altercation?'

'On the contrary, doctor. I *rarely* get into an argument. And I don't believe I have been involved in an altercation since I was ten.'

The psychiatrist nodded, scanned his checklist, and said, 'Finally, about sexual adjustment, captain. When was the last time you slept with a woman?'

The captain deliberated. '1958 . . .'

'1958?!' The psychiatrist gasped. 'Good lord, captain! That long ago?'

The pilot seemed puzzled. 'But, doctor – ' he glanced at his watch ' – it's only 22:10 now.'

                                    ↪

Irish foreplay: 'Bessie, brace yourself.'

French foreplay: 'The food will get cold . . .'

British foreplay: 'Would you mind terribly? You *can* think of the garden . . .'

Jewish foreplay: Two hours of pleading.

American foreplay: 'Hi.'

WASP foreplay: Drying the dishes.

೧

Pretty Maureen Feeny, sleeping next to her husband, was having a marvellous dream. A handsome stranger was making passionate love to her. In her sleep, Mrs Feeny sighed and moaned in ecstasy, then blurted: 'Oh . . . good God! I hear footsteps. . . . Go! Fast! It's my husband!'

Mr Feeny jumped out of the window.

೧

As the groom embraced the bride, holding her in a long, fervent kiss, the whisper of a child in the front row of the chapel was clearly heard: 'Daddy, is he spreading his pollen on her now?'

೧

Young Simpkins wrote a long letter to his mother, a week after his arrival at Annapolis, to tell her of his exciting new life, his friends, his courses. 'And next week they are going to teach me how to use a sextant.'

Mrs Simpkins telephoned her minister. 'Reverend Dean, do you *know* what the navy is teaching our young men?!'

೧

'Say, laddie, an' have y' seen Casey O'Hare in recent days?'
'Nay.'
'He's in hospital, with many a broken bone.'
'Is he now? What happened?'
'Well, laddie, Casey always said sex on the TV is pretty awful. An' it is, me boy, it is. Casey fell off.'

೧

Deep in the night, Brecher shook his wife. 'Lena . . . Lena . . .'
She mumbled, 'Mmh. . . . What?'
'Darling, I got you two aspirins and a glass water.'
Lena sat up. 'What's with you, Nat?'

'For your headache, Lena.'
'Who has a headache?'
'You don't have a headache?'
'No.'
'Great. Let's make love.'

See also **Bachelors, Hanky-panky, Love, Marriage**

Shadchens

Note: Jewish marriages were customarily arranged by the heads of families. In Eastern Europe, the professional matchmaker, or *shadchen*, performed a very important social function. Not only did he travel from village to village, to scour communities for available boys and nubile girls; he was a purveyor of news, gossip, rumours; he gathered information about eligible mates, weighing their family backgrounds, noting individual qualities, matching personality factors in an undertaking that today is assigned to computer-dating services.

L. R.

'I can't believe it!' exclaimed Shlissel the Shadchen. 'A young man like you – intelligent, attractive, making a good living ... such a good Jewish boy isn't *married?!*'

'True, true,' sighed the young man. 'And don't think I wouldn't like to get married ...'

'So think of all the nice girls I awready brought to your attention!'

'I know. But the truth, Shlissel, is this: whenever I meet a girl who would make a good wife – take care of me, share my joys and sorrows, even cook like my mother ... she *looks* like my father.'

Sigmond Shlossberg, having patiently borne with Feivel the Shadchen's hyperbole, said, 'But in all the wonderful things you told me about the girl, you left out one important thing!'

'Me? Feivel? Never! ... What did I leave out?'

'She – limps!'

'Only when she *walks!*' protested the *shadchen*.

⌒

In a certain town, there was a grievous shortage of marriageable young men. One of them, Beryl Chodovitch, quite ugly and equally conceited, came to Baruch the Shadchen and said, 'I am finally considering getting married. But I warn you – I'll accept nothing but a very *special* match. And the dowry has to be plenty!'

Baruch studied young Chodovitch, then said, 'Fortunately, I have just the girl for you! Her father is rich, and she is beautiful, well educated – '

'Wait a minute,' said Chodovitch. 'Why isn't such a girl married?'

The *shadchen* raised his hand, 'You want to know why such a girl is not married? I want you to know – that's why her rich father may accept someone who is not – excuse me, Beryl – the most attractive young man in the world. I will be perfectly frank. This beautiful, educated, charming girl has one affliction: once a year, she goes crazy.'

'She goes *crazy?*'

'Yes. Sad, but true. But that doesn't have to bother you, Beryl! She doesn't make any trouble – she just goes quietly *meshugge* – for only one day. Then she's absolutely charming and normal for another year.... And her *dow*ry!'

Beryl Chodovitch smiled. 'Let's go see her right now.'

'Not yet,' said Baruch. 'This match must wait.'

'Until when?'

'Until the day she goes out of her mind again.'

⌒

Muttel Metchnik, a marriage broker, having sung the praises of a female client, brought his excited young man to see her.

The prospect took one look at the damsel, paled, said, 'Glad to meet you,' and signalled to Metchnik.

'What's the matter?' asked the *shadchen*.

The young man whispered, 'You said she was young, and she's almost forty! You said she was attractive, and she looks like a chicken! You said she was – '

'You don't need to whisper,' said Muttel. 'She's hard of hearing, too.'

⌒

Pincus Ofek, an extremely resourceful *shadchen*, was impressing
his young prospect, Hi Winkel, with the boundless virtues and
charms of the unmarried Ruchel Bernitz, ending, 'And to look at,
that alone – my boy, Ruchel Bernitz is like a painting!'

Hi Winkel could hardly wait for his blind date. . . .

When Pincus Ofek came to the young man's flat the next morning, he beheld a frosty Winkler.

'You didn't fall head-over-heels with Ruchel?' the *shadchen*
inquired.

'*Fall* for her?! Why, her eyes are crossed; and her nose is
crooked, and when she laughs, one side of her mouth – '

'Stop!' Pincus Ofek presented an open palm. 'Why didn't you
tell me you don't like Picasso?!'

⌒

Ezra Karper confronted the *shadchen*, scowling, 'You lied to me!'

'Me? Lie? *Never!*' retorted the *shadchen*. 'Isn't she pretty? Well
educated? Loves music?'

'Yes, yes,' said Ezra, 'but you also told me she comes from a
famous family! You said her father is dead – and I just learned *he's
in jail* – '

Sneered the *shadchen*. '*That* you call living?'

⌒

'Listen, Mr Greenblatt,' the *shadchen* complained, 'I'll be glad to
look through my files – and even make a special trip to certain
places – to find a suitable husband for your Etta.'

'If only that could come true!' sighed Mr Greenblatt.

'But frankly – I have to tell you, your daughter looks like she's
forty years old!'

'Looks, looks,' scoffed Greenblatt. '*Who* goes by looks? Some
teenagers look like mature matrons and some middle-agers – '

'Wait.' The *shadchen* raised a minatory palm. 'You specifically
told me that your daughter is only twenty-nine years old!'

Mr Greenblatt gazed into the distance.

'Mr Greenblatt – *twenty-nine* years old? . . . Is that true?'

Greenblatt replied, 'Partly.'

⌒

Asa Schwartz was twenty-nine, attractive, well spoken, well off –
and leading a bachelor's dream life.

For such a marriageable young man to remain single (nay, to persist in refusing to consider marriage) struck Shimen the Shadchen as an offence in the eyes of the Lord. 'Who ever heard a nice Jewish boy of twenty-nine, shouldn't at least be going steady?!' the astounded *shadchen* asked Asa.

'*I*,' said Asa, 'don't go steady, because *I* don't want to get married.'

'Why not?' demanded Shimen. 'Give me awready one good reason! Just one!'

'Because I'm having the time of my life,' smiled Asa. 'No ball-and-chain around my neck. No nagging. No whining. No fancy clothes to pay for. And I come when I want, I go where and when I want, I can date a different girl every night of the week! . . . Tell me, *shadchen*, what in the world can be better than that?'

'I'll tell you what in the world can be better than that!' exclaimed Shimen. 'The life of a happily married man can be better than that! A man with a loving, giving, devoted wife – like I have. How can you know what joys are in a home? Look, Asa. Think about this. Every single night when I come home – tired out, hungry, even depressed from the long day's work – my dear partner in life, my darling Rosaleh, gives me such a warm hello, a hug, a little kiss, takes off quick my coat, makes me sit right away in the big chair, takes off my shoes, puts on my feet comfortable slippers, brings me the paper, a little glass wine. . . . Then she serves me a dinner – ai, ai, ai! Fit for Count Potofsky! For a *king*, even. . . . And after we eat, we maybe go take a walk, maybe see friends, maybe take in a movie. . . . And then we come home – to a nice, warm bed. And we lie there, under the clean sheets, close together, man and wife – so contented, and my Rosaleh tells me what happened to her all day – the shopping, the cleaning woman, the sink needs fixing, the dropping in by her sister, the call on her mother. . . . She talks, I listen, the house is cozy, I feel my eyes getting heavy. . . . And my Rosaleh talks some more – and talks, and talks, and talks until one day – so help me God! – that woman is going to drive me right out of my aching *mind!*'

Salo Shimshom, a veteran *shadchen*, highly regarded in the orthodox community, was touting the charms of a Malka Janine to Josiah Zetan, a confirmed bachelor.

'Malka?' asked Josiah. 'The blondie?'

'The same.'

'You must be cuckoo, *shadchen*. She's almost blind!'

'That you call a failing?' cried Shimshom. 'That's a blessing – because she won't see, half the time, what you're doing.'

'She also stutters!'

'Lucky you,' sighed the *shadchen*. 'A woman who stutters doesn't dare talk too much, so she'll let you live in peace.'

'But she's deaf!' complained Josiah.

'*I* should have such luck! To a deaf wife you can shout, you can bawl her out – '

'She's at least twenty years older than I am!'

'Ah,' sighed the *shadchen*, 'I thought you were a man of vision. *I* bring you a marvel, a woman you can spend a lifetime with, and you pick on one little fault!'

An eager *shadchen* brought Shlomo Kantrovich, his young male prospect, to the Vishner home to meet unmarried Lena Vishner and her parents.

On their walk back, the *shadchen* said, 'Well, Shlomo, did I exaggerate? Isn't that Lena some girl? And think what a big *dowry* she'll bring you! Did you see the furniture in that house? The silverware? The rugs . . .'

Said the young man uneasily. 'But her father seemed so *eager* . . .'

'Don't let that fool you!' exclaimed the *shadchen*. 'That Lena has two dozen boyfriends!'

'And her mother,' said Shlomo, 'kept pushing . . .'

'That's only your imagination!'

'Look, for all I know, they *borrowed* the fine rugs and all that silver just to impress me!'

'*Borrowed* it?' echoed the *shadchen*. 'Shlomo, are you out of your mind? Who would lend a *nickel* to such deadbeats?'

See also **Aplomb, Bachelors, Chutzpa, Ingenuity, Love, Marriage**

Shaggy Dogs

Harlan and Evans were at the bar, where they had been for two hours, paralyzing their gray cells. Finally Harlan hiccuped. 'Bob, do you know what time it is?'

Evans yawned. 'Yes, I do.'

'That's good,' said Harlan.

∽

Rinaldo the Great, magician *extraordinaire*, came to the office of the manager of a vaudeville circuit. 'Sir, I have perfected a new act that will be an absolute sensation. I saw a woman in half!'

The manager eyed Rinaldo with disdain. 'You call that *new?* My God, man, where have you been? Magicians have been sawing women in half for three hundred years!'

'Lengthwise?'

∽

'That turtle certainly is nearsighted!'

'A turtle *near*sighted? How on earth can you tell?'

'He fell in love with an army helmet.'

∽

The tall, bronzed man in the safari jacket walked into Malachy's Bar – with a magnificent parrot perched on his shoulder.

'Saints alive!' exclaimed Malachy. 'That is a magnificent bird if ever I did see one. Where in the world did you then get it?'

'Brazil,' yawned the parrot.

∽

'Oh, man, did *I* have a dream last night!' said Peter Joyce. 'I was in Atlantic City, at Caesar's Palace, and every time I rolled the dice I hit a seven. Every number I bet at roulette came up. Every time I dropped a quarter in a slot machine – bang! Jackpot!'

'Hey-hey!' exclaimed Terence McPhail. 'Did *I* have a dream last night! But frustrating! I dreamed two of the most beautiful models in the world walked into my apartment and without a word began to take off their clothes. *Two* of them. What could I *do?* It was the most frustrating – '

'Wait a *minute*, pal. Why the hell didn't you phone me to come right over?!'

'I *did*, Peter, but you were in Atlantic City.'

೭

Simon Hassenfeld, a widower, lavished all his love on his new dog, Hinteleh. He taught Hinteleh to stand on his hind legs, his front paws folded across his breast, for as long as half an hour. Then he taught Hinteleh to wear a *yarmulka* and sway back and forth, as if in prayer. Then old Hassenfeld got a small prayer shawl and taught Hinteleh not to shrug it off his shoulders.

Came the High Holy Days. Hassenfeld hastened to the synagogue with Hinteleh, whom he sat on the bench between himself and his customary neighbour, Svetlow.

At the right time, Hinteleh rose to pray along with the entire congregation. He swayed back and forth, made grunting, grumbling noises – until Mr Svetlow cried out, 'Hassenfeld! Am I going crazy, or is this dog *praying*?!'

'He's praying,' said Hassenfeld.

Svetlow gasped, gulped, stared at Hinteleh, then exclaimed, 'Hassenfeld, I tell you, with this little dog you can make a million dollars on television!'

'You're telling me? But try and tell that to him. *He* wants to be an accountant!'

೭

The bartender at P. R. Fogarty's Bar and Grill showed a large lobster in front of Emmet Clancy. 'For you, Emmet, me lad. Compliments of the house for your bein' the most regular client of Fogarty's all this year!'

'That's wonderful,' said Emmet. 'The perfect thing for dinner!'

'Naw,' grimaced Fogarty. 'He just had his dinner. Why don't you take him to a movie?'

೭

The phone rang on the desk of the president of the Algonat bank. He picked it up. 'Yes?'

'This,' growled a man's voice, 'is a stickup!'

'What kind of a joke is this?' snorted the president.

'It's no joke! Mail me fifty thousand dollars or I'll blow your brains out!'

ↄ

Ike Bushkin often ate at Garber and Gulovitz's Tasty, a self-service restaurant on West 72nd Street that specialized in delicacies from the counter marked APPETIZING.

One night, Mr Bushkin chose a fine, plump 'chubb' whitefish, picked up two bagels, a slab of cream cheese, and a bottle of Dr Brown's Celery Tonic. He sat down at a table for two, cut a bagel in half, smeared each side with cream cheese, lifted his fork to insert under the skin of the smoked fish and lift it off, when he noticed the glazed eye of the whitefish staring at him in a bitter, accusatory manner. This completely unnerved Ike Bushkin. . . . He looked out of the Tasty's window for a moment, observing the stream of passersby. Then he lifted his knife, and with his fork, returned to the task of skinning the whitefish. And again he *felt* the accusatory stab of that cold, unwavering, uncondoning eye.

Ike Bushkin was now so unnerved that he put down his knife and fork and left Garber and Gulovitz's.

Ten days later, Ike returned to the Tasty, again chose a fine, fat whitefish, and again, as he began to lift the skin, the reproving glare from the plate drove all hunger from Ike Bushkin's mind. He left the fish unskinned, uncut, uneaten – and departed.

More than a month later, Ike found himself on the Lower East Side. He went into 'Kasha' Kipnin's Lone-Star. To the waiter he said, 'A couple of your best bagels – plain bagels, no sesame seeds or onions on them; a good portion your own cream cheese – not Philadelphia; a bottle Dr Brown's Celery Tonic; and a nice, plump, juicy – make sure it's not dried out – smoked fish.'

The waiter assembled these items and deposited them on the table before Ike Bushkin.

Ike cut the bagels in half, smeared cream cheese on them, poured some Celery Tonic into the glass, lifted his knife and fork – and stopped, paralyzed by the icy glare of the fish's eye. Before Ike could even lower his implements, he heard the whitefish sneer: 'What's the matter, mister? You don't eat at Garber and Gulovitz anymore?'

ↄ

Angus Donaldson, travelling from Aberdeen to Blackpool, could not believe that the conductor, collecting fares, was telling him the right amount of the fare to Blackpool. The two men argued with heightening emotion – until the conductor yelled, 'There's nae use arguing with a stooborn, jug-headed mon like ye!', picked up Donaldson's suitcase, lowered the window, and, as the train was crossing a bridge, threw the suitcase out of the window. 'And ye can get off next stop, too!'

'Ye lyin', no-good Welshman!' cried Donaldson. 'Firrst y' try to rob me iv the price of a ticket – and now y've gone an' drowned m' only son!'

⌒

'Big Mac' McGonigle, the newest prisoner, walked into the exercise yard. He saw a group of men sitting in a circle. . . . Suddenly one convict said, 'Thirty-nine!' and the circle broke into laughter.

A second prisoner said, 'One hundred and nine.' Everyone in the circle laughed.

A third man cried, 'Eighty-five!' and a wave of laughter swept across the ranks.

'What in hell's goin' on?' asked McGonigle.

'Well,' a prisoner explained, 'we been here so long, and tell the same jokes over and over – so we all know them so good, now we just call out the numbers. Go ahead . . . try one.'

McGonigle said, 'Forty-six.'

No one laughed.

'Sixty-two!' cried McGonigle.

Grimaces, shrugs.

'One hundred and eighty!'

A few groans, a few grunts.

'What the hell's wrong?' asked McGonigle. 'Ain't them jokes funny enough f'r ye?!'

'Oh, sure, those are funny jokes. But, man, the way you *told* them . . .

See also **Dummies, Just Jokes, Shlemiels, Tall Tales**

Shlemiels

Note: Shlemiel is a priceless word because it embraces such a mélange of simpletons, luckless souls, misfits, patsies, pigeons, pipsqueaks, suckers, born losers, milquetoasts, *et alia*. I know no better way to pinpoit the characterization than by these classic definitions:

A shlemiel falls on his back and breaks his nose.

A shlemiel takes a bath, and forgets to wash his face.

A shlemiel is always knocking things off tables – and a *nebech* always picks them up.

A shlemiel rushes to throw a drowning man a rope – both ends.

If it rained soup, a shlemiel would have only a fork.

When a shlemiel wants to hang himself, he grabs a knife.

A shlemiel measures water with a sieve.

A shlemiel has accidents that start out to happen to someone else.

A shlemiel doesn't know how to find a notch in a saw.

Shlemiels are usually regarded with pity, not scorn: they cannot be blamed for the infirmities of their judgment, the folly of their choices, or the naïveté that governs their hapless course through life.

ᔕ   L. R.

Jack Benny, a grand master at portraying the shlemiel, upon receiving a cherished national award, accepted the honour with these memorable words: 'I don't really deserve this beautiful award. But I have arthritis, and I don't deserve that either.'

ᔕ

'Doc, doc!' Merkin cried into the phone. 'It's my Dotty! She's startin' them labour pains! Just like you said!'

'Now calm down, Mr Merkin. Get yourself together.'

'Sure, doc, sure. What should I do?'

'First,' the doctor said, 'tell me: How far apart are the pains coming?'

'Uh – they're all in the same place, doc!'

ᔕ

'Does a slice of bread,' asked Max, 'fall with the buttered side up or down?'

Jacob said, 'With the buttered side down!'

Max said, 'With the buttered side *up!*'

So they made a bet.

Jacob buttered a slice of bread, raised it, and let it drop. It fell – buttered side up.

'I win!' cried Max.

'Only because I made a mistake,' protested Jacob.

'What mistake?'

'I buttered the wrong side.'

G

Three shlemiels were in a bed, trying to sleep, but it was so crowded none could doze off. Finally one man said, 'I've got an idea. It's so crowded in here, I'll get out.'

He got out and stretched on the floor.

In a moment, one of the men in the bed said, 'Listen, Moishe. I think you can come back to bed: there's plenty of room now.'

G

Two shlemiels were at the rail of the great ocean liner, staring at the vast, limitless sea.

'Just look at all that *water!*' exclaimed the first shlemiel.

'You bet,' said the second. 'And don't forget – that's only the *top.*'

G

Two shlemiels were drinking tea. In time, one looked up and announced portentously: 'Life! What is it? Life – life is like a fountain!'

The other pondered a few minutes, then asked, 'Why?'

The first shlemiel thought, scratched his chin, then shrugged, 'Okay, so life *isn't* like a fountain.'

G

(*Note:* Shlemiels certainly do not have to be Jewish.)

Scene: St Wilby's Club, London

'Rupert, old man. I must take you into my confidence...'

'Of course, Ellsworth.'

'Well, last night, after a very late directors' meeting, I went home. I crept up the stairway so as not to awaken Sheila, stole into our bedroom – and there, by God, in *bed* with her, naked as a frog, was Leonard Saville!'

'Good Lord!' gasped Rupert. 'What did you do, old man?'

'I stared coldly at Saville for a good two minutes, then, without a word, I turned on my heel and walked out, down to the kitchen, and made myself a proper pot of tea!'

Rupert nodded gravely; after a long moment, he said, 'I *say*. . . . But – what about Saville?'

'Humph!' huffed Ellsworth. 'I thought to myself, By God, let the bounder get his own tea!'

∽

'The best way to keep from getting constipation,' said Dr Hockner, 'is to drink warm water an hour before dinner every night.'

'I'll certainly do that,' said Mr Erd.

The next time he saw Dr Hockner, the doctor asked, 'Well, how are you feeling now?'

'Terrible.'

'Do you drink warm water an hour before dinner every night?'

'Doctor, I tried!' Erd's sigh came from the depth of his being. 'But who can keep drinking for more than ten minutes at a time?'

∽

Henry Graver, an indubitable shlemiel, came home early one afternoon to find his wife and his best friend in bed. 'Omi*god!*' cried Henry. 'What are you two doing?'

His wife turned to her bed partner: 'See, didn't I tell you he was a dummy?'

∽

The foreman at the Steuben Glass Factory came over to the new hand. 'Nice day work you've done, Lenski. I see you marked and stacked all those crates very neatly.'

'Yes, *sir!*'

'Good. . . . Did you stencil the important "*This Side Up*" on the top of each crate?'

'Oh, yes,' said Lenski. 'And to protect them double good, I put the notice on the bottom, too.'

See also **Dummies, Jews, Just Jokes, Nebechs**

Shnorrers

Note: Every Jewish community once had at least one shnorrer, and often a platoon. The shnorrer was no run-of-the-mill mendicant. He was not apologetic; he did not fawn or whine. He regarded himself as professional. He did not so much ask for alms as *claim* them.

For shnorrers considered they had a licence from the Lord: after all, they were *helping* Jews discharge solemn obligations to the poor and the unfortunate. Through these noble acts, a good Jew could accumulate *mitzvas!* Shnorrers seemed to know that they were both exploiting and assuaging one of the most powerful psychological forces in the psyche of Jews: guilt.

The shnorrer 'recoiled from demeaning himself . . . from sheer arrogance and vanity. Since he was obliged to live by his wits,' writes Nathan Ausubel, 'he developed all the facile improvisations of an adventurer. . . . He would terrorize his prey by the sheer daring of his importunities, leaving him both speechless and wilted.'*

On the part of the Jewish community, shnorrers were regarded as performing some sort of social function. Exactly what this function was, I could never fathom as a child; but everyone seemed to take it for granted – and took it for granted that no explanation was necessary. (Maybe shnorrers served this purpose: often excellent *raconteurs*, they circulated stories, jokes, gossip.)

In Chicago, when I was walking with my parents, Izzy, 'our shnorrer' (as my parents thought of him), would come up to us, extend his palm, receive his nickel or dime, and proceed to his next 'clients'. Not a word was exchanged: no greeting, no *'Shalom'* or *'Sholem aleichem'*, merely a nod from the mendicant, a sigh from my father, a smile from my mother.

One Sunday, the shnorrer was nowhere to be seen. After we walked the length of the shnorrer's usual territory without encountering Izzy, my mother said, 'I wonder what's happened to our shnorrer? I hope he's not sick.'

'Sick?' My father snorted. 'He's as healthy as a horse.'

'Then why isn't he on the street?'

'He's probably in Florida,' said my father, 'taking his vacation.'

*Treasury of Jewish Folklore, pp. 267–68.

L. R.

∽

The blind man stood on the corner in Whitechapel, jiggling his tin cup.

A woman stopped and dropped a shilling into the cup.

The blind man said, 'May the good Lord shine His face on ye, ma'am. I knew ye had a kind heart the minute I seed y' comin' down th' road.'

∽

A shnorrer came to the back door of the Winkel house on his bi-weekly rounds. 'I haven't a penny in the house,' apologized Mrs Winkel. 'Come back tomorrow.'

'Tomorrow?' The mendicant studied her sharply. 'Lady, I hope you don't let this happen again. A man can lose a *fortune*, extending credit.'

∽

A beggar stood each morning in front of the World Trade Centre, with a box of cheap pencils. 'Pencils ... only ten cents a pencil...' the beggar chanted.

One wealthy Wall Streeter each morning dropped a dime into the beggar's box, saying, 'Good morning,' without ever taking a pencil.

Ond day the rich man dropped his dime with his usual 'Good morning,' started to enter the building, but felt a tap on his shoulder.

'Mister,' said the beggar. 'I've had to raise my prices. Inflation. A pencil now costs a quarter.'

See also **Chutzpa, Jews, Retorts, Sarcasm**

Signs

In a students' dormitory in Sweden

Italians are not allowed to sing after midnight.

Germans are not permitted to get up before 5 A.M.

In a Kowloon tailor shop

CUSTOMERS GIVING ORDERS
WILL BE
SWIFTLY EXECUTED

On a boarded excavation site in New York

DANGER!
COMPLIMENTS OF
VITIELLO BLASTING MAT CO.

First prize: Sign pinned to dress of pregnant woman at masquerade ball:
I SHOULD HAVE DANCED ALL NIGHT

Menu   **TODAY'S SPECIAL**
                          Barely Soup

Sign in deli   **Try Our Special Swiss Cheese:**
                      24% less cavities

In fancy food store   **We sell the finest**
                      home-made imported caviar

⌒

Above a bin containing flyswatters, in a hardware store

The hand is quicker
Than the eye is

Beneath this, a cynical customer had printed:

But often slower
Than the fly is.

Sign on bench   **WHET PAYNT**

PASSERBY: You spelled 'wet' wrong.
PAINTER: I know: but when I spell it right no one pays attention.

Sign in Rome: **SPECIALIST IN WOMEN
AND OTHER DISEASES.**

On house painter's truck

LOVE THY NEIGHBOUR!
PAINT THY HOUSE.

In an elevator in a Belgrade hotel

To move the cabin, push button for wishing floor. If
the cabin should enter more persons, each one
should press number of wishing floor. Driving is
then going alphabetically by national order.

thanks to DONALD CARROLL

Chalked on a post-no-bills wall:

DOWN WITH GRAFFITI!

Sign on car bumper:

BAN BUMPER STICKERS

On door:

PLEASE DO NOT READ THIS

Label on package

**Please notify us at once if this
label fell off in transit**

On a menu

Ice cream	70c
Pie (like Mother made)	50c
Pie (like Mother wished she could make)	$1.50

Sign in butcher shop

THIS WEEK ONLY
T-BONE – $1.00

Pedestrians had to step much closer to read the type underneath:

With meat: $6.00

In Austrian hotel

IN CASE OF FIRE
PLEASE DO UTMOST
TO ALARM HALL PORTER

On door to hospital ward

VISITORS:
HUSBANDS ONLY.
ONE PER BED

Sign I saw in Tokyo (in English)

COMING SOON
HOTEL AND OFFICES
BIGGEST ERECTION IN TOKYO!

On Sunnyvale Sanitarium:

NOBODY LEAVES HERE MAD.

Mrs James Morse Thirkall
is pleased to announce
the arrival of
Mary Nelly – 6 pounds 8 ounces –
and
the loss of twenty pounds

Tag on parka

Material	
Wool	20%
Unknown	70%
Other	10%

Notice in window of Jurgenson's Skin-Diving Equipment Store

We carry a complete
line of under ware

Over bed in guest room

**Be it ever so humble,
There's no place like home.**

See also **Advice, Graffiti, How's That Again?, Typos**

Snafus

Mrs Blitzstein dialled her daughter's number and sang out, 'Hello, darling. This is your mama. So, how's everything?'

'Everything is just *awful*, mama. The children are acting crazy, the house is a mess, I have a bad back – and we are having three couples for dinner!'

'Stop! Your worries are over! I'm coming right over,' said Mrs Blitzstein. 'I'll calm down the children, I'll clean up your place so every corner shines, and I'll cook a dinner for you and six guests no one will never forget!'

'Oh, mama, you angel! That's just marvellous of you! ... How's Papa?'

'What? Papa? ... Darling, have you gone mad? Your papa – may his soul rest in peace – died seven years ago!'

A pause fell upon the line. 'Er – what number are you calling?'
'Alton-six, four, four, nine, one,' said Mrs Blitzstein.
'This is Alton-six, four, four, nine, *four*!'
'Omigod! I dialled a wrong number!'
'Wait! *Please!*' the voice wailed. 'Does that mean you're not coming over?!'

∽

A seventh-grader was so late coming home from his suburban school that his mother was frantic.
'What happened to you?' she cried.
'I was made traffic guard today, mama, and all the kids have to wait for my signal, after I stop a car, before they can cross the street!'
'But you were due home two *hours* ago!'
'Mama, do you know how long I had to wait before a car came along I could stop?!'

∽

Mr Feibleman called Sanchez and Battista ('Awnings, Shades, Venetian Blinds – Reasonable Prices, Expert Work'). 'Listen, do you fix blinds?'
'*Sí,*'
'I mean, just fix. I don't need a new one.'
'*Sí.*'
'So come to Forty-six Forley – '
'You no can bring in?'
'Who could bring in such a big, clumsy thing?' Mr Feibleman gave the man his address. 'How soon can you come?'
'*Martes,* Tuesday. I pick up.'
'Not sooner?'
'Señor, am very, very busy.'
The following Tuesday, while Mr Feibleman was at work, Sanchez came to the Feibleman apartment. He rang the bell.
Mrs Feibleman, whom her husband had totally forgotten to tell of the repairman's visit, opened the door. 'Hello,' she said.
'I am Sanchez.'
'So?'
'Lady, I come collect – venetian blind.'
'Aha.' Mrs Feibleman opened her purse and gave the man a dollar. 'May God help your good work. Goodbye.'

○

TRUE

When I learned that three English friends had been trying to reach us at our London hotel, leaving their numbers (we had received not a single message, nor one phone call), my wife said, 'Go down to the lobby. Pick up a house phone. Ask for Leo Rosten. . . . I'll bet they don't know we're registered!'

I did as instructed. 'Leo Rosten, please.'

'*Would* you mind repeating the name?' a duchess crooned.

I repeated my name.

Pause. 'How is that spelled?'

I spelled my name.

Fifty-three moments later, I heard: 'Awfully sorry, sir, but no one of that name is registered.'

'I *know* he's registered!'

A sniff skewered my self-esteem. 'Are you certain?'

'I am *quite* certain. I happen to be Mr Rosten.'

The phone went dead. It stayed dead. . . .

I stepped to the next house phone. 'Mr Rosten, please. Leo Rosten.'

A Caribbean refugee replied, 'Could you please spell thot?'

I did.

'One *moment* please. . . . Sir, I must inform you thot name does not appear on our guest register.'

I accosted an assistant manager. 'I'm afraid your operators don't understand my American accent. Would you mind phoning the room of Mr Leo Rosten? . . .'

'Are you *shaw* your party is in the hotel?'

'Absolutely *shaw*,' I said. 'In fact, you are looking at him.'

He flinched. 'Do you mean you are trying to ring *your*self, sir?'

'I am trying to get my wife, who is waiting in our room.'

The man's face burst into ecstasy: 'Ah, then you know your room number.'

I showed him my key: 416.

He lifted the phone. 'Room *faw*-one-six, please.' He handed me the receiver.

'Hull-o-o,' came a hoarse African bass.

'Is this room four-sixteen?' I asked.

'No! Thees room is foh-foh-seven.'

I replaced the phone. The assistant manager had evaporated. . . . I lifted the phone yet once more. 'Would you take an important message, from the Foreign Office – for room four-one-six? For Leo Rosten. . . . Just tell him that Prince Peregrine Hapsburg of Albania telephoned.'

And that night, for the first time, a chit from the Telephone Message Centre was slipped under our door. It read:

> Foreign Office phoned Mr Leo from Boston. He should call Prince Barry Green Hamburg in Rumania.

from my The 3:10 to Anywhere

Slocum Barnes was frightened of his own shadow. When he moved to a new town, the first thing he did was build a big storm cellar. He put in two kerosene lamps, a week's supply of drinking water, canned soups, vegetables, etc.

A week after the storm cellar was completed, a terrific wind came up, the sky darkened, and Slocum ran into the storm haven, slamming down the overhead door and the steel bars.

They found Slocum, a day later, buried in the rubble of the earthquake.

See also **Can you Believe it?, Dummies, Embarrassing Moments, True Tales**

Squelches

Shortly after the Nazis came to power, a restaurant in Berlin put this sign on its door:

HORST WESSEL RESTAURANT

ARYAN CLIENTS ONLY

One day, a distinguished-looking man entered the restaurant. The owner bowed and scraped, the cloakroom girl helped the man off with his fine coat and hat, and the headwaiter led him to a table.

As the man sat down, the headwaiter noticed he was wearing –

Gott in himmel! – a *yarmulka.* The *maître d'* turned pale and signalled to the owner, who hurried over. The headwaiter pointed to the skullcap.

'Sir!' the owner thundered. 'We do not serve Jews!'

'That's good,' said the customer. 'I don't eat them.'

☙

'All right, Victor, I know I'm not the perfect wife for you. I'm just outspoken.'

'By whom, dear?'

☙

During complex naval manoeuvres, a small ship, hit by a wave, scraped against a huge battleship. Very soon the captain of the small ship received this radio message from the commander of the big one:

IF YOU TOUCH ME THERE AGAIN
I'LL SCREAM

☙

The proud proprietor of Smolinsky's Superb, a restaurant on lower Broadway, was making his rounds among the tables full of diners. 'Hello. . . . Glad to see you. . . . Everything okay?' At one table, occupied by a lone, sour-faced customer, Smolinsky said, 'Are you enjoying?'

'Enjoying what?' asked the stranger.

'My food,' said Smolinsky.

The customer stared at the proprietor. 'Mr Owner, frankly: I could get more nourishment biting my lips!'

☙

'A lot of men,' she said, 'are going to be *miserable* when I marry!'

'How many,' he asked, 'are you going to marry?'

☙

The young rabbi finally summoned up enough courage to say to Mr Benenson, one of the elders of the community: 'I trust you won't mind my mentioning it, but I can't help noticing that – you always fall asleep when I'm preaching.'

Replied Benenson, 'Would I sleep if I didn't trust you?'

∽

At a meeting in China's capital between the Greek premier and the Chinese Communist leader Mao Tse-tung, the latter asked how many people there are in Greece.

'Eight million!' the premier proudly replied.

'Really,' said Chairman Mao. 'And what hotel are they staying at?'

∽

'Freddy,' said Mrs Wainwright, 'we're giving a small party to celebrate my husband's birthday. I'm anxious for you to come.'

'Fine, Maggie. When is it?'

'On the eighteenth. Seven o' – '

'The eighteenth?' said Freddy. 'Do you mean this month or last month?'

'This month.'

'Maggie, darling, today is the nineteenth. The eighteenth was yesterday.'

'I know,' said Mrs Wainwright. 'And where the hell were you?'

∽

A man with a roving eye and a permanent leer got into a crowded hotel elevator operated by a very pretty, very shapely girl.

After they deposited people at several floors, the Don Juan was the only passenger left. He said to the operator, 'Sweetheart, I imagine you must be pretty tired after a day of all these stops and starts.'

'The stops and starts,' she replied, 'don't bother me. What I can't stand is the jerks.'

∽

The traffic on 28th Street was bumper to bumper. The cross-streets were clogged. Cars and trucks inched ahead, stopped, waited, inched on. . . . The passengers in the taxi leaned forward and called to the driver, 'For God's sake, isn't there some way you can go *faster?!*'

'Yep,' said the driver, 'but I'm not allowed to leave the cab.'

∽

The *maître d'* of a very posh French restaurant in New Orleans beheld, to his horror, a tourist at one of the tables tucking his napkin into the collar of his shirt. After taking thought, the *maître d'* went over to the customer and, with the utmost politeness, asked, 'Do you want a shave or a haircut, sir?'

In Hernando's Estrella Bar in Miami Beach, José Vitali, watching television's lottery, leaped to his feet, shouting, '*Numero* t'ree-forty-seex! I ween! I ween! Ten t'ousan' doellar!'

The others sang out their congratulations. But one sourpuss called, 'Hey you, Vitali! How you peek soch a *numero*? T'ree-forty-seex?'

'From *ensueño* [dream]!' laughed José. 'I am by horse race. Horses ron. Wins a *numero* one hondred. Second, comms *numero* twanty. Next, is ninaty-four.'

The sour-faced man closed one eye. 'One hondred, twanty, ninaty-four?'

'*Sí, sí!*'

'These *numeros* no add op t'ree-forty-seex!! They make two hundred forateen!'

José ruminated and then shrugged. 'I choose t'ree-forty-seex, *amigo. You* be da *mathematico!*'

An earnest first-term congressman sent out a long questionnaire to his constituents, asking for their opinions on the economy, military expenditures, school prayer, etc. The final question was: 'In the light of all the complex problems that face our nation, what do you suggest Congress do?'

Several answers read: 'Adjourn.'

A rogue I know likes to discombobulate barbers who never stop yakking. When they finish their ministrations and hold the mirror behind his head for approval, he studies the reflected image, then says, 'N-no. A little longer in back, please.'

ACCOUNTING OFFICE

TO: George Strand

FROM: Comptroller

We cannot approve your latest expense account.

R. Jackson

P.S. How much would you take for the fiction rights?

Ꮹ

Whenever Zvi Meyer rose to speak in the Knesset, even the members of his own party groaned. Meyer gave the dullest, most soporific speeches in the assembly. But one day, he rose and delivered an absolutely brilliant – indeed, a scintillating – oration. So astounded were the members of the assembly that, the moment Meyer finished, they rose as one, applauding furiously.

When their fervour had run its course, and the members sat down, a sardonic voice from the gallery called: 'Author! Author!'

Ꮹ

```
Israel Ortov
28 Broadway
New York, N.Y.


Dear Israel:

    Knowing of your interest in the work of
our committee, I am putting your name down
for  a  pledge  of  $1,000  in  our  current
drive for funds.

                    Yours,
                    Les Alderman



Les Alderman
806 Fourth Ave.
New York, N.Y.


Dear Les:

    Thanks for advising me that you put me
down for a pledge of $1,000 in your current
drive for funds.
    I am interested in the work of another
fund.   So  I  am  putting  you  down  for  a
```

```
$1,000 pledge there.   In this way, Les,
no  money  has  to  pass  between  us.
```
Yours,
Israel

CS

At a very exclusive London club, a lord of the realm kept complaining to his waiter about the uncommonly slow service. His complaints did not help. In exasperation, the lord exclaimed, 'My God, man, do you have any idea at all of who I am?!'

The waiter responded, 'No, sir. I have not been employed here very long. But I shall inquire at the desk, sir, and inform you without delay.'

CS

Scene: Kumpelmeyer's Bakery

MRS WEISHAUPT: Listen, Mr Kumpelmeyer, every roll I bought in here yesterday vas so stale I couldn't eat vun of zem!

KUMPELMEYER: Mrs Weishaupt, I sink you are crazy! Zere's abzolutely nossing wrong wiz mine r-rolls. Vhy, sixty years ago, during ze Depression, people vould have go down on zeir knees and sanked ze *Lieber Gott* for r-rolls like zese!

MRS WEISHAUPT: Sixty years ago, I vould, also. Zese rolls vere frash zen.

See also **Groucho, Repartee, Retorts, Sarcasm, Waiters, Wit**

Stock Market

The day after the stock market plummeted to a new low, two brokers were sharing a taxi from Wall Street to Penn Station. 'Oh, Lord, what a day!' groaned Wilmott. 'And there's not a sign of relief in sight. All the indices are terrible: unemployment, loan demand, interest rates – Charley, to tell you the truth, I can't remember when I last had one good night's sleep!'

'Really?' said Charley. '*I*, for one, sleep like a baby.'

'*What*? Do you mean that?'

'Absolutely,' said Charley. 'Every night, I get up every two hours – and cry.'

See also **Business, Stratagems**

Stratagems

A mother in Montana simply could not get her ten-year-old to tuck in his shirt-tails – until, one night, as he was sleeping, she sewed a lace edge on the bottom of each of his shirts.

∽

'Hello. Is this the Rectory of Saint Matthew the Evangelist?'
 'That it is.'
 'May I speak to Father Shannon?'
 'I am Father Shannon.'
 'Well, father, my name is Homer Swaith. I am the assistant deputy director of the Manhattan branch of the Internal Revenue Service. I'm calling, confidentially, about the tax returns of Aloysius Byrne, a member of your parish . . .'
 'Y-yes?'
 'Mr Byrne has claimed a ten-thousand dollar tax deduction for a contribution he says he made, in *cash*, to your sodality. . . . In strict confidence, Father Shannon, do you remember receiving such a sum from Mr Byrne?'
 There was a moment's silence. Then Father Shannon said, 'Well, now, Mr Swaith, if you will call me tomorrow – just about this time – I *assure* you, the answer to your question will be – yes.'

∽

Hans Schwebel, in West Berlin, said to his wife, 'I think those Communists are opening every letter I send to our Brunhilde, working as she is for the German embassy in Moscow. I have a plan to fool them. In my next letter I will say: "I have put in a tiny hair – so if a censor opens this envelope, the hair will fall out."'
 Two weeks later a letter from Brunhilde arrived. Frau Schwebel opened it and read aloud: "'Dear Papa, stop such foolish worries about the Russians opening your mail. Your hair was still in the envelope when I opened it!' . . . Ah, Hans, see how wrong you were!'
 Schwebel chuckled so that his whole body shook. '"Foolish worries"? "How wrong I was!"? *Liebchen*, my fears are true!'

'What are you talking about?'
'I didn't put a hair in the letter to Brunhilde.'

‿

'Well now,' said Ferguson to the American visitor to Glasgow, 'coom around siven, if that's convenient for ye – '
'Fine. And where do you live?'
'I'll gie ye m'card. . . . Now, ye push th' button with y'r elbow, an' when – '
'My elbow? Why can't I press the button with my finger?'
'Och mon!' snorted Ferguson, 'Ye're not plannin' t' coom empty-handed, are ye?'

‿

William Collier opened a play, *The Patriot*, on December 30.
On January 2 a full-page ad blared:

SECOND YEAR ON BROADWAY!

‿

A woebegone panhandler, unshaved and bleary, accosted Ned Harrigan and mumbled, 'Can y' spare a good Irishman a quarter for a cup of java?'
Harrigan surveyed the derelict with care. 'Mac, if you answer me truthfully I might give you five bucks.'
'Hey, *man*,' gulped the bum. 'Shoot.'
'Do you drink?'
'Never touch a tot of the filthy stuff!' cried the panhandler.
'Do you smoke?'
'Not one cigarette since me blessed father died of the filthy weed!'
'Do you gamble?'
'Gamble? May the Lord strike me blind if it ain't ten years since I rolled a pair of dice!'
'Do you spend one night a week with men friends?'
'None of my friends wants to spend ten *minutes* with me!'
Harrigan chortled. 'Come with me.'
The two men hastened to Harrigan's flat around the corner. Just before Harrigan unlocked the door, he gave the bum a five dollar bill, flung open the door, and the panhandler stepped in.

Harrigan's wife called, 'Hello, dear,' and gave a shriek.

'Don't be alarmed, darlin',' beamed Harrigan. 'I just want you
to see what happens to a man who gives up drinking, smoking,
gambling, and going out with the boys one measly night a week!'

TRUE

The lady with a child in her arms, another holding her left hand,
another holding her skirt, raised her free hand, shouting: 'Taxi!
Taxi!'

The Yellow Cab pulled up to the curb beside her.

The lady opened the back door and put one child after another
inside, closed the door, and said, 'Start your meter. I'll be back in a
jiffy. Forgot my purse.' She hurried back in the house.

It was a good eight minutes before the lady returned, smiling
broadly. She opened the back door but instead of getting in, she
proceeded to take her three offspring out. 'How much do I owe
you, driver?'

The driver said, 'A dollar forty. . . . But I don't get it, lady! Did
you change your mind – ?'

'Oh, no.' The lady gave him two dollars. 'You see, I had to make
an important call to a lawyer, long distance, and these three have
been driving me crazy!'

See Also **Business, Ingenuity, Rabbis, Revenge, Salesmen, Tact**

Tact

Adolph Zukor, the long-lived head of Paramount Pictures, was re-
puted to be the most courteous producer in the world. He would
with the utmost regret suspend the services of an employee. His
notices were famous:

> Dear Charley:
>
> You're fired.
> Warmest regards,
>
>   ADOLPH ZUKOR

⌒

'Now, Mr Harkness,' asked Mrs Walton coquettishly, 'how old you think I *am*?'

'Mrs Walton,' replied Harkness, 'you certainly don't look it.'

⌒

Phineas Fitzgerald was a compulsive gambler. Again and again he drove his devoted wife to despair with his losses. One night, as Phineas was about to leave for a poker game, his wife, Katherine, said, 'Me darlin', this is y'r last poker game w' the boys. Ye will never gamble again an' remain Katy Shaw's husband!'

That night, Phineas played like a genius. So great was his luck that he won pot after pot. On the last play, he held four queens – and he put his entire stake, winnings and all, on his final bet. His opponent, Donald Casey, met the bet. Phineas, chortling, laid down his four queens. Casey placed his cards face up. He had four aces.

Phineas rose, turned purple—and dropped dead.

Now the other players debated who should go to Phineas Fitzgerald's house and inform his wife, Katy. 'What about you, Charley Croly?'

'No, no, not him!' exclaimed another player. 'Last time this happened to Jimmy Rafferty, may his soul rest in peace—you, Charley Croly, knocked on th' poor woman's door and asked, "Do I have the pleasure of addressin' the widow Rafferty?" She fainted. . . . Not you.'

'How about Muldoon here?'

'Not on y'r life!' blustered Muldoon. 'I could not bear to glance upon poor Phineas's bereaved woman.'

'McManus! You, Ryan McManus! Nerves of iron y' have, man, and a steadfast purpose . . .'

And the words were true. So it was Ryan McManus who strode to the Fitzgerald's flat on 83rd Street, walked up the stairs, knocked on the door.

Katy Fitzgerald opened the door. 'So, Phineas – ' Her jaw was set, her arms akimbo, but when she saw McManus, she said, 'Ryan McManus, is it? What brings y' at such an hour?'

'Katy Fitzgerald, I have to tell y' somethin' most unusual. Suppose I should tell y' that in the last pot tonight, your good husband held four queens – *four queens*, mind you, bet the whole works, fixin' to win a *lot* of money – an' it turns out that that stumble-bum Donny Casey had four *aces!* Can you imagine that, Katy Fitzgerald! Supposin' this happened. What would y' say?'

'I would say,' the indignant woman said, drawing herself to her full height, 'may the good Lord teach that Phineas of mine a final lesson! May that man o' mine drop dead!'

'He did, Katy,' said McManus. 'Goodnight.'

○

The same story is told about a Jewish gambler, Label Trupin, who lost his all playing blackjack – and dropped dead. His friends consulted and agreed that Morty Somech was the best man to break the news to Alma, Label's wife, whom he had never met.

Morty Somech took a taxi to the Trupin apartment house, walked up two flights of stairs, and knocked on the door. A comely woman opened it.

'Do I have the pleasure and privilege,' asked Morty, 'of addressing the *almoonah* [widow] Trupin?'

'Absolutely not!' said Alma.

'I'll betcha,' said Morty.

○

Elsa Maxwell, the celebrated party-giver, once revealed her formula for making her guests feel good: 'When they arrive, I say, "At last!" And when they start to leave, I say, "Must you – already?"'

See also **Aplomb, Diplomacy/Diplomats, Rabbis, Salesmen, Stratagems**

Telegrams

Two Frenchmen, Raoul Spero and Maurice Vauté, old enemies, had such a violent falling-out that Spero challenged Vauté to a duel.

Promptly at six thirty the next morning, Spero and his second appeared at the designated place in the Bois de Boulogne. Maurice Vauté had not appeared.

At six forty, Vauté's second, Jacques Seligson, came out of a taxi, carrying the pistol case.

By seven, Vauté had still not appeared.

'The man has stained his honour!' scowled Raoul Spero.

'No, wait. Look!' cried Seligson.

The men saw a bicycle swiftly pedalling toward them. But the figure on the bicycle turned out to be not Maurice Vauté but a messenger with a telegram – for Spero.

He ripped open the envelope.

```
SORRY.  DELAYED.  HATE TO
DISAPPOINT YOU.  WAIT NO LONGER.
SHOOT.
                              Vauté
```

```
JAMISON AND KENNY
14 WAYNE ST.
SECAUCUS, N.J.
YOU ARE NOW THREE MONTHS LATE IN DELIVERING
OUR MERCHANDISE.  CANCEL ORDER AT ONCE.
                              HANSON BLAIR
                                    TOLEDO
```

```
HANSON BLAIR
709 WENTWORTH
TOLEDO, OHIO.
CANNOT CANCEL ORDER AT ONCE.  YOU HAVE TO WAIT
FOR YOUR TURN.
                              JAMISON and KENNY
```

```
N. SIMMONS
PRESIDENT
ANCOLA CORPORATION
COMPLETELY SNOWED IN.  ALL FLIGHTS CANCELLED.
NO CHANGE IN WEATHER PREDICTED.  PLEASE ADVISE.
                    TOM GROBAN
                    HOTEL MANSFIELD
                    BUTTE, MONTANA
```

```
TOM GROBAN
HOTEL MANSFIELD
BUTTE, MONTANA
   START SUMMER VACATION AT ONCE.
                    N. SIMMONS
```

Father of newborn boy to wife

```
        MRS STELLA MARCH
        PASSEVANT HOSPITAL

        EVERYONE TELLS ME YOU HAD A BOY IN
        YOUR ROOM LAST NIGHT.
```

See also **Graffiti, Ingenuity, Signs**

Texans

'You say you've lived in Dallas all your life?'
  'Yep. I was born here. So was m' pappy.'
  'You must own a lot of cattle.'
  'Nope.'
  'Well, I imagine you have a few gushing oil wells?'
  'Nope.'
  'Uh – do you own some land?'
  'Land? Yep.'
  'A lot?'
  'We-ell, three and a half acres.'
  'That's *all*?'
  'That's all.'
  'Three and a half acres – that isn't much of a ranch for a Texan.
Tell me, what do you call it?'
  'Downtown.'

A jeepload of GIs in Iowa approached a very small horse, tethered
to a fence. The jeep stopped. 'My God,' said the first GI. 'That's
the smallest damn horse I ever seen.'
  'It looks more like a big dog –'
  'Must be the smallest horse in the world – a breed all its own.'
  'Maybe it's a small Shetland pony.'
  Along came a farmer.
  'Are you the owner of this goldurn animal?'

'Sure am.'

'Well, what is it – a pony, a dog, or a horse?'

'It's a horse, all right. No doubt about it. I've got papers back in the farmhouse authenticatin' that this is the smallest true horse in the world!'

'Aw, shucks,' drawled a soldier. 'Why, back home in Texas we got horses that's as small as two of that one put together.'

See also **Boasts, Can You Believe It?, Just Jokes**

Traffic

Sign at school crossing: GIVE OUR KIDS A BRAKE!

An out-of-town woman, in a hurry, took a cab in mid-town New York. After a few blocks, the taxi was stuck, immobile, in a fierce traffic jam. The cab sat, absolutely still, then crawled for a few feet, then stopped again.

'Driver,' called the out-of-towner, 'is it always this bad?'

'Nope.'

'I see by my watch – it's almost ten o'clock.'

'Yep.'

'I suppose I should be grateful that I didn't get caught in the nine o'clock jam!'

'Lady, this *is* the nine o'clock jam.'

Sign at bottom of steep incline in Colorado:

RESUME BREATHING

On a city bus: TAKE TWICE A DAY – TO RELIEVE CONGESTION.

Traffic lights: Clever devices that safely get pedestrians halfway across a street.

Cry a bit
For Buck Le Mott.

He was lit,
His lights were not.

Travel

The Frankfurt-am-Rheim Travel Society was going by bus through
the countryside of England. Being Germans, they appeared punc-
tually each morning, returned to their bus on the minute after visiting a castle or ruin, and chafed if the tour guide ever fell a minute
behind schedule.

Now, as the bus pulled up to the meadow at Runnymede, the
guide announced through the loudspeaker, '*Meine Herren und
Damen*, there is no need to get off here. It is enough to see the
meadow and that historic oak tree – for under that tree was signed
the historic document from which come all the freedoms Englishmen today enjoy: the Magna Carta!'

'Ven did zat hoppen?' one Frau asked.

'1215.'

The president of the Travel Society glanced at his watch and in a
reprimanding tone told the guide, 'You missed it by twenty-four
minutes!'

Radio travel programme in Iowa: . . . I shall never forget the beauties
of Rome, that glorious city of fallen arches.

True Tales

The late great pianist, Leopold Godowsky, loved to tell friends of
the time he was having a formal swallowtail suit made for a forthcoming world tour. To spare the impresario's time and energy,
the tailor would come to Godowsky's apartment on Central Park
West. This tailor (whose name is, alas, not preserved for history)
was a superb, meticulous craftsman, a master of cut and needle-

work, and a perfectionist of the highest order. And Leopold Godowsky was notoriously impatient.

Week after week, the tailor appeared in Godowsky's apartment, fitting, draping, pinning, marking. Each time Godowsky would fret and scold. '*Another* fitting? Good God, tailor, when will you be *done*?!'

At the sixth such session, Leopold Godowsky lost his temper. 'Tailor, in the name of heaven!' he cried. 'You have already taken six *weeks* – '

'So?' the tailor responded.

'"So?" "So?!" Six weeks for one suit?' Godowsky fumed. 'Listen, man. It took God only six *days* to create the entire *world!*'

The tailor nodded. '*Nu?* Look at it . . .'

☙

Overheard in the foyer of one of our grandest hotels:

> Young lady to old lady seated on a shooting stick:
> 'But, Granny, why not sit in one of the large, soft chairs?'
> Old lady: 'One *never* sits on a hotel chair, my dear. One never knows who has been sitting here before.'

Daily Telegraph

☙

Some years ago, Leopold Godowsky, star pianist and irrepressible wit, was being pressed by a friend. 'You mean to say you would rather take a train for three nights and four days to get to California – instead of taking an aeroplane that gets you there in ten hours?'

'I would,' said Godowsky.

'Are you that afraid of crashing?' asked the friend.

'I don't like aeroplanes, I don't trust aeroplanes, I don't *need* aeroplanes!'

'But, Leopold, I have gone over the cold, hard facts about flying: the actual statistics! Do you realize you are safer in an aeroplane than in a bathtub? Or riding in an automobile! Or riding on a train – '

'Enough with facts,' said Godowsky. 'You can do anything with statistics!'

The friend paused. 'Well, perhaps you are right, Leopold. After all, every one of us has something of the mystic in him – '

'Mystic? Why "mystic"?'

'I mean, deep down, I guess, we all feel that when all is said and done, wherever you are, when it's your time . . . It's all a matter of when God calls you!'

'Right, my friend. Right.'

'Well, there you are, so you may as well fly . . .'

'One minute. Not me.'

'But you agreed that it's all a matter of when God calls you!'

'Absolutely,' said Godowsky. 'So why should I be twenty thousand feet in the air when God calls the pilot?!'

See also **Can You Believe It?, Embarrassing Moments, Shaggy Dogs, Snafus**

Typos

Note: I have for years collected typographical errors. Considering the billions of words printed each year in newspapers, magazines, leaflets, weeklies, house organs, it is quite remarkable, in sheer statistical terms, that 'typos' are so infrequent.

I am overjoyed whenever my eye falls upon a serendipitous misprint. To list the sources (Elgin, Illinois, *Courier*; Chicago *Herald-Examiner*; Owensburg, Kansas, *Observer*) would simply encumber the text without increasing the pleasure.

L. R.

To curry good luck, he always carried a rabbi's foot.

The proprietor said he would allow no woman in the bra without a man.

WANTED: Lawyer is searching for accomplished, well-recommended deceptionist.

Miss O'Hayer has been raising birds for many years and is credited with having the largest parateets in the state.

Lola Carlisle, a budding author, said she had circulated her navel among various Hollywood producers.

... Sergeant Alfred Blaine is a twenty-year veteran defective on the police force.

(next day)

Correction: ... Sergeant Blaine is a twenty-year veteran detective on the police farce.

He is a student in the Episcopal Seminary at Cambridge, which is afflicted with Harvard University.

He heard himself assailed as a self-centred financial executive who buttered his own beard.

The major was overtired because of his many official cuties.

He got up, dressed, took a shower, and ...

He clung to the sill by his fingerprints.

The new bride is twenty feet wide and forty feet long.

The bride was upset when one of her flower girls stepped on her brain and made a big tear in it.

Dorothea: I've learned my lesson. Please come home. It was just a passing fanny. Love ... Harold.

Picking up his hammer, nails, and two broads, he went back into the cabin.

In college catalogue

English 406: Three plays by Shakespeare. Intensive analysis of *Hamlet, Macbeth, Anatomy and Cleopatra.*

In bakery window: Cakes iced in white, brown, pink, and glue.

Menu: Dreaded Veal Cutlet.

To remove a fresh grease spot on a rug, cover the spot with blotting paper, then press with a hot flatiron. Cover the spot with magnesia, let it remain for 24 years, then brush off.

Correction: It was 'Whistler's Mother,' not 'Hitler's Mother' (as reported in yesterday's *Courier*), that Professor Bixly lectured on. Nothing is to be gained in trying to explain how the error occurred.

See also **Bloopers, Boo-boos, Definitions by Children, Geography Revised, Headlines, History Revised, Malaprops, News Items, Signs**

Waiters

When you go to a restaurant, be sure to choose a table near a waiter.

☞

Epitaph on a waiter's tombstone

Here lies Ephraim Teshler, Waiter
'God finally caught his eye.'

☞

In a delicatessen on 14th Street, Abe Tamkin called his waiter over. 'Listen, waiter. What is this sandwich I am eating?'

'Just what you ordered: a pastrami on rye.'

'Look, I'm half through already – and I haven't hit even one tiny piece of pastrami!'

'So take another bite,' said the waiter.

Mr Tamkin took a bite, chewed, swallowed, and declaimed, 'Still no pastrami!'

'You went right past it!' retorted the waiter.

☞

Nothing in New York is unique as its waiters. They are independent, thin-skinned, cynical, and incorrigibly sardonic. After prolonged research, I have come to the following unkind conclusions:

1. A New York waiter hates to tell anyone the correct time. Once, I asked a passing menial, 'Can you please tell me what time it is?'

He answered, 'You're not my table.'

2. When taking your order, the New York waiter grunts or

growls; this makes it impossible for you to know whether he really understood you – which is part of the pledge he took during his initiation into the Society of the Dissemination of Ulcers.

3. He hands you the menu upside down. This is done in order to exercise the customer's wrist, toning up your muscles for tipping.

4. He asks you exactly how you like your meat done, so he can tell the misanthropes in the kitchen how long to overcook it.

5. He writes your order down in a secret code. In this way, he can give you the wrong bill, which is always larger than it ought to be. You would think that *once*, at least, a wrong bill would be smaller than your rightful one, but this never happens. Economists explain this as the Law of Irreversible Gain.

from my The 3:10 to Anywhere

Mr and Mrs Jorge Camoza, from Madrid, visiting New York for the first time, entered the Diego Café and Brasserie and sank wearily into a booth near the entrance.

A waiter came over and handed each of the Camozas a menu. Señora Camoza sighed. 'Jorge, my feet they are killing on me.'

'I also,' said her husband. '*Camarero* – 'scusa. I do speak Sponish.'

'*Señor, yo comprendo*,' said the waiter.

'Ah! *Maravilloso!*' beamed Señora Camoza.

'Waiter,' said Señor Camoza, 'We are both exhaust. New York is so noisy, so busy, so impolite . . .' He glanced at the menu. 'I'll have soup with – what is that?'

Said the waiter, 'Dumplings, stuffed with meat.'

'I, too,' said Señora Camoza. 'And waiter, with the soup – *por favor*,' she smiled, 'just one kind word to a tired tourist!'

Soon the waiter returned with two bowls of soup. He placed them before the Camozas.

As he started to leave, Señor Camoza sighed, '*Camarero*. Did you not forget something?'

'Eh? What?'

'The kind word,' smiled Señora Camoza.

'Ah *si, si*, señora.' The waiter bent down, and into her ear whispered, 'Don't eat the dumplings.'

Scene: Pattashik's 5-Star Restaurant

'Waiter!' called a customer. *'Waiter!'*

A waiter ambled over to the table. 'What,' he yawned, 'can I do for you?'

'For me, you can make like a waiter! Ten minutes I've been sitting here, calling for a waiter. The service in this place is absolutely terrible!'

'How do you know?' said the waiter, blinking. 'You haven't had any.'

At the great Café Royale on Second Avenue in New York, I first heard this ever-green classic:

WAITER: So, gentlemen, what will you have to drink?
FIRST CUSTOMER: I'll have tea.
SECOND CUSTOMER: I'll have tea, too. But waiter, be sure the glass is clean!
(*Waiter exits, returns*)
WAITER: Two teas. . . . Which one of you asked for the clean glass?

My interest in the New York waiter began when I was seventeen and visited Manhattan for the first time. My uncle, who had survived four years on Devil's Island, took me to his favourite restaurant.

As we entered, the waiter, spying my uncle, promptly smote himself on the forehead and cried, 'He's back!'

UNCLE: 'Back?' You eat here once, who has the strength to go any-place else?
WAITER: There are ten thousand waiters, at *least*, in New York. Why does God have to pick on me?
UNCLE: Maybe He's trying to teach you a lesson – to be polite, once, to a customer.
WAITER: That's not a lesson, that's a jail sentence. Besides, I am an atheist.
UNCLE (*to me*): In this restaurant, they give you ulcers *before* you eat. (*To waiter*) For the sake of my nephew here – a boy with a future, with a right to live – tell me honestly: how is the chopped liver?
WAITER: The chopped liver is no worse than the pickled herring.

UNCLE: I don't like pickled herring.

WAITER: Let me be the first to congratulate you.

UNCLE. Is the gefilte fish, through some oversight on the part of the management, fresh?

WAITER: To my enemies, I wouldn't recommend it.

UNCLE (*to me*): That means, that to his *friends*, it's delicious. . . . I'll take it. And, assuming that we survive, do you recommend the pea, vegetable, or chicken soup?

WAITER: Mister, are you ordering a meal or voting in an election?

UNCLE: I'm hoping, fool that I am, to get a *hint* about the food.

WAITER: For that, ask a chemist; I'm only a waiter.

UNCLE: You hide it beautifully. . . . Let me ask you, man to man: If you were in my place, what would you eat?

WAITER: If I was in your place, I'd kill myself.

UNCLE: That, I'll do on my way *out*. . . . I'll have the chicken soup.

WAITER: Better take the barley. . . . Mr Nephew, what do you want?

I: I'll have the borscht, please.

WAITER Don't be a fool; take the vegetable. (*The waiter brought us our fish, then the barley soup for my uncle and the vegetable for me.*)

UNCLE: That vegetable soup smells delicious! . . . Waiter, why didn't you recommend it to me?

WAITER: *You* didn't ask for the borscht!

L. R.

See also **Can You Believe it?, Chutzpa, Conversations I Cannot Forget, Restaurants, Retorts, Sarcasm, Squelches**

Weirdos

MY FRIEND WILBUR

I first began to wonder whether Wilbur was some kind of nut when we were in high school. We were walking along one afternoon when Wilbur, without warning, announced: 'Schatzski's Ring is a constriction of the lower œsophagus.'

I stopped. 'Is anything wrong with your œsophagus?'

'No.'

'Then why did you tell me that?'

'What?'

'About Schatzski's Ring.'

'I don't know,' said Wilbur. He blinked, 'I thought it would interest you.'

Or take the time our gang was hanging around the corner, discussing you-know-what and Wilbur suddenly declared: 'A conger eel can lay fifteen million eggs a season!'

'Willy,' said Zack Pinchik, in a voice that dripped disgust, 'you are the type who one-a-these days they are gonna throw a net over his head so's you will spend the rest of your life playing "Chopsticks" for doctors in white coats ... Eels,' he echoed. 'F' cryin' out loud, why *eels*?'

Wilbur flushed. 'I – thought it would interest you ...'

Or take the time Wilbur went into a fit, shouting: 'Yes, sir! Yes, siree! Carpathian peasants trim their bunions only under a new moon! How about *that*? Huh? Wow!' (I checked the source Wilbur gave me and he was absolutely right: peasants in Carpathia simply shun podiatry unless a full moon is shining.)

I often wondered what quirk in Wilbur's nature made him store up such weird odds-and-ends. After long contemplation I came to the conclusion that Wilbur must have discovered, early in life, that ideas confused him – so he began to collect information. There's nothing wrong in that, mind you: some boys collect stamps, others coins, grownups gather matchbook covers. Well, Wilbur collected trivia. In that way, he was able to substitute facts for conversation. Wilbur's brain was not deep, but it *was* retentive. He desperately wanted to be liked, and he gave you the only treasures he possessed. He was so eager to make friends, and so clumsy in the ways he went about it, that he reminded me of the old Chinese proverb: 'He is like a man in a barrel of rice with his lips sewed up.' Come to think of it, I heard that from Wilbur.

I think God had chosen Wilbur to be one of his *shlemiels* – well meaning, generous, and hopelessly inept. When you took a walk with him, for instance, you found yourself bumping into him, even though you were both in the normal, side-by-side arrangement for walking. And when you introduced Wilbur to someone, he would pump the other person's hand as if there was a water shortage.

After high school, Wilbur went to work in the basement of a department store, selling curtain rods. Inside of a month, his sterling character, zeal, and erudition gave the basement manager a nervous breakdown.

Now, Wilbur started door-to-door selling. He swiftly progressed from touting ironing-board covers to extolling cemetery plots. He neither shone or starved in his new profession, since he took plenty of time 'breaking the ice,' he told me, employing smiles, chuckles, and friendly small talk – about things like the origin of the word 'bloomer' or the mischievous tributaries of the Tallahassee River.

One day I lunched with Wilbur at a vegetarian restaurant. (The sight of red meat made him faint.) We had no sooner sat down than Wilbur beamed, 'I recently had geographic tongue!'

'What?'

'Geographic tongue,' said Wilbur. 'That's when your tongue has entire areas of blotches that differ in colour like a map.'

'How did you get it?' I asked.

'I don't know,' said Wilbur. He plopped sour cream into his borscht. 'That's one of the most interesting things about it. *No* one knows what causes it or what makes it disappear! Look.' He stuck his tongue out. I had never realized what a long tongue Wilbur had, but it looked perfectly normal: pink, moist, and in no way like a map.

'Your tongue looks perfectly normal,' I said, 'pink, moist, and in no way like a map.'

'That's because it disappeared,' said Wilbur.

'What was the treatment?' I asked.

'What treatment?' asked Wilbur.

'The treatment for geographic tongue.'

'Oh ... None. It just went away. That's because it was a benign, *migratory glossitis!*'

I ate my blintzes thoughtfully.

'Thank God it wasn't the *rhomboid type!*' Wilbur blurted. 'How about you? Have *you* had any unusual ailments since we last met?'

I felt a genuine twinge of regret. 'I'm afraid not, Wil.'

Among other nuggets of data with which Wilbur dowered me were these:

In Borneo, they call 1.36 pounds of anything a Catty.

The sawfly is often wingless.

The zip code of Yum Yum Tennessee is 38390.

In Blowing Rock, North Carolina, *snow falls upside down!* (Because a wind sweeps up through the rocky flume below, in the immense cliff that overhangs a gorge in the Blue Ridge Mountains, making a very powerful updraft.)

I often wondered if Wilbur would ever get married. His cousin Oscar once fixed Wilbur up with a blind date. Wilbur was to pick the girl up at her apartment at seven o'clock. At 7:19 the girl phoned Oscar and said, 'I am going to break every bone in your body!'

You can imagine how astonished I was when I spied Wilbur, one Saturday afternoon, on a bench in Central Park with a girl. He leaped to his feet and hopped up and down in delirium as he introduced me. 'Hey! Say! Listen! This is N-Naomi Spredforth!' She was a thin, pleasant waif of a girl, slightly bucktoothed. Her eyes were navy blue. 'Naomi comes from Comfort, Texas!' boomed Wilbur, who had never been good at keeping a secret.

'You don't have a Texan accent, Miss Spredforth,' I said.

'That,' said she, 'is because I was only born in Comfort; financial reverses compelled my father to take us to live with his sister Mineola, who lives in Cos Cob, which is a tiny community five miles from Stamford, Connecticut. . . . Do you mind if I tat?' She opened her tote and removed a tiny hand shuttle with a needle stuck in some embryonic lace.

Wilbur suddenly blurted, 'Did you know that in Burma, girls born on a Sunday are supposed to marry only boys who were born on a Tuesday?!'

Naomi's mouth stayed open wider than is customary. A knowing expression crept into her eyes. 'The Greeks,' she lilted, 'think Tuesday, not Friday, is the unlucky day of the week.'

'*Really?*' gasped Wilbur. 'The Burmese drive bamboo stakes into the ground so that their spirits will have a place to sit!'

Naomi laughed as her fingers deftly tatted. 'Did you know that there is a tree in Florida called the Gumbo tree – and it can reach a height of *sixty-three* feet?'

They were married three weeks later. And I don't have to see Wilbur any more.

from my *People I Have Loved, Known or Admired*

Wills

Old Mr Fitzhugh, as crotchety as he was shrewd, finally went to Tolliver's to buy a hearing aid. 'Ay'm wantin' the finest hearin' aid y've got,' he said. 'In fact, Ay'm wantin' one that's so wee not a soul in Dundee will know Ay'm wearin' one.'

A month later, Mr Fitzhugh stopped in to tell Mr Tolliver how good the hearing aid was. 'It's a *mira*cle, mon, it is!'

'And, Ay'm thinkin' how happy your family and friends are that you have it,' said Mr Tolliver.

Mr Fitzhugh broke into a cackle. 'Hoot, mon. They dinna *know* I have it: Why, jist this past week, Av've changed my will fourteen times!'

See also **Lawyers**

Wit

No man ever forgets where he buried the hatchet.

'KIN' HUBBARD

Wagner's music is not as bad as it sounds.

MARK TWAIN

When it comes to giving, some people stop at nothing.

GEORGE JESSEL

Keeping a secret from his wife is like trying to sneak the dawn past a rooster.

FRED ALLEN

He was so skinny he looked like he'd been pulled through a key-hole.

FRED ALLEN

He looks like a dishonest Abe Lincoln.

WOLCOTT GIBBS (of Harold Ross)

> You certainly have a ready wit.
> Tell me when its ready.
>
> HENNY YOUNGMAN

There usually is an answer to any problem: simple, clear, and wrong.

H. L. MENCKEN

Out of snow, you can't make cheesecake.

How is it possible that the clod who wasn't good enough to marry your daughter is the father of the smartest grandchild in the world?

The man who marries for money will earn it.

When two divorced people get married, four get into bed.

The longest road in the world is the one that leads from the pocket.

Don't call a man honest just because he never had a chance to steal.

YIDDISH SAYINGS

When Mark Twain started to register in a hotel in Canada, he placed his signature under the entry above it, which read: Sir Edmund Lee and valet. He wrote: Mark Twain and valise.

I would rather go to bed with Lillian Russell stark naked than with Ulysses S. Grant in full military regalia!

MARK TWAIN

Statisticians

Men who know that if you put a man's head in a sauna and his feet in a deep freeze, he will feel pretty good – on the average.

The higher a monkey climbs, the more you see of his ass.

GENERAL JOSEPH STILLWELL

Diogenes, 'tis said, went around the known world, holding his bright lamp in his noble quest to find an honest man. When he got to Romania, someone stole the lamp.

Cleanliness is almost as bad as godliness.

SAMUEL BUTLER

When a man brings his wife a gift for no reason, there's a reason.

MOLLY MCGEE

Partner, I suppose that you learned how to play bridge only yesterday. But may I ask: what *time* yesterday?'

GEORGE S. KAUFMAN

George Moore, Irish author, was asked on his eightieth birthday what accounted for his long and exceptionally healthy life. 'I have thought a good deal about that,' said Moore, 'and I am convinced that both my age and my health are to be explained by an obvious fact: I never touched a cigarette, a drink, or a girl until I was almost ten years old.'

Cornelia Otis Skinner opened in a New York revival of Bernard Shaw's *Candida*. The next morning she received this cable:

EXCELLENT! GREATEST!
SHAW

Bowled over by such superlatives from a notoriously acidulous critic, the actress cabled back:

A MILLION THANKS. BUT UNDESERVING SUCH PRAISE.
CORNELIA OTIS SKINNER

Within two hours came this reply:

I MEANT THE PLAY.
SHAW

To which the incomparable actress responded:

SO DID I.
SKINNER

The difference between truth and fiction is that fiction has to make sense.

MARK TWAIN

See also **Cynics' Dictionary, Graffiti, Groucho, Old Saws Sharpened, Repartee, Retorts, Reviews of Note, Signs, Typos**

Women's Lib

At the Amazon Garage, Ms Maude Crawford, an ardent women's rights advocate, comes up to a customer's car at a gasoline pump, asking, 'Fill him up?'

W. C. Fields, who was a misanthrope no less than a misogynist, was once asked by a matron to address her garden club. As Fields hemmed and hawed, the matron said, 'I am *sure* that a man of your wide experience favours clubs for women.'

'Indubitably, madam, indubitably,' declaimed Fields. 'But only if every other form of persuasion fails.'

See also **Applications, Hanky-panky, Love, Marriage, Sex**

Wordplay

Postcard from Jackson Hole, Wyoming

Dear Phil:
We both miss you as much as
if you were right here.

On her first trip to London, Mrs Crowley could hardly wait to go shopping at Yardley's, the world-famous soap emporium. The sales girl asked, 'Madam, do you want it scented or unscented?'

'I'll – uh – take it with me.'

⌒

The very vain actress shook the latest photograph in the face of the photographer furiously. 'This picture is a disgrace, a caricature, a – Leslie, tell me the truth. Do you really think this godawful photograph bears any resemblance to me?'

'Darling,' replied Leslie, 'the answer is in the negative.'

⌒

Scene: Atheneum Club, London

'Terrible mess, our young,' said Lord Stonehurst.

'Ghastly, my dear Stonehurst, simply ghastly!' said Lord Chadwyn.

'No standards. No morals. Pop into bed with anyone. *I* didn't sleep with my wife until we were married. What about you?'

Lord Chadwyn pondered for a moment, downed some whisky, then sighed, 'Can't remember, old chap. What was her maiden name?'

⌒

'I sy, guv,' said the panhandler, 'd' ye 'appen t' 'av a bob for a cup o' java?'

'No, I don't. But you need not worry about me. I'll manage, I will. I'll manage.'

⌒

NOTICE TO ALL EDITORS

From: Bernard Kilgore, chairman.

If I see the word 'upcoming' in the *Wall Street Journal* once more, I shall be downcoming, and some copy-checker will be outgoing.

⌒

NOTICE TO WRITERS

From: Harold Ross, editor, *The New Yorker*

I am damn annoyed by the careless, cozy way 'pretty' and 'little' are beginning to pop up all over the magazine!

In the next issue appeared a column by James Thurber, containing:

'. . . observers agree that the building is pretty ugly and a little big for its surroundings.'

↶

Little Lila Griffiths was lost in her homework, when her grandfather said, 'An' what be ye readin', me darlin'?'

'It's about how the South changed, grampa, after a man named Whitney invented the cotton gin.'

'The *what*?!' astounded grampa asked.

'The cotton gin.'

'Faith, an' can ye believe somethin' like that, me girl? That them southerners actually drink *cotton*?!'

See also **Cynics' Dictionary, Groucho, How's That Again?, Repartee, Retorts, Sarcasm, Waiters, Wit**

Yiddish

Yiddish is the Robin Hood of languages. It steals from the linguistically rich to give to the fledgling poor. It shows not the slightest hesitations in taking in houseguests – to whom it gives free room and board regardless of genealogy, faith, or exoticism.

Never in its history has Yiddish been so influential – among Gentiles. (Among Jews, alas, the tongue is running dry.) We are clearly witnessing a revolution in values when a Pentagon officer, describing air-bombardment pattern, informs the press: 'You might call it the bagel strategy.' Or when the London *Economist* captions a fuss over mortgage rates: *Home Loan Hooha*. Or when the *Wall Street Journal* headlines a feature on student movements: '*Revolution, Shmevolution*.' Or when England's illustrious *Times Literary Supplement*, discussing the modern novel, interjects this startling sentence: 'Should, schmould, shouldn't, schmouldn't.'

My earliest awareness of the marvellous resilience of my mother tongue came when I was quite young. An old woman, bowed under the weight of shopping bags, stopped me:

'*Yinger mon, ir farshteyt Yiddish*?' ('Young man, do you under-
stand Yiddish?')
'*Yaw*,' I answered.
'Vat time is it?'

Words and phrases are not the chief 'invasionary' forces Yiddish
has sent into the hallowed terrain of English. Much more signifi-
cant, I think, is the adoption by English of Yiddish linguistic
devices:

1. Blithe dismissal via repetition with an *sh* play-on-the-first-
    sound: 'Fat-shmat, as long as she's happy.'
2. Mordant syntax. 'Smart, he isn't.'
3. Sarcasm via innocuous diction: 'He only tried to shoot him-
    self.'
4. Scorn through reversed word order: 'Already you're discour-
    aged?'
5. Contempt via affirmation: 'My *son*-in-law he wants to be.'
6. Fearful curses sanctioned by nominal cancellation: 'A fire
    should burn in his heart, God forbid!'
7. Politeness expedited by truncated verbs and eliminated pre-
    positions: 'You want a cup coffee?'
8. Derisive dismissal disguised as innocent interrogation: 'I
    should pay him for such devoted service?'
9. The use of a question to answer a question to which the
    answer is so self-evident that the use of the first question (by
    you) constitutes an affront (to me) best erased either by (a)
    repeating the original question or (b) retorting with a question
    of comparably asinine self-answeringness.

Or consider the Ashkenazic panoply in which insult and
innuendo may be arrayed. Problem: Whether to attend a concert
to be given by a neighbour, niece, or friend of your wife. The same
sentence may be put through manoeuvres of matchless versatility:

1. '*Two* tickets for her concert I should buy?' (Meaning: 'I'm
    having enough trouble deciding if it's worth one.')
2. 'Two *tickets* for her concert I should buy?' ('You mean to say
    she isn't distributing free passes? The hall will be empty!')
3. 'Two tickets for *her* concert I should buy?' ('Did she buy tickets
    to *my* daughter's recital?')
4. 'Two tickets for her *concert* I should buy?' ('You mean to say
    they call what she does a "concert"?')

5. 'Two tickets for her concert *I* should buy?' ('After what she did to me?')
6. 'Two tickets for her concert I *should* buy?' ('Are you giving me lessons in ethics?')
7. 'Two tickets for her concert I should *buy*?' ('I wouldn't go even if she gave me a complimentary!')

Who has not heard or used phrases such as the following, which are literal translations from the Yiddish:

> Get lost.
> You should live so long.
> My son, the physicist.
> I need it like a hole in the head.
> Who *needs* it?
> So why do you?
> All *right* already.
> It shouldn't happen to a dog.
> OK by me.
> He knows from nothing.
> From that he makes a *living*?
> How come only five?
> Do him something.
> *This* I need yet?
> A person could bust.
> He's a regular genius.
> Go hit your head against the wall.
> You want it should sing, too?
> Plain talk: he's crazy.
> Excuse the expression.
> With sense, he's loaded.
> Go fight City Hall.
> I should have such luck.
> It's a *nothing* of a dress.
> You should live to a hundred and twenty.
> On *him* it looks good.
> It's time, it's time.
> Wear it in good health.
> Listen, *bubele* . . .?

What other language is fraught with such exuberant fraughtage?

from my *Joys of Yiddish*

Yinglish

Accusing someone of asininity by echoing a question
The true *maven* of Yinglish knows the sweet uses of scorn:

Q. Don't you want to meet a wonderful boy, get married, and have a fine family?

A. No, I don't want to meet a wonderful boy, get married, and have a fine family. (Meaning: 'How stupid can you be to ask such an idiotic question?')

Accusing someone of idiocy by denying the obvious
This deadpan ploy is typical of Jewish sarcasm:

Q. How would you like an all-expense-paid trip to Hawaii?

A. I prefer to spend the winter in a foxhole in the Bronx. (Meaning: 'How can you even *ask* such a stupid question?')

Affirming indignation by repeating a question in the form in which it was asked, with varying intonational emphasis
This is a favoured ploy in Yiddish, and a major contribution to the scornful persiflage of Yinglish. Note the dramatic effect achieved by the shift of stress, *seriatim*:

1.

Q. Did you send your mother flowers on her birthday?

A. *Did* I send my mother flowers on her birthday? (Meaning: 'Are you implying that I could forget an important occasion like that?')

2.

Q. Did you send your mother flowers on her birthday?

A. Did *I* send my mother flowers on her birthday? (Meaning: 'What kind of monster do you think I am – not to send my mother flowers on her birthday?')

3.

Q. Did you send your mother flowers on her birthday?

A. Did I *send* my mother flowers on her birthday? (Meaning: 'And suppose I didn't send them? Suppose I brought them in person? Is that a crime?')

4.

Q. *Did you send your mother flowers on her birthday?*

A. Did I send *my* mother flowers on her birthday? (Meaning: 'Have you forgotten that I sent *your* mother flowers on her birthday? If I sent flowers to your mother would I forget to send flowers to mine?')

5.

Q. *Did you send your mother flowers on her birthday?*

A. Did I send my *mother* flowers on her birthday? (Meaning: 'You know that I always send flowers on their birthdays to my wife, my sister, my aunt, my cousins in New Jersey, so are you implying that I am the kind of *paskudnyak* who would send flowers to them and not to my own *mother*?')

6.

Q. *Did you send your mother flowers on her birthday?*

A. Did I send my mother *flowers* on her birthday? (Meaning: 'Flowers were just the *beginning* of what I gave my mother on her birthday!' which suggests anything from a round-trip ticket to Israel to a condominium in West Palm Beach.)

7.

Q. *Did you send your mother flowers on her birthday?*

A. Did I send my mother flowers on *her* birthday? (Meaning: 'If I always send my mother flowers on *my* birthday, what kind of *grubyan* would I be not to send her flowers on hers?')

8.

Q. *Did you send your mother flowers on her birthday?*

A. Did I send my mother flowers on her *birthday*? (Meaning.

'Flowers you don't have to send your mother on New Year's or the Fourth of July – but on her *birthday*?!')

All right already
From Yiddish: *genug shoyn*

1. Enough!
2. Say no more, for God's sake!
3. Will you please shut up?
4. I can't *stand* any more!

'All right already,' a thriving export from the Bronx, is, to be exact, a version of 'Enough already!' And in that context 'All right already!' signifies exasperated agreement:

5. Okay, okay, just stop nagging me!
6. You win: save your voice.
7. I give up: you shut up.

Big deal!
This withering dismissal comes right from Yiddish: *A groyser kunst!* ('Some big art!') or the sarcastic *Khokhma!* with the accent on the *ma* ('Stroke of genius!').

I can hear the auditorium ring with objections: '"Big deal" is English!' and 'What is Jewish about "Big deal"?' So I'll tell you what's Jewish about 'Big deal.' The phrase is sarcastic. The mood is derisive. The phrase is not descriptive, but deflative. It is uttered with emphasis on the 'big', in a dry, disenchanted tone.

In such usage (as against, say, 'He signed a big deal today'), the exclamation was launched in the 1940s (see Wentworth and Flexner, *The Dictionary of American Slang*). It swiftly gained popularity as a blasé retort among the young, especially on our high school and college campuses:

'He made the ping-pong team!'
'Big deal.'

Cockamamy

1. Confused, mixed up.
2. Implausible, ludicrous.

3. Farfetched, offensive to credulity.
4. Imitation, fraudulent.
5. Cheap, not worth much.
6. (As an epithet) Silly! Absurd!

The number of definitions suggests the utility of this admirable concoction, a linguistic gem from the Lower East Side, cherished in Brooklyn, pampered in the Bronx, and now indispensable to the argot of urban life. I, for one, have found no pejorative synonym so pungent.

7. Decalcomanias: dye pictures transferred to the back of the hand, after wetting, rubbing, and peeling off the paper.

The slang coinage seems inevitable: How many children on Broome Street or Flatbush Avenue could pronounce, much less spell, the forbidding 'decalcomania'? True, the word became shorted to 'decal'; but can 'decal' hold a candle to *cockamamy*? Never.

Contempt via reiteration, plus the scathing 'sh – ' gambit

'Who says she's not clean? Clean-shmean, let her shave off her moustache.'
'Honest-shmonest, he sings like a frog.'
'Nice-shmice, did they give a penny to charity?'

Could be

From Yiddish: *Es ken zayn*, pronounced *'s ken zyn*.
1. It may be; it may come to pass.
2. But maybe not.
3. Time will tell.
4. Anything is possible.
5. Wait and see.
6. *Who* knows?

The following illustrate the denotations numbered in the definition above.

1.

A: Darwin said that man is descended from animals.
B: Could be.

2.

A: Do you think Pfaumbach is telling the truth?
B: Could be.
A: You don't sound confident.
B: I'm not.

3.

A: I wonder if Schultz will pay that bill.
B: Could be. . . . How long do you expect to live?

4.

A: Will Dora really marry a man forty years older?
B: Could be.
A: It's hard to believe.
B: With *Dora*?

5.

A: I don't think Mishkin will have the *nerve* to show up. What do you think?
B: Could be.
A: Could be what: yes or no?
B: Neither.

6.

A: You think *she* was the one who tipped off the police?
B: Could be.
A: Or do you think *he* did?
B: Also, could be.
A: You certainly like to straddle the fence!
B: I know how to say, *Who* knows?

಄

Don't ask!

From Yiddish: *Freg nit* (or *nisht*). 'Don't ask *me*' is English; 'Don't ask' (or 'Dun't esk!') is Yinglish.

1. Things are bad.
2. The answer would be so disheartening I prefer not to give it to you.
3. The answer is obvious.
4. Absolutely!

This laconic imperative contains a symphony of signals:

'Don't ask me to tell you (whatever it was you asked me) because I would rather not even *mouth* the answer.'

Or: 'Were I to answer your question instead of putting you off with a "Don't ask!," it would depress you so much you'd be sorry you inquired!'

Or: 'Take a hint: do me a favour; desist.'

'How's your wife?'
'Don't ask.' (She's in bad shape.)

'It will be the best party of the year! Are you coming?'
'Don't ask.' (Absolutely!)

'You look terrible, Joe. How's business?'
'Don't ask!'
'Ah . . . Listen, for this time of year, that's not so bad.'

'*Shalom*, Teddy. How's your wife?'
'Still sick.'
'And your children?'
'*They*, thank God, are fine.'
'And your *gesheft*?'
'I can't complain. Excuse me, Henry, I have to go – '
'Wait a minute. Has it ever occurred to you, Teddy, that in all the years we've known each other, it's always *I* who asks the questions – never you. Have you ever *once* asked how I am, how's my Shirley, my job?'

'Migod, Henry, you're right. How thoughtless have I been! From today on – Henry! How are things with you?'

Sighed Henry: 'Don't ask.'

Fancy-shamancy
    100 per cent pure Yinglish.

1.   Overly ornate.
     'Did you ever see such a fancy-shmancy reception?'
2.   Pretentious, affected.
     'That fancy-schmancy Maurice Vermont. I knew him when he
        was Morris Greenberg.'
3.   Attempt at style that fails, hence is vulgar.
     'Their decorator is classy, but their furniture is fancy-
        schmancy.'

The employment of the sardonic *shm* (*q.v.*) must have been among the earliest reduplications adopted by Lower East Side Jews. 'Fancy-shmancy' came to the attention of cosmopolitan New York when it appeared in the very popular vaudeville sketches of Potash and Perlmutter, Smith and Dale, *et alia*.

C

... give!
Yinglish.

Slang imperative for:
1. Talk!
2. Tell!
3. Open up!

This colloquial command is familiar to any moviegoer:
'Who paid you, Lefty? C'mon, *give*.'
'Who killed her, pal? . . . *Give!*'

C

Go know ...
Yinglish. From Yiddish: *Gey vays*.

1. How could I know?
2. How could you *expect* me to know?
3. How could *anyone* know?

This vivid disclaimer shifts blame from one's self to the universe; it is matchless as a stratagem of self-exculpation: 'Go know my line was tapped.'

C

Hoo-ha

1.   An exclamatory flourish that accentuates sentiments ranging from aspirated admiration to hoarse scorn.
2.   A big to-do; confusion, complexity.
'That was some *hoo-ha* in Times Square!'
'What was I supposed to do in the middle of such a *hoo-ha*?!'
3.   A fuss, 'stink', a stir, an issue magnified.
'Did she make a *hoo-ha* about the service!'
'I'll give them a *hoo-ha* they'll never forget!'

As an expletive, this immensely versatile declamation serves to express:

1. Admiration: 'His new wife? *Hoo-ha!*'
2. Envy: 'Is he well off? *Hoo-ha.*'
3. Deflation: 'That you call an actor? *Hoo-ha.*'
4. Skepticism: 'It's a foolproof deal? *Hoo-ha.*'
5. Astonishment: 'He joined the Navy? *Hoo-ha!*'
6. Scorn: 'Does she gossip? *Hoo-ha.*'

Do not for a moment think that this sextet exhausts the affective possibilities of this hyphenate. Facial and vocal counterpoint will register other sentiments with distinctive piquancy or dubiety:

7. You can't mean it! ('You'll leave home? *Hoo-ha!*')
8. Imagine! ('He moved to Japan? *Hoo-ha.*')
9. Wow! ('The party? *Hoo-ha!*')
10. Like hell. ('I should donate to his campaign? *Hoo-ha.*')
11. Who do you think you're fooling? ('Do I believe you? Every syllable, *hoo-ha.*')
12. Well, I'll be damned! ('In the chapel, in the middle of the eulogy, she just stood up – *hoo-ha* – and walked out!')
13. I'd like to live long enough to see that! ('He's going to win the Kentucky Derby? *Hoo-ha.*')

DISCIPLE: Master, do you believe that money isn't everything?
SAGE: *Hoo-ha.* It isn't even enough.

... know from nothing ...
From Yiddish: *fun gornisht (gornit)*

> In Yiddish, double negatives are both proper and common: e.g., *Zie hot nit keyn mon* (she has not no man). What I find even more piquant is that in Yiddish one can use a *triple* negative: *Keyner hot nit keyn vort gezugt* (No one had not no word uttered) – which in English would be 'No one uttered a word.'

'He don't know from nothing' emphasizes meaning by mocking English grammar triply: 1) in using 'don't' instead of 'doesn't'; 2) in adding the unnecessary 'from'; 3) in doubling the negatives.

Look who's talking

Yinglish: analogue of the Yiddish *Kuk nor ver s'ret!* ('Just take a look at who's talking.')

This imperative is not intended to make you direct your eyes to the speaker. It is intended to announce to the world that the speaker is:

1. Utterly unqualified to make the statement.
2. Incompetent, even if qualified.
3. Shamelessly biased in the matter.
4. A well-known liar, not to be trusted in *any* matter.
5. Off his/her rocker.
6. The very person who loused everything up in the first place.
7. The pot calling the kettle black.

DOLLY PARTON: Look at the *bust* on that girl!
ANYONE: Look who's talking.

$\backsim$

Nu
nu(?!)
nu-nu

> Rhymes with 'do.' From Russian: well; so; and german *nu* and *nun*. Cognates of *nu* are common in Indo-European tongues; but in which is *nu* put through such prodigious acrobatics as glorify it in Yiddish?

> A huffy/whimsical emphasizer, qualifier, interjection, sigh, aside, lament, expletive, or comment.

Nu and *oy* are quintessential Yiddish and sturdy Yinglish. These versatile utterances are the sonic equivalents of a moan, a groan, a nod, a sob, a grin, a grunt, a sneer, a complaint. . . . Consider the nuances of this two-lettered arsenal:

1. '*Nu?*' (How are things? What's new?)
2. 'Should we go? *Nu?*' (What do *you* say?)
3. '*Nu.* What could I do?' (Well . . .)
4. 'I saw her leave your apartment at three A.M. *Nu* . . . ?' (So – o – o? Explain.)
5. ' – he ran out! *Nu?*' (Can you beat that?)
6. 'Listen, I want the money. *Nu?*' (Will you or won't you pay?)

7. A.: 'I'm going to a funeral.'
    B.: '*Nu*?' (So what's the hurry?)
8. 'They raised the rent again! *Nu*.' (Nothing can be done.)
9. 'They liked the book. I – *nu*?' (I did not, but I leave it to you to
    guess why.)
10. ' – so buy the damn thing. *Nu*?' (Put an end to the shilly-
    shallying.)

When used in tandem, *nu* becomes a sentence:

'Can you imagine how I felt? *Nu-nu*.' (I know you can, so I'll
skip an elaborate description.)
'They argued, they fought – *nu-nu*.' (Why go on?)
'She says you're an animal! *Nu-nu*?' (You've got to respond to
that.)
I should warn the unwary that to ask a Jew '*Nu*?' invites the
frustrating, even infuriating, reply: '*Nu-nu*?'
Other uses:

1.

'Would you like a Danish?'
'*Nu-nu*?' (Of *course* I want a Danish.)

2.

'Listen, Jerry. The whole building knows . . .'
'*Nu*?' (So what?)
'Don't give me with the "*Nu*?" Jerry! *Nu-nu*?' (Open up. Talk.)

3.

'Hector, are you Jewish?'
'*Nu*? (What else?) Are you, Claude?'
'*Nu-nu*?' (Of course I am.)

Labedz wrote out this wire to Kuznets:

> HOW ABOUT PAYING ME BACK?
> I LENT YOU 200 DOLLARS.
> ALREADY FOURTEEN MONTHS.
> LABEDZ

Labedz reread the message, then struck out the first line, then the
second. Then, after scratching his chin, the third. Instead of the

whole kit-and-caboodle of words, he wired Kuznets:

NU?

LABEDZ

That afternoon he received this reply:

NU-NU?

KUZNETS

Oy

Oy is not a word; it is a vocabulary. It is used to express:

1. Simple surprise. 'When she saw me, she said, "*Oy*, I didn't expect you!"'
2. Startledness. 'She heard a noise and exclaimed, "*Oy!* Who's there?"'
3. Small fear. '*Oy!* It could be a mouse!'
4. Minor sadness (sighed). 'When I think of what she went through, all I can say is *o-oy*.' (Note the *oy* prolonged, to indicate how sensitive one is to the troubles of others.)
5. Contentment. '*Oy*, was that a delicious dinner!'
6. Joy. '*Oy*, what a party!'
7. Euphoria. 'Was I *happy*? *Oy!* I was dancing on air!'
8. Relief; reassurance. '*Oy*, now I can sleep.'
9. Uncertainty. 'What should I do? *Oy*, I wish I knew.'
10. Apprehension. 'Maybe he's sick? *Oy!*'
11. Awe. 'He came back alive yet? *Oy!*'
12. Astonishment. '*Oy gevalt*, how he had changed.'
13. Indignation. 'Take it away from me. *Oy!*'
14. Irritation. '*Oy*, is that some *metsieh!*'
15. Irony. '*Oy*, have you got the wrong party!'
16. Pain (moderate). '*Oy*, it hurts.'
17. Pain (serious). '*Oy, Gottenyu!*'
18. Revulsion. '*Feh!* Who could eat that? *O-oy!*'
19. Anguish. 'I beg you, *tell* me! *Oy!*'
20. Dismay. '*Oy*, I gained ten pounds!'
21. Despair. 'It's hopeless, I tell you! *Oy!*'
22. Regret. '*Him* we have to invite? *Oy!*'
23. Lamentation. '*Oy*, we cried our eyes out.'
24. Shock. 'What? Her? Here? *Oy!*'
25. Outrage. 'That man will never set foot in this house so long as I live. *Oy!*'
26. Horror. ' – married a dwarf? *Oy gevalt!*'
27. Stupefaction. 'My own partner ... *o-o-oy*.'

28.   Flabbergastation. 'Who ever *heard* such a thing? *Oy!* I could
      plotz!'
29.   At-the-end-of-one's-wittedness, or I-can't-*stand*-any-more.
      'Get out! Leave me alone! *O-O-O-o-o-oy!'*

Mrs. Fishbein's phone rang.
   'Hul-lo,' a cultivated voice intoned, 'I'm telephoning to ask
whether you and your husband can come to a tea for Lady Win-
dermere – '
   '*Oy,*' cut in Mrs Fishbein, 'have *you* got a wrong number!'

Repetition – to escape the obvious and maximize persuasiveness

   'I'm going, I'm going.'
   'I know, I know.' (Usually 'I know, I *know.*')
   'You'll like it, you'll *like* it.'

This kind of repetition is a staple of Jewish communication and
illustrates the propensity of Yiddish to employ irony for the
banishment of the banal. The difference between 'You'll like it'
and 'You'll like it, you'll *like* it' is as monumental as the difference
between 'I don't know,' which is bloodlessly phatic, and 'I don't
know, I don't *know!*' which is a defiant assertion of ignorance.

Sarcasm via the use of innocent adjectives/adverbs in malefic contexts

   'She wasn't depressed: she merely tried to hang herself.'

   'He knocked out only four of my teeth.'

   'I doubt that he ate more than fifteen sandwiches.'

   'Was that much to ask: ten million dollars?'

Shmegegge
   Rhymes with 'the Peggy.' Derivation: unknown (alas).

1.   A drip, a *shlepper,* a jerk.
2.   A clumsy *klutz.*
3.   A sycophant.

This admirable, disdainful neologism, an epithet for a class of human nerds, is a gem in the coronet of Yinglish. It won my heart when I first heard it in New York. I had never heard *shmegegge* in the Jewish enclaves of Chicago, Washington, or Los Angeles. I have never been able to find so much as a hint of a spoor of its origin.

There's no one here to talk to
Hyperbole from Yiddish: *Nito tsu vemen tsu reydn!*

1. It's useless for me to talk; you refuse to listen.
2. You are not *capable* of understanding!
3. You are too stubborn, too prejudiced to listen, so why waste my breath trying to reason with you?

The words are English and the syntax ordinary: what then makes the content Yinglish? The rhetorical murder of everyone except the aggrieved speaker.

What's with . . . ?
From Yiddish: *Vos iz mit . . . ?*

1. What's wrong with . . . ?
2. Please explain that.
3. Why are you (he, she) acting this way?

The proper English phrasing would be 'What's the matter with . . . ?' or 'What's wrong with . . . ?' or 'What's bothering . . . ?' The syntax of 'What's with . . . ?' is distinctly Yiddish; its popularity in American and British slang has made it Yinglish.

Who knows?
From Yiddish: *Ver veyst?*

1. I don't know.
2. Maybe someone, somewhere, knows the answer, but I doubt it.
3. You may search the whole world for an answer to that question but – believe me! – there is none.

Any language contains the neutral interrogation 'Who knows?' But as rendered in Yinglish ('*Who* knows?' or, with umbrage,

'Who *knows*?'), the phrase is not interrogatory; it is declarative. It is also accusatory ('Why do you ask me for an answer to a question that is clearly unanswerable?'), or sarcastic ('What a dope you are to think I can answer something like that!'), or philosophical ('Beware the surface innocence of the question; to answer is to risk entrapment in epistemology').

The ironic ploy of 'Who knows?' may be transferred to any number of pseudointerrogative asseverations: 'Who *cares?*' 'Who could?' 'Who should?'

4.   It's Greek to me.

. . . you should excuse (the expression; me; my frankness)
From Yiddish: *Zolst mir antshuldigen*: You should excuse me. Please excuse . . .

This genteelism, a long feature of New Yorkese, takes on a satirical note in conversation among the sophisticated:

'He is a Good Humor (you should excuse the expression) salesman.'

Intramural aspersions are more easily expressed in this barbarism than in naked disdain:

'Professor Montzer is a (excuse the expression) Keynesian.'

'Professor Tunkel is a (pardon the expression) monetarist.'

'He wants to play rock-and-roll (excuse the expression) music.'
                                        from my *Hooray for Yiddish*

Postscript
How Not to Tell a Joke

A friend has asked me if I can teach 'the ordinary reader' how to tell a joke. It is much easier to tell a reader what *not* to do.

1. Don't begin by saying, 'I may botch this up' or 'I'm not good at telling jokes.' A prefatory warning of incompetence invites your listeners to be on the alert as to exactly how and where you will fulfil your prophecy.

2. Don't begin with 'Do you want to hear the funniest, most *hilarious* joke I've ever heard in my whole life?!' or 'This is going to have you rolling in the aisles!' or even 'I thought I would *die* laughing!' Such hyperbole challenges disagreement, framed in such unspoken retorts as 'The hell it is' or 'Like hell I will.'

3. Never start with 'This man,' 'This nurse,' or even 'This undertaker.' Since 'this' requires prior identification, you may be well into your joke while your audience is still preoccupied with wondering 'Which man?' or 'Why an undertaker?' They will surely miss part of your narration while groping for a clue or an answer.

4. As you talk, look directly into your listener's/listeners' eyes – not at your napkin, his/her ear, or the birdcage in the corner.

5. Act as if you *enjoy* telling the joke, which suggests you know how to do it.

6. Smile, grin, chuckle (in moderation), this cues your audience into doing likewise.

7. Don't hem, haw, clear your throat or honk your sinuses – unless it is to mimic the conduct of a character in your joke. Mimicry is marvellously effective, if you have a talent for it; if not, don't try it. Poor mimicry induces wincing.

8. The same is true of dialect. It is superb, if delivered with mastery. But such skill is rare – even among professional comedians. Do not use dialect unless you have a faultless ear, an acute

larynx, and a sensitive sense of the tremulous line between the affectionate and the derisive. You would be surprised by how many Jews are sensitive to 'Yid' accents, how many Italians resent imitations of the superabundant vowels that attend their presumptive solecisms, how many Poles, Greeks, or Germans ('Chermans') think it condescending for anyone to imitate their particular articulations.

9. Do not digress. Stick to the central narrative thrust. Focus full attention on the story. Intrusions such as 'Incidentally, my husband and I visited that part of Louisiana five – maybe six – years ago and we *loved* it!' or 'That reminds me, be sure to ask me for the name of a great restaurant we discovered in Acapulco last year.'

10. Do not introduce irrelevant details. If the breed of dog is not essential to the joke, do not give it. If the height, weight, posture, or pockmarks of a character do not tie directly into the crucial 'payoff', do not introduce such distractions.

11. Be very careful of your choice of verbs. It raises the hackles of your audience to be told '"Certainly!" he demurred.' Or '"It's a mile farther," she told.' Or even '"Drop that child or I'll blow your brains out!" the parson hinted.'

12. When what is spoken is plain, do not deploy the overly energetic: '"I'm not at all certain that the doctor meant me to tell you this," he shouted at the top of his lungs.'

13. Conversely, when vigorous action is described, do not undermine it with coy attempts at subtlety: 'He kicked the wrestler in the face and then in the groin, explaining, "And those are for Aunt Matilda."' Or, '"I will not stand by and see an old lady tied up, strapped to a wheel, and tortured!" the sheriff admitted.'

14. If you are unsure of your command of an audience, choose brevity over length. Patience is never exhausted by swift narration. The shorter the yarn, the less opportunity for irritating padding or unintended boo-boos. A sparse wit is better than a fat bore.

15. At all costs, deliver the final, climactic line without a smidgeon of uncertainty – no fumbling or floundering or lame self-correction. The wording of a punch line (which includes its rhythm, pace, pauses, emphasis) is the final and decisive factor in inducing laughter.

Let me illustrate these points (themselves worth the price of this volume) with a *miserably* executed joke:

God, Jack! I heard the most hil*a*rious joke last week – no, it was the week before – at the party Joe and Sue Nifkin (you know Joe, don't you?) gave to celebrate their tenth wedding anniversary. What a *bash* that was! At least forty, maybe fifty people – and did we get loaded! . . . Anyway, here goes – and I hope I get it right, because telling jokes is not exactly my dish. . . . Anyway, there was this big, big husky man – he could maybe be a Wall Street banker or the chairman of IBM, which is the largest and most profitable corporation in the world, comes out of a fancy hotel – like, say, the Ritz in Paris. (There isn't a Ritz in New York, is there? No.) Let's see, where was I? Oh, yes, this big, husky man comes out of a fancy hotel, let's say the Regency in New York, or – yes! – Claridge's in London!

Well, the doorman, who is Irish to the core, naturally tips his hat – I mean, touches the visor, you know the cap of his uniform, politely – and asks, 'Begorrah, mon, an' kin I be helpin' ye?'

The big, husky man, who is a German or Austrian from Berlin, I guess, replies, '*Ach*, I belief you *can* help me, doorman.'

'How, sir? Jist ye say the worrd and it's as good as doon.'

So the big, husky man (he's not wearing a hat, by the way) says, 'Vell, yust call me a taxi.'

So the Irish doorman does a 'take', I guess they call it in movie lingo – you know, he looks like he ate a green apple and is wondering about the consequences – so, as I was saying, the doorman says, 'Okey-dokey, gov'nor.' Then he straightens up – like this, see, bracing his shoulders – and hollers, 'You are a taxi!'

> (*Reluctant note:* The entire joke should go:
> 'Doorman, call me a cab.'
> 'Yes, sir. You're a cab.')

Bye now.